Rural Women's Power in South Asia

Gender, Development and Social Change

Series Editor: **Wendy Harcourt**, Associate Professor in Critical Development and Feminist Studies, The International Institute of Social Studies, Erasmus University, The Hague, The Netherlands

Series Committee: **Lydia Alpizar**, Executive Director of the Association for Women's Rights in Development, São Paulo, Brazil; **Srilatha Batliwala**, India-based feminist activist and Scholar Associate with the Association for Women's Rights in Development, Bangalore, India; **Yvonne Underhill-Sem**, Associate Professor of Development Studies, University of Auckland, New Zealand

The 'Gender, Development and Social Change' series brings together path-breaking writing from gender scholars and activist researchers who are engaged in development as a process of transformation and change. The series pinpoints where gender and development analysis and practice are creating major 'change moments'. Multidisciplinary in scope, it features some of the most important and innovative gender perspectives on development knowledge, policy and social change.

The distinctive feature of the series is its dual nature: to publish both scholarly research on key issues informing the gender and development agenda as well as featuring young scholars and activists' accounts of how gender analysis and practice is shaping political and social development processes. The authors aim to capture innovative thinking on a range of hot spot gender and development debates from women's lives on the margins to high level global politics. Each book pivots around a key 'social change' moment or process conceptually envisaged from an intersectional, gender and rights-based approach to development.

Titles include:

Wendy Harcourt (*editor*)
WOMEN RECLAIMING SUSTAINABLE LIVELIHOODS
Spaces Lost, Spaces Gained

Pashington Obeng
RURAL WOMEN'S POWER IN SOUTH ASIA
Understanding *Shakti*

Rekha Pande (*editor*)
A JOURNEY INTO WOMEN'S STUDIES
Crossing Interdisciplinary Boundaries

Gender, Development and Social Change
Series Standing Order ISBN 978–1–137–03413–7

You can receive future titles in this series as they are published by placing a standing order. Please contact your bookseller or, in case of difficulty, write to us at the address below with your name and address, the title of the series and the ISBN quoted above.

Customer Services Department, Macmillan Distribution Ltd, Houndmills, Basingstoke, Hampshire RG21 6XS, England

---

Rural Women's Power in South Asia

Understanding *Shakti*

Pashington Obeng
Associate Professor, Wellesley College, MA, United States

palgrave
macmillan

First published 2014 by
PALGRAVE MACMILLAN

Palgrave Macmillan in the UK is an imprint of Macmillan Publishers Limited, registered in England, company number 785998, of Houndmills, Basingstoke, Hampshire RG21 6XS.

Palgrave Macmillan in the US is a division of St Martin's Press LLC, 175 Fifth Avenue, New York, NY 10010.

Palgrave Macmillan is the global academic imprint of the above companies and has companies and representatives throughout the world.

Palgrave® and Macmillan® are registered trademarks in the United States, the United Kingdom, Europe and other countries.

ISBN 978–1–137–32075–9

This book is printed on paper suitable for recycling and made from fully managed and sustained forest sources. Logging, pulping and manufacturing processes are expected to conform to the environmental regulations of the country of origin.

A catalogue record for this book is available from the British Library.

Library of Congress Cataloging-in-Publication Data
Obeng, J. Pashington.
Rural women's power in South Asia : understanding *shakti* / Pashington Obeng (associate professor, Wellesley College, MA).
pages cm
Summary: "This book investigates how women's power and caste cleavages often continue to transcend and crosscut the boundaries of caste/tribe, gender, age, class and religion in India, Pakistan and Bangladesh. Building upon recent formulations of South Asian gender discourse, it explores the ways that perceived notions of women and castified geographies are not only structured in complex and localized relationships of dominance, but are also constituted by practices of the state and central governments. By examining both the particularities of local women's efforts to improve themselves and the ways that power is mediated, the author addresses the multiplex ways individuals both adapt and contest the hegemony of the dominant structures"—Provided by publisher.
Includes bibliographical references.
ISBN 978–1–137–32075–9 (hardback)
1. Rural women—South Asia—Social conditions. 2. Rural women—Government policy—South Asia. 3. Women in rural development—South Asia. 4. Power (Social sciences)—South Asia. 5. Dominance (Psychology)—South Asia. 6. Caste—South Asia. 7. Social structure—South Asia. 8. South Asia—Rural conditions. I. Title.

HQ1240.5.S64O24 2014
305.420954—dc23 2014019767

Typeset by MPS Limited, Chennai, India.

For Amelle Naana Amma Obeng

Contents

Preface

As we drove from Trojillo to Santa Fe in Honduras on 15 July 2007, our Garifuna companion Stefan Vasques, on seeing a group of elderly women sitting under a tree, said, "There sit the ancestors, the *agubidas*." Garifunas are also called Black Caribs who live in Honduras, Belize, Guatemala, and Nicaragua in Central America. Later, I learned that elderly women are sometimes called ancestors among the Garifuna communities of Honduras. On arriving in Santa Fe, we saw some children playing on the streets. Suddenly Stefan alerted my cousin Tete and me to how the children ran away from where they were playing because they had seen their grandmothers. The grandmothers expected the children to be at home and not playing outside. This incident made me appreciate Kerns' (1997) analysis of Belizean elderly women and their status and influence among the Garifuna of Belize. Kerns addresses how marginalized women are able to shape their personal and collective realities in the face of racism, patriarchy, and ageism. It is not only in Belize that apparently marginalized women create strategies to advance themselves despite the odds.

For instance, Gopal Siddi, African Indian and a 63-year-old widow in Chipgeri, was the lead ritual woman when she was possessed by her late husband's spirit to perform *puja* (religious rite) four months after her husband's death in a community of about a hundred people on 19 June 2009. Though a widow in a socially and economically depressed area of Karnataka, India, she used the occasion of a feast to honor her late husband's memory to deploy sacred capital to perform a ritual that benefited her household, community, and those who attended the feast. Besides the practical aspect of feeding people who were part of the feast, Gopal took on the role of a ritual specialist as she blessed all those who were present. She played a role that only a widowed senior woman could perform.

Janubai Gauri Kokre is a 38-year-old Gowli, an OBC (Other Backward Class, Category 1) woman from Jogeshwarhalla in North Karnataka. She is a social worker who uses a motorcycle to visit, empower, and convey battered women to police stations and hospitals. Though a rural Indian woman of the Gowli group, her newly gained power as a social worker in Karnataka enables her to perform roles that were not open to her, her peers, and her parents about 15 to 20 years ago. Gowlis are traditionally cow herders and milk sellers in parts of North Karnataka. Today as a result of the support of nongovernmental organizations (NGOs) that trained her to become a social worker and bought a motorcycle for her, Janubai's sphere of influence has enlarged beyond her traditional profession and "domestic" duties.

The incident in Santa Fe, Honduras; insights from Kerns' (1997) findings on Belizean women and Cliggett's (2005) work in Zambia; and insights from Batliwala (1996), Basu (1998), Kabeer (1999), and Subramaniam (2006) on social power in South Asia inspired me to raise questions that pushed me to examine rural women's power (that I term *shakti*) and influence in South Asia.

Not all women wield equal social and political *shakti* in their communities. Further, though through widowhood, divorce, senior women's status is perceived as disadvantaged, there are times when some women create or use resources to actualize themselves. Thus, there are rural women who do not simply reproduce their marginality as thoughtless, dispirited, and helpless people, but find ways of constructively using their disadvantage to advance themselves.

There is a growing body of literature on women, yet there is no critical study of the details of the cultural and historical contexts in which rural young and senior women exercise varying degrees of power and influence in Pakistan, Bangladesh, and India. International and national policies in transnational discourses tend to reflect how the most vulnerable such as women are disenfranchised in their respective societies.

I locate my findings within a long tradition of categorization of people according to age groups, castes, and tribes, in order to explore sites of differences among women and how they respond differently to opportunities and constraints in present-day Pakistan, Bangladesh, and India. This work focuses on women in their apparently marginalized positions in South Asian sociopolitical and economic hierarchies. Also, it illumines how rural women see themselves and rework their forms of power and status by manipulating social categories and power systems to negotiate and mediate notions of power and roles.

Theoretical framework of the study

This study examines how South Asia rural caste and tribal women who are a part of Indian, Bangladeshi, and Pakistani communities use notions of gender, tribe, caste, and age to publicly articulate new forms of power in South Asia. I investigate the public expression of forms of *shakti* among rural women between the ages of 20 and 60 and "senior" women of 60 years and above (1) to assess the sociohistorical impact on women's status and roles; (2) to analyze how the women understand and embrace new government and NGO opportunities, and information and technological advances to rework their roles through interpretations of their past; and (3) to use the findings to clarify and develop a conceptual framework of intersectionality for understanding varying constructions and articulation of women's power and influence in South Asia. This conceptual tool enables us to understand the influence of interlocking and overlapping spheres of economics, caste, social ideologies, sexual hierarchies, and politics and how they are subject to

(Bourque and Warren 1981: 211) rural women's manipulation in their everyday social interactions. *Shakti* uses a theoretical formulation that addresses "the voices and causes of differently situated women" (Shaheed 2010: 95) in rural South Asia. As I focus on the lived experiences of senior women, I am able to unearth the details of their settings and how they exercise varying degrees of power and influence (cf. Cliggette 2005: ix–x). The analysis illumines the different constructions of being senior and how some seniors use resources to articulate their power and influence. The work expands our understanding of power beyond concepts that focus solely on how the dominant may exert control over marginalized people. For instance, patriarchy has received much attention for how it is used to subordinate women (Bourque and Warren 1981; Basu 1992; Paul 1992; Visaria and Visaria 1996; Jejeebhoy 2002). My approach to power extends the discourse on hierarchies to include sociocultural forces that create and reproduce power inequities in South Asia. It explores forms of power centers and patterns of relationships with their embedded "hidden transcripts" (Scott 1990). Further, the work explores how rural women create social spaces and formulate discourses based on their notions of matters of exclusion, economic and political participation, and access to resources (Bourque and Warren 1981).

As caste and tribal women, the South Asian society defines the communities to which the women belong as possessing habits, behavior patterns, beliefs, dress code, and practices that mark them as different from the normative dominant society. Their "ascriptive characteristics" (Cohen 1999: 38) are used to objectify such communities as others.

My study was made possible by research grants from the Mellon SIRT, through Wellesley College and the Faculty awards from the College, funds from Harvard University and Brandeis University where I served as the Madeleine Haas Russell Visiting Professor.

A project of this nature also benefited immensely from my research assistants and conversation partners such as Lauren Lorincz (MFVGF), Anna Alissa al Qatab alHusein Hitzmann, Gauri Subramani, Dhivya Perumal, Courtney Ackeifi, Natalie Maddox, Sharre Brooks, Terrika Duckett, Asha Sundararaman, Joy Clarke, Caroline Moore, Leah Hamilton, Kirstin Yarnish, Moriah Smith, Victoria Cheng, Brittany Long, the Kamios, Kelly Ford, Nena Radtke, Linda Lago-Kass, Bonnie Scott Jelinek, Jodi Baier, Dahlia Rawji, Bhagyashree R. Bhat, J&J Rossetti, Valerie von Rosenvinge, the Ackeifi family, the Ashiagbors, the Cobblahs, Chris and Fiona Almeida, John Williams, Clark Andrews, Eric Marriot, Dr. Prema Ama, Bani, Janak and family and the Ansahs. I thank Carl Novotny and Judy Swhanberg, the Epsteins, Debbie Thornton and Bill, Greta Sarginson, the Raverets, the Garlands, the Hoffmanns, the St. Clairs, the Wilsons, the Ottens, Fr. Francis, Fr. Arun, Sunil Siddi, Ramnath Siddi, Jairam Siddi, Mohan Siddi, the Lindseys, Nancy Glynn, Don Frederico, the Hills Church office staff and clergy, Susan Langer of Wellesley College, the Petrovichs, the Robinsons, and Elyse and family for all their support and inspiration throughout the work. Thanks also to the Dishmans, Liz & Ray Stevens, the Kingstons, Carolyn Sheild, Chelsey Baturin, Allison Parker, Manavalan BhuvanaRaj and the generous rural women of *shakti*.

Sisters Stella, Reeta, Isabella, Rafael, Shaila, Felcy, Leena, Edith, Jesse, and Valentine, you all have been a source of support and inspiration for me, and I thank you. Thanks to my boss Pramod Shirali who translated, drove, hosted, and made sure that all members of my research team were well and safe. My deep gratitude to Amanda McGrath, Ambra Finotello, and Christina Brian of Palgrave Macmillan for their support and the anonymous reviewers who provided helpful suggestions on the draft of the manuscript.

And to the amazing family that planted and watered the seeds for this work, I say *sukryia, thumba upakara* to Professor Vai, Mr. Kwasi, Mr. Kwaku, Mr. Kofi, Connery, Pastor Pash Adu Kumi and family, Mrs. Obenewa and family, Mrs. Afua and family, Mrs. Amma and family, and Mr. Kwadjo and family.

Series Editor's Preface

Rural Women's Power in South Asia: Understanding Shakti is an important contribution to the series in its challenge to western centric views of gender and development and understanding of social change. In focusing on the *Shakti* of rural women, Pashington Obeng redefines power from a generational, gender, and South Asian perspective in a detailed study of how feminine power is embodied in economy, society, and culture.

The book moves us far away from the dominant view of the violated, downtrodden, vulnerable "third world woman" to a nuanced look at how women of rural South Asia of different generations live with, transcend and subvert gender power relations. In a fascinating set of case studies Obeng shows how women use their gender, tribe, class, caste, and age to articulate their own specific forms of power as they negotiate the systems of oppression around them.

The book is a welcome contribution to the series as an invitation to gender and development scholarship and policy makers to think again how to understand complex and far from simple experiences of poor rural women in their daily economic and social interactions.

Wendy Harcourt
Associate Professor,
Institute of Social Studies,
Erasmus University, The Netherlands

1
Introduction

Over the past two decades in India, Bangladesh, and Pakistan, economic expansion and rapid changes in industrial, agricultural, and information technology have led to a reconstitution of these countries' social hierarchies, a reconstitution that has also affected class, caste, and (particularly germane to this study) gendered divisions of labor in the rural communities of South Asia.

In this book, I explore how rural South Asian women of various ages use the social and material resources available to them to respond to, transcend, or subvert those hierarchies and the power structures that support them. I also examine, through a series of individual profiles and case studies, how such women use their gender, tribe, class, caste, and age to publicly articulate forms of power and negotiate with or challenge systems of oppression around them. The framework I use will benefit policy makers and social theorists because it takes the experiences of poor rural women in their daily social interactions seriously.

Scholarship on the highly pluralistic societies of India, Pakistan, and Bangladesh tends to group citizens by their countries' major and minor religions. It often ignores or minimally addresses people's "contested role[s], status, and legal rights" (Lawrence 1994: 163).

In the present work, I explore some of these very issues, in particular the ways that rural women in South Asia craft and deploy their power at the intersections of, on the one hand, their countries' efforts to create equality for their respective citizens and, on the other, entrenched countervailing forces of caste, ageism, class, gender, and religion. In addition, the women profiled in this work are divided into two groups: those between the ages of 20 and 60 and those aged above 60 (referred to as "seniors" by India's Ministry of Labour and Employment).

Through research into India's democratizing efforts, their impact on rural women, and the women's differing responses to those measures and to similar efforts in Pakistan and Bangladesh, this comparative study on the deployment of South Asian women's power (called *shakti* in this book; see my explanation below) focuses on women's lived experiences and how the women studied mobilize the new resources now available to them for personal advancement.

Shakti is the Sanskrit word for the embodiment of female divine creative power and the agent of change and nurturing (Harish and Harishankar 2003); *shakti* also connotes the power of the female deity of motherly strength and energy and the force to restore balance. A person who holds power is considered to be a *shaktiman* (Woodroffe 1918). In this work, I use the term *shakti* to mean "female power," and I investigate the various forms of *shakti* in the contemporary context of rural South Asia to

(1) assess sociohistorical impacts on women's status and roles there,
(2) analyze how women understand and embrace new governmental and nongovernmental (NGO) opportunities, as well as information and technological advances, to rework their roles, and
(3) use these findings to clarify and develop a conceptual framework for understanding various constructions and articulations of the power and influence of rural women in the Global South.

I begin with a brief survey of relevant theories of power in order to explore rural women's lived experiences and notions of women's power (*shakti*) within the multiple centers of patriarchy and other social inequalities in South Asia. The study illuminates an array of rural women's negotiations to deploy local manifestations of female power within the broader context of South Asia.

Foucault (1977) argues that power is "diffuse" and "productive" and that it relies on social relations and diverse points of resistance. Giddens (1984), following Foucault, contends that power plays out in a complex social context in which human agency and social structures have intertwining relationships. The interconnection between agency and social relations requires that we understand how the powerless may resist their exploitation or acquiesce because they have internalized a distorted consciousness that favors a dominant individual or group (Lukes 2005). Bourdieu (1977) also contends that, though marginalized people may not wield formal power, they have the capacity to disempower those who hold traditional power and influence; in some cases, for example (he argues), the marginalized choose not to obey the powerful. Hence, he points to the power of the powerless who use forms of resistance.

Powerlessness, according to Gaventa (2006), is rooted in social inequality and failed or ineffective social solutions. In the same paper, Gaventa proposes a theory of power that I find fruitful for my discussion of how South Asian rural women deploy various forms of formal and informal power. Gaventa (2006: 23–33) points out that

> *[p]ower "over"* refers to the ability of the powerful to affect the actions and thought of the powerless. The *power "to"* is important for the capacity to

act; to exercise agency and to realise the potential of rights, citizenship or voice. *Power "within"* often refers to gaining the sense of self-identity, confidence and awareness that is a precondition for action. *Power "with"* refers to the synergy which can emerge through partnerships and collaboration with others, or through processes of collective action and alliance building.

I use Gaventa's categories of power to inform how I explore the ways in which power unfolds in people's social relationships and the extent to which women manifest their transformative power (Giddens 1984). For example, I draw attention to rural women's ability to choose, amidst obstacles, resources for consciousness-raising to unlock their capacity to empower themselves as well as those who benefit from the services they offer.

I also use Clegg's (1989) theory of power, which addresses the dispositional, episodic, and facilitative dimensions of power, to investigate the different grades of strength, determination, and capacity to achieve results, honor, dignity, and courage, as women put up resistance, in order to elucidate *shakti* as it is crafted and made manifest by the women profiled. According to Clegg (1989), there are three forms of power: the episodic, in which rules, forms, and resources are changed in social interactions; the dispositional, which entails the social construction of meaning attached to roles and membership in an institution; and the facilitative, which deals with how resources, networks, and the environment may be used to empower or disempower an agent.

In this work, I further use a theoretical formulation that addresses "the voices and causes of differently situated women" (Subramaniam 2009; Shaheed 2010: 95) in rural India. This conceptual tool enables us to understand the mutual influences of the interlocking and overlapping spheres of economics, caste, social ideologies, and sexual hierarchies and politics, and how they are subject to (Bourque and Warren 1981: 211) rural women's manipulation in their everyday social interactions.

I also draw insights from Oommen (1970) to address power as expressed by community leaders and segments of society called "power reservoirs" that shape decision-making processes, though not necessarily in the same ways as those who have formal public power. Based on Oommen's views, I investigate how rural women use their informal networks as a critical resource to advance their goals. I also explore forms of power centers and patterns of relationships, including embedded "hidden transcripts" (Scott 1990), among rural women.

The present work also focuses on how women create social spaces and formulate discourses based on their notions of matters of exclusion, economic and political participation, and access to resources (Bourque and Warren 1981). The discussion on resistance benefits from Mbembe (2001: 110), in his *On the Postcolony*, where he argues that resistance be understood and conceptualized as "the dynamics of domesticity and familiarity." By implication, Mbembe argues that a person who resists articulates ways in which the dominant and the dominated vie for power within the same cultural space (Edmondson 2007: 6).

Although Mbembe contends that the dominated tend to avoid direct confrontation with their oppressor, it is also important to include Nyamnjoh's perspective of "domesticated agency, whereby the person is engaged in negotiation, concession, and conviviality over maximization of pursuits by individuals or particular groups in contexts of plurality and diversity" (Nyamnjoh 2002: 116). The above perspectives help us understand how counterhegemonic actors express multiple notions of agency as they engage others in diverse domains of influence.

I now turn to local understandings of female power (*shakti*) that open up new ideas for constructing and classifying notions and processes of power based on diverse social relations.

1.1 Caste and tribal *shakti* (power)

Shakti describes the primordial female principle that pervades the universe. This work uses the *shakti* notion to provide an alternative way of conceptualizing power, gender, and caste relations in South Asia. *Shakti* is understood as the force that animates the universe and therefore all living entities. In humans, *shakti* is the ability to act, be compassionate, and have the courage to end injustice. The divine female principle, *shakti*, is a source of energy for *shiva* (Rajan 1998). In Shaktism it is equated with Brahman, the highest spiritual reality that pervades all existence. Also, in Shaivism (with devotion focused on Shiva) and Vaishnavism (with devotion focused on Vishnu), *shakti* is the feminine energy of the male divinities. According to Woodroffe (1918), *shakti* and *shiva* are twin aspects of one and the same reality. *Shiva* is the masculine unchanging aspect of divinity, while *shakti* is the fluid and changing aspect. In the text Devi Mahatmaya, *shakti* is manifested in all women. Therefore, they have the power to both nurture the world and destroy evil forces. Thus, in the face of certain aspects of Brahminic traditions that are perceived as being oppressive in terms of caste and gender, it is the philosophical construct of the primordial female and nonpatriarchal traditions that has been deemed liberating throughout Indian religious history. *Shakti* can dwell in people; therefore every person's total freedom can be achieved when she or he develops and uses the female principle. The process of reaching this is described as the union between *shiva* and *shakti* (Rajan 1998). The unmanifest *shiva–shakti* is knowable only in the ecstasy of yoga.

In some contexts *shakti* is manifested in both destructive and creative ways to "sustain the universe" (Gold 1994: 26). It is a form of dynamic power that unfolds within social relations (Foucault 1977; Dowding 1991; Allen 1999) and structures to generate ongoing self-empowerment and empowerment for others as it calls attention to systemic challenges.

It is in the lives of the ordinary rural women discussed in this work that the divine, creative energy takes its concrete form and shape. While *shakti* can be attained through austere living or ascetic practices, the women profiled in this study actualize their *shakti* by their courageous actions, determination, and insistence on justice for all. When *shakti* is drawn upon by these women of lower-caste communities and religious minorities, they are able to enlarge the concept of the female power as they manifest their own agency to improve their conditions in contemporary South Asia. The feminine transformative force, according to Rajan, can be appealed to and used to contest and subvert religious and patriarchal hierarchies (Rajan 1998: 38). *Shakti* as used in this work, though a Hindu religious idiom, does not privilege one religion over another in the struggle for women's emancipatory efforts. Rather, *shakti* is used as a metaphor to describe and interpret the multiple ways in which women may deploy their influence to advance themselves in their communities (Rajan 1998: 34–38). Thus, in the current study, I borrow from notions of *shakti* to comment on how South Asian women embody the animating feminine principle by being strong leaders and teachers, bearers, and transmitters of culture and knowledge. In tangible ways, the women symbolize the energy and spiritual power present in the divine procreative act between *shiva* and *shakti*.

In the present work, "power" embraces respect, honor, dignity, courage, the capacity to get things done, and "weight," such as positive influence. Power, *shakti*, connotes a powerholder, a *shaktiman* (as already mentioned). Depending on contexts, *gaurava* (Sanskrit for respect, importance, pride, power), *vajen* (Marathi for "weight" or courage), *izzath* (in Hindi/Urdu), and *manndenscho* (respect) and *dairadith* (courage) are words that are used to describe power. The last two are in Konkani, a language spoken in parts of Goa, Mangalore, Bangalore, and areas in North Karnataka; they are words some rural Karnataka Indians use to describe power and influence. For example, in describing the power of a woman in one village, the Siddis speaking Konkani used the words *dairadith* and the Muslims *izzath*.

The publicly articulated policies of empowerment in India, Bangladesh, and Pakistan seem to suggest that political power is conferred rather than achieved or acquired. The interlocutors of power are often not chosen by women and in general are imposed on the people being assisted. So it is important to use a fruitful model for exploring rural women's power in order to unearth the rich and complex *shakti* that has historically been situated at the formal or informal sociopolitical and economic locations of present-day South Asia.

1.2 Literature review

Scholars of South Asia have used various theories of social hierarchies to address the complex and multiple domains of power at work in India, Bangladesh, and Pakistan (Agarwal 1994; Chowdhry 2004; Bhatt 2006). Batliwala (1996) and Kabeer (1999) have also called attention to "social power" that embraces "internal strength and confidence, collective organization, reflection and analytical skills, information, political participation, and knowledge" (Subramaniam 2006: 7).

The current work builds on these scholars' insights to illuminate local notions of social power and the processes and systems within which women forge forms of *shakti*. It is here that I extend the discourse to include power structures and women engaged in constructing notions of honor, dignity, courage, respect, and authority to distribute power. This work, based on rural people's understanding and practice, further helps us to reconceptualize social and private power as extensions of each other. Also, I examine specific ways in which some women perform a delicate dance as they expand and assert their *shakti* while operating within local understandings of femininity (Sa'ar 2006). (There are times, however, when some women in the exercise of *shakti* are seen and treated as deviants for overstepping the boundaries of socially acceptable behavior for women.)

Patriarchy has received much attention for how it is used to subordinate women (Bourque and Warren 1981; Basu 1992; Paul 1992; Visaria and Visaria 1996; Jejeebhoy 2002). In India's highly stratified society, gender oppression is linked with other forms of exploitation based on caste, class, community, tribe, age, and religion. In such multiple hierarchies it is important to examine the complex articulation of different forms of patriarchy. Thus, Sangari and Vaid (1989) distinguish between the modern ways by which patriarchal systems subordinate women and the "democratizing of gender relations" to illuminate the potential and inherent contradictions in South Asian central governments' democratizing and reform efforts.

I use gender analysis to compare information on the power relations between men and women in order to explore how social myths, legends, rituals, symbols, and language are used by the dominant to obtain an advantage in social relations (Clegg 1989; Lukes 2005). I then situate the discussion in the larger context of power as a complex and multilayered phenomenon that shifts in form and intensity (Gaventa 2006).

I also interrogate the discursive terms in which legendary women are folklorized and celebrated institutionally and in religious festivals as part of a community's identity. I interpret and examine ways in which female heroic legends are contested in light of violence against women, covering all forms of coercion, including physical, sexual, verbal, and mental abuse. It is here that I draw insights from Bourdieu (1977), Giddens (1984), Clegg (1989),

Agarwal (1994), and Gaventa (2003) to focus on women's power to mobilize symbolic and real power to resist injustice.

The women profiled in this work include presidents of *panchayats* (a local system of governance) and members and leaders of self-help groups (SHGs) called *sanghas*; they include hostel wardens, social workers, and healthcare providers. I also address women involved in informal economic activities such as agriculture, basket weaving, pottery, shop keeping, and sewing. This work also examines questions of community and solidarity, the power of female friendships, and the sense of belonging as important issues that inform and transform the cultural politics of gender, caste, and tribe in South Asia today.

Studies on gender and caste in South Asia often portray women as disempowered within sexual hierarchies and by social marginalization (Visaria and Visaria 1996; Farzana 2008; Bhattacharyya et al. 2010), and they tend to conflate the roles and statuses of young and senior women. In most writings, young and senior women are defined as lacking access to economic, social, and political resources enjoyed by men and other dominant groups, such as upper-caste over lower-caste women and mothers-in-law over daughters-in-law. For instance, Brinton Lykes et al. (1996) speak to the ways, subtle and overt, in which social and sexual hierarchies are constructed in institutions and through social interactions and discourses by dominant groups to exploit women and other minorities.

Jejeebhoy (2002: 229–300) mentions some of the shortcomings of studies that have been conducted on rural South Asian women. She points out that such studies highlight women's limited access to and control of material resources, their lack of access to knowledge and information, their limited authority to make independent decisions at home or in the community, and their general inability to create and foster equal power relations in their families and in society (Basu 1992; Paul 1992; Visaria and Visaria 1996). She also states that most scholars do not address the differing opinions between husbands and wives about the supposed autonomy or power of women (Jejeebhoy 2002: 229).

My study includes the views expressed by husbands and wives when the women profiled are married, as well as comments from focus groups of men and women. Also, I situate women's power within various social relationships to provide a broader and deeper understanding of women's competing and overlapping forms of power.

Women and power in South Asia: This section addresses selected literature about rural women and power in South Asia and how this book addresses concerns that are raised in that literature. Chowdhry's (2004) book examines the historic exclusion of Indian women from the control of critical resources by patriarchal systems and how women in North India are beginning to assert themselves in response to the Indian central government's interventions.

My work explores, in detail, the lives and stories of rural Bangladeshi, Indian, and Pakistani women to address the intertwining relationships between entrenched ideologies and the material conditions that have prevented women from advancing themselves. I also examine how women of various ages respond differently to government and NGO interventions in their lives. Further, this book pays attention to how some women are able to create and use resources for self-empowerment.

Bhatt (2006) focuses on the ways Indian women in the informal economy have drawn on Gandhian philosophy to struggle with and challenge social and economic hierarchies for personal advancement. Although Bhatt looks at the success of the Self-Employed Women's Association (SEWA), she also focuses on inadequacies in the implementation of women-directed reforms in India. I explore ways in which rural women educate themselves to make use of reform laws or use strategies to effect policy changes at local levels. I also look at the politics of various age groups and focus on senior women by addressing ageism in Indian, Pakistani, and Bangladeshi society.

Commenting on the causes of communal and ethnic clashes in India, Bhattacharyya's (2010) book addresses the Indian government's efforts to include communities that have been excluded from politics and economic activities that in the past have principally benefited the rich and powerful. My work discusses the Indian government's efforts to provide opportunities for women to engage in political processes. It also pays attention to how some women have been able to create and use resources for self-empowerment by analyzing how they have translated their personal force/power into public status and influence.

Mullen's (2012) book explores 30 years of India's decentralization of its governmental structure, which has aimed at allowing rural people to participate in local government. This is a timely addition to the discourse on local and national politics because it explores the relevance of local governance systems. My work builds on Mullen's work by focusing on local governing authorities such as *panchayats* and economic organizations such as *sanghas* and by examining how differently situated women of various ages use female power to build mutually supportive political and economic friendships. I detail how women either embrace or ignore the new opportunities ushered in by governments and NGOs.

Advancing the argument on women's empowerment, Subramaniam (2006) addresses "situated contexts" such as *sanghas* (SHGs that include both men and women) that serve as networks for women to improve themselves in order to challenge gender, religious, and caste norms in India's state of Karnataka. While Subramaniam focuses on rural women and their networks as a base to interrogate injustices, my work expands the discourse beyond political activism. I build on her work to address the ways in which women express *shakti* in their daily lives, beyond public political activism. My book examines the ways rural women of different castes, tribes, and religions deploy *shakti* for capacity building and making political protests for the economic and social development of their communities and themselves.

There have also been a number of relevant studies addressing Pakistan and Bangladesh. For instance, Weiss and Gilani (2001) examine the different domains of power in Pakistan. They argue that, in the political and economic history of Pakistan, there have been many power players. Weiss' essay in that work, on gendered power relations, helps to elucidate how Pakistani women confront a myriad of challenges as they try to assert influence.

Kelkar and Krishnaraj's (2013) book presents a hopeful note on how the different power players in Pakistan may succeed in that country's floundering democracy.

Bennett's (2010) work on prominent women leaders in Islamic countries such as Pakistan and Bangladesh sheds light on how, in Islamic societies, culture rather than religion can be deployed to benefit at least some women. The women in this case—Benazir Bhutto, prime minister of Pakistan, 1988–1990 and 1993–1996; Sheik Hasina, prime minister of Bangladesh, 1996–2000; and Khaleda Zia, prime minister of Bangladesh, 1991–1995 and 2001–2006—are examples of Muslim women leaders who seem to be the exception to the rule in Islamic countries. These women belonged to political families either by birth or by marriage, but they also had skills, talents, and abilities of their own that they applied effectively in becoming leaders of their countries.

Sathar and Kazi (1997) focus on women in rural Punjab in Pakistan and the ways in which they manifest various kinds of power. Their book draws on data from married women and their husbands, addressing women's employment patterns, their autonomy in marriage, and their perceptions of fertility and contraception. Some of the women are also engaged in agricultural or nonfarm employments, or in some cases both.

The above works present various perspectives on how women deploy power in their respective countries. These studies do not tackle how rural women of varied ages in different geographical areas assert their influence. My book, however, addresses women in rural communities who belong to different age groups and manifest formal and informal *shakti* in context-specific domains of their lives. In addition to discussing women of various ages of South Asia and their display of power, my book examines the processes, ideologies, and social hierarchies they encounter in their respective communities.

The challenges that women on the local *panchayats* and union *parishads* (Bangladeshi village/local governance structures) face in Bangladesh are the focus of Panday's (2008) work. In this work, Panday describes one of the key obstacles faced by women such as "representation without participation." A case in point is what Panday calls the "mobility obstacle." In such cases, women are prevented from taking part in decision-making processes or attending emergency meetings when they are called, deliberately, at times inconvenient for the participating women (Panday 2008: 502). This analysis is fruitful because it shows how entrenched some of the cultural practices are in Bangladesh.

Das et al. (2002) discuss how sexual hierarchy shapes reproductive practices. They state that there is intersectionality between women's control over their bodies, their increased autonomy, their roles in their households, and women's empowerment in general. Their work is insightful because it gets to the heart of the debate on sexual violence against women. However, their work's theory of power does not cover women's *shakti* and how women's friendships and other informal networks are deployed to counteract sexual hierarchies.

Other scholars have focused on how urban women use power in techno-economic settings of South Asian metropoles (Ghadially 2007). Urban-based women's activist organizations have also received attention (Basu 1992). These scholars have addressed how educated, urban middle-class women use modern information and communication technologies to advance themselves and participate in their respective local politics.

Rege's (2004) work includes a Dalit (i.e., "the broken/oppressed") feminist perspective on social hierarchies. Her study is important because it calls attention to the disempowered voices of marginalized caste, class, and religious communities.

Agarwal (1994) argues that the gender gap between men and women is sharply manifest in the lack of ownership of land by women. Landlessness has a serious economic impact on women especially in rural South Asia. In South Asia, Agarwal argues, access to arable land (at the time of her study, controlled by men) determines a person's economic well-being, and she examines the barriers to women's land ownership and control and how these might be overcome. Agarwal's argument is very insightful because the rural women of India, Pakistan, and Bangladesh profiled in my work may not necessarily draw on land ownership as a source of power for personal advancement (Agarwal 1994) but, nevertheless, value land ownership as a critical identity marker.

My work examines women's various sources of power and how women negotiate with or challenge systems of oppression, including when they are dispossessed of land resources.

Some rural women draw on resources such as informal networks of female farmers, entering into local politics on *panchayats*, or opening shops to sell condiments for personal advancement. As Kabeer and Huq (2010) have argued, love and solidarity among landless women in rural Bangladesh have become powerful tools that women have deployed to improve their lives, change entrenched social structures, and challenge injustices they have encountered.

I use some of the examples described in the studies cited above for my comparative discussion on rural women's *shakti* in South Asia. However, I go beyond describing the obstacles to show how women advance themselves and, in some cases, subvert age-old cultural practices.

The significant contributions of the present work lie in their specificity. I pull apart the particulars of institutional and ideological matrices at work at a given moment in a given place to identify the ways rural women of various ages understand, mobilize, perform, or subvert gender, age, caste, and other social hierarchies in South Asia.

I investigate the extent to which both women of childbearing age and those beyond that age have redefined and used symbolic and literal centers of power to enhance the well-being of themselves and their families while increasing their own power and status. In the chapters that follow, individual women of childbearing age, such as the Muslim 40-year-old Ramijabi Siddi, affectionately called *mohabbathse* (Hindi/Urdu for one who loves and cares for others), and women beyond that age, such as 70-year-old Sumbai Nagubai, a Gowli, express different levels of agency and power in the overlapping spheres of private and public, age, gender, caste, and religion.

1.3 Relevance of the work

Shakti: Rural Women's Power in South Asia will intervene in the debates on women's power by foregrounding how rural women deploy power while also elucidating the structures that prevent some women from participating in processes aimed at women's empowerment.

This book focuses on the different effects of the Indian, Pakistani, and Bangladeshi governments' policies and interventions on their respective and distinct groups of rural women. The study addresses India through its ongoing efforts to empower women, the formation of scheduled castes/scheduled tribes (STs/SCs) to equalize social disparities, and the significant growth of India's economy (though not many citizens have yet benefited from this). The work also examines Bangladeshi liberalizing programs and Pakistan's experiment in democracy (Mumtaz and Shaheed 1987).

This book has broad significance for readers interested in understanding the play of power in tribal society and beyond. The above South Asian countries' central and state governments' efforts at social inclusion, support of human rights, and women's empowerment necessitated the classification of communities into STs/SCs and other backward castes (OBCs), classifications for people granted recognized statuses that can help them access certain government benefits for education, employment, and health care. Also, the respective governments assert they are implementing programs that will empower women and other citizens that have been disenfranchised; such programs include enterprise creation through income-generating projects and the forming of *panchayats* or the equivalent of local communicating governing bodies.

Not only will the findings of this study contribute to public policy, and to broader social and political issues that enhance or restrict people's daily life in South Asia, but they will also elucidate how new forms of governance and projects that promote equity and fairness are playing out in a range of overlapping settings.

This work explores how women acquire new roles to increase the arenas of their self-determination in South Asia's burgeoning public and private spheres. I also detail how various political brokers, villagers, and women navigate social life in uneven social spheres by examining the perceptions of these stakeholders of the newly gained opportunities taking shape as a result of the growth of NGOs and state, central, and subdistrict (*taluk*) government institutions in all three countries.

The study will add to our knowledge of forms of power and deepen the growing literature on women in caste and tribal societies that has developed in the past 20 years (see Jeejebhoy 2002; Waerness 2004; Subramaniam 2009; Sharma 2011). My work also contributes to rethinking theorizing notions of gender, age, politics, and agency, as well as reconsideration of the broad contemporary research on indigenous and rural populations in South Asia.

As this work addresses the entrenched social hierarchies that women constantly face as they seek personal advancement, it also pays attention to the different ages of the women studied. My work specifically focuses on the differences between women who are between 20 and 60 and those who are over 60, in a range of caste and tribal (socially and economically deprived and isolated) rural communities.

Research shows that, in addition to gender- and age-based identity, power structures are formed through social relationships (Kumar 1994; Kasturi and Mazumdar 1994; Gardner 1995). For instance, the multiple power centers formed in South Asia are articulated differently, and at times they contain competing notions of age, gender, religion, and local customs. A focus on outward signs of age and gender does not help us to comprehend fully how young and old rural women create, use, or share power. This work contributes to the growing interest in the study of women's lives as lived in societies with a high percentage of citizens living in rural communities.

This study will challenge and expand prevailing scholarship that either overstresses the success stories of women from the Global South or undervalues women's status, influence, and power there. This historicized and contextualized study shows that arenas of power and status articulation are mediated and negotiated beyond the obvious "gender asymmetry," caste logic, and economic and political marginalization (Gardner 1995: 201) of the women studied. While some senior women seem to be leading more fulfilled and empowered lives now than when they were young and married, there are some young women who, by dint of their enterprising spirit, personal strength, initiative, persistence, and determination, create and share power within their families and communities. Such women then work for self-fulfillment and control resources to improve themselves and others.

1.4 Methodology

This work is a multi-sited, sustained, in-depth ethnographic analysis based on interviews, primary documents from India, and secondary sources from Pakistan and Bangladesh that focus on the profiled women's personal narratives, the women's biographies, and detailed analysis of the status and power of women in the three countries of the study. Additional information is based on participant observation, census data, interviews of focus groups and officials of *panchayats*, and documents from *panchayat* offices.

Between June 2009 and August 2012, I started to investigate the historical phenomenon of rural women's status and power, exploring how caste, tribe, age, and social hierarchies play out, and what efforts to promote or hinder women's empowerment by government, NGOs, communities, families, and individuals were meant for women. I interviewed young and senior women and men from 50 communities in North Karnataka, India, to unearth and interpret their understandings of the roles, power, and behavior of women in their societies. I use these data to clarify women's agency in appropriating and shaping new forms of power and status while they interpret their actions in light of the importance of their heritage. In order to understand the historic changes of rural women's role and status and how these changes have come about, I focus on biographies of women from Siddi, Lambani, Vaddar, Korovar, Gowli, and other OBC communities in Karnataka, India, and in communities in Bangladesh and Pakistan.

With the help of census data, I analyze information about women who work in the organized and in the unorganized labor sectors. I combine census analysis with in-depth interviews of women and men to verify if the women are performing roles similar to or different from their traditional ideal roles, and I analyze the sociohistorical roles and role norms in rural India to discover local notions of women's ideal roles and status. This approach enables me to examine whether those ideals are changing or tend to be rigid. As I explore this, I also examine the social contexts in which those roles and status are shaped.

Further, by collecting data on individual women, I use their biographical information to analyze the specific moments in their lives when they took on new roles and how these new roles have affected their status in their families and communities. I also used the data collected to explore forms of individual and community power structure and how *budavantas* (Telugu or Kannada), *jantos* (Hindi), and *hiriyarus* (Kannada) for elders, wisemen, or ancestors (as in some cases when used by Siddis) acquire and use their power. Also, I examine the roles, activities, and influence of economic elites, such as moneylenders, wealthy landowners, and religious leaders with high ritual status, to verify the extent to which their decisions allow or constrain women's access to and use of power.

For example, an NGO member named Loyola Vikas Kendra, in Mundgod, trained Renuka, a 30-year-old Vaddar woman from Mainalli, to become a vermin compost farmer (Vaddars are traditionally the stonecutter caste). Renuka was at first successful as a compost farmer. She took a loan to construct pits for her compost project and began to sell her product to farmers in Mainalli and its neighboring communities. When her production increased, she became the target of some men politicians who wanted their cronies to be more successful than she was. Renuka said, "One day, the men who sell the earth worms suddenly increased the price of the worms," and when she said she could not buy worms for any more than 400 rupees per kilogram, the men threatened to sell the worms to other compost farmers. Without the worms she could no longer continue farming. When her clients could no longer get compost supplies from Renuka, they found other sources; as a result, Renuka's business began to fail. She later learned that friends of local politicians (the politicians were Havik Brahmins) wanted to start their own compost farm, and those politicians influenced the worm suppliers to take business away from Renuka.

Despite Renuka's training and the loan she took to play a new and empowered role in present-day India, long-standing social hierarchies and cronyism obstructed her and obstruct other women's exercise of entrepreneurship. Renuka's case helps us understand social hierarchies that create and reproduce power inequities in India's rural communities.

I admit that these selected women do not represent all rural women in South Asia. At the same time, as I compare the case studies from diverse tribal/caste communities of women who use and express multiple forms of power, my data elucidate the historical contexts in which these women live, as well as the women actors themselves, who are concrete examples of how an understudied community of women play complex and important roles to articulate their new rights to equality in South Asia.

1.5 Summary of chapters

This introductory chapter presents the current study's theoretical framework, methodology, and relevance, as well as the new perspectives it provides on South Asian rural women's power and influence. It also includes a literature review.

Chapter 2 addresses the complexity and variety of the lived experiences of women from different religious and cultural backgrounds. I begin by focusing on the historical context in which these women live, and the social classifications and conceptions of caste identity for SCs, STs, OBCs, and other minority groups to which these women belong. I also examine the different impacts of the partition of the British-ruled Indian subcontinent after independence in 1947 on large communities in the three subject countries. This chapter illuminates these complex and varied historical events and the sociopolitical systems in which minority groups in Pakistan and Bangladesh, and Indian caste and tribal rural women, live and work.

In Chapter 3, I explore the interventions and policies of the central, state, and district governments of Bangladesh, India, and Pakistan in providing social and political rights and other resources to women. It is here that I address NGOs and how they engage in development programs for rural people. I explore examples such as inheritance systems and the reservation of seats for women on *panchayats* and other local governing bodies.

Chapter 4 examines the varying impacts of recent social and economic changes on women between the ages of 20 and 60, and how they tap resources to participate in local politics and economic activities to effect change in their lives as they help to transform their societies and, at times, their culture's values. The women's roles range from presidents of *panchayats* to members and leaders of *sanghas*. Other women are hostel wardens, social workers, and healthcare providers (also called Accredited Social Work Activists, or ASHAs, in India). I also address women involved in informal economic activities such as agriculture, basket weaving, pottery, small-shop ownership and tailoring. The analysis shows how young women marshal different resources to enable them to advance themselves and help improve the social and material conditions of their communities.

Chapter 5 focuses on the complex ways that individual rural women aged 60 and above draw on social, sacred, and other cultural resources to advance themselves and provide for others. In this chapter, I discuss the importance of cultural values that combine with economic and social change either to constrain or to open women's access to public influence and community life. Further, I investigate the extent to which senior women mobilize resources, including social services and material resources, for personal advancement.

Chapter 6 discusses how my study contributes to a new understanding of ways in which rural women view themselves and leverage their power, status, and influence by drawing on new opportunities and resources available to them provided by their governments, local civil societies, and international organizations. I address how some women have emerged on the local and subdistrict (*taluk*) political landscape to deploy varying forms of *shakti*. I also call attention to how the women profiled function within powerful institutional constraints that have underpinned and sustained systems of patriarchal politics.

In the study as a whole, I stress the role of women in both the formal and informal economies in their respective communities, and point out rural women's creative solutions and imaginative activities in the face of years of subordination under the entrenched patriarchal and other social hierarchies in South Asia.

2
History and Identity

This chapter focuses on the diverse groups of people occupying minority or marginalized status in South Asia. I explore the various impacts that the British-led Indian subcontinent's partition into India and (originally) East and West Pakistan had on large numbers of such people as well as on communities that live in socially, economically, and politically marginalized areas. While dividing people through the partition along religious, caste, and tribal lines created minority groups in South Asia, the partition further reinforced the marginalization of the people displaced by the partition itself and the hardships that followed.

This chapter also examines the sociohistorical contexts in which communities have been classified according to caste, tribe, and class. The discussion thus elucidates the social values and the religious and political structures that either enhance or restrict women's lives and their economic and political participation in Pakistan, Bangladesh, and India and addresses the interplay between women's desires and aspirations, on the one hand, and the traditional expectations for women, on the other, in the rural areas of the three countries.

I also provide a brief comparative gender analysis of some of the castes and tribes to highlight power relations between men and women in order to link the discussion to the complex ways in which power plays out in rural societies.

Since the partition had different impacts on the countries that emerged, I will start by commenting on how Pakistan was affected before I touch on Bangladesh and India.

2.1 Partition and castified structures in Pakistan

The partition of the Indian subcontinent in 1947 fractured cultures, faiths, and families. Zahoor (2009) describes ways in which the Urdu word *muhajir* (immigrant/outsider) is often heard in the Punjab area in Pakistan since partition. One may hear a person say, "I am a son/daughter of this soil," to differentiate the speaker from the audience. Then the speaker may ask, "Mein koi muhajir haan?" (Am I a *muhajir*?) or "Tu muhajir tan nahin?" (Are you a *muhajir*?). This apparently innocent statement masks years of history in which large numbers of peoples on the subcontinent have suffered and continue to suffer acts of discrimination on the basis of faith, gender, caste, tribe, or geography.

Gooptu (2002) states that the categories of insider/outsider that occasioned the partition experience also created, in the local and national imagination, debates and attitudes about the inclusion or exclusion of religious and linguistic groups. Thus, in the national politics across South Asia, there has been a concern about aliens and legitimate citizens.

Some South Asian scholars have recently turned their attention to forms of marginalization that can be traced back to the partition of the subcontinent. Scholars of the partition all agree on the various challenges and opportunities that those who were displaced had to contend with. For instance, Mehdi (2007: 55–84) argues that the partition was traumatic and daunting for millions of people. Mehdi gives examples: "Among the displaced, approximately seven million Hindus and Sikhs were forced to leave their home in Pakistan and migrate to India and nearly seven million Muslims were uprooted from their homes in India and forced to migrate to Pakistan" (2007: 55–56). These people had become aliens in their own land. Mehdi continues, asserting that the partition impacted the political, cultural, social, economic, and religious landscape of South Asia. The immense impact on millions of the inhabitants resulted in ways in which people were "stripped of their historical, geographical and cultural identity. The only identity that mattered during partition's violence and after was religious" (Mehdi 2007: 55).

Kaur (2007) examines the "human face" of the experiences of Punjabi Hindu and Sikh migrants from Pakistan who resettled in Delhi. Kaur provides detailed studies of the lives of refugees in both new-built localities, such as Lajpat Nagar, and areas that had formerly been Muslim, such as Karol Bagh.

An estimated 75,000 women were abducted and subjected to sexual violence in Pakistan in 1947 (Gooptu 2002). Other forms of violence were also committed against women. Gooptu's analysis highlights differentiated refugee experiences resulting from social status and gender. The satellite towns and refugee housing colonies provided different amenities for different classes of refugees. "The class differences visible during the population movement," Kaur (2007: 166) states, "became further entrenched when permanent housing projects were undertaken on such basis. This ensured that refugees were reinvented in their old class of social stratification." The social dislocation of partition-related migration created conditions in which social hierarchies remained more or less intact (Kaur 2007).

Pakistan's economy, though making some improvements, until the last ten years, was based on agriculture that was controlled by village elders

(Kaur 2007). The government's political, economic, and social interventions have often been thwarted by political instability, natural disasters, including serious earthquakes, and religious militancy.

The Indian and Pakistani governments also attempted to bolster patriarchy in the wake of partition. During partition, both formal and informal victimization of women took place. Kaur reveals that a separate refugee colony for young widows was established in Lajpat Nagar, Pakistan, in which the state closely monitored its inhabitants' social behavior. The women were not allowed to go outside its boundaries without the permission of the female social workers. "The state," Kaur argues, "reproduced [familial] notions of honour through abstinence and seclusion by fulfilling the role of the patriarch. The honour at stake was no longer that of an individual or family, but rather that of the Indian nation ... the state had to restore 'normalcy' by reproducing familiar practices. Thus the state attempted restoration of all that was lost during Partition, including the restoration of the social landscape" (2007: 252). Research on refugee resettlement in Lahore (Talbot 2006) reveals a similar guardianship role, with the state like a family patriarch controlling female sexuality through arranging early marriages of young female orphans.

2.2 Autonomy and minority groups in Bangladesh

At the time of partition, present-day Bangladesh was called East Pakistan, a Muslim majority nation that became independent Bangladesh in 1971. When Bangladesh gained its autonomy, Biharis (ethnic Muslims often called stranded Pakistanis, living in Bangladesh) were given the option of staying or being repatriated to Pakistan (Mehdi 2007). It is believed that about 529,669 Biharis chose to go to Pakistan. In 1976, the Bangladesh Foreign Ministry offices indicated that 47, 550 Biharis were still living in Bangladesh. Among them, about 18,000 were reportedly repatriated to Pakistan in 1979 (Farzana 2008). A further 9,000 were repatriated in 1982 and 325 in 1993. Since then, the process has virtually stopped.

The Biharis who remained in Bangladesh live in 66 camps scattered across Dhaka, Chittagong, Saidpur, Rangpur, Khulna, and other districts. Farzana (2008: 1–19) adds the Chakma, Marma, Rakhain, Kol, and Vil to the minority groups in Bangladesh. Many were born in the camps also inhabited by Biharis, almost all of the inhabitants of which suffer because of lack of water, sanitation facilities, community care, and education (Haider 2003; Farzana 2008). Most Biharis, according to Farzana (2008), are confined to their camps, do not own land, and tend to be daily wage laborers. In the Millat Camp in Mirpur, some of the Biharis are sari makers, while some of the seniors beg to support themselves and some of the unmarried girls are forced to engage in prostitution to support themselves (Farzana 2008).

Despite its internal conflicts from religious extremism, Bangladesh has made some dramatic political, economic, and social improvements for its citizens. The country has benefited from the services of NGOs and the United Nations. The central government has also been aggressive in implementing reform programs aimed at creating development opportunities for Bangladeshis.

Since 1971, the Bangladeshi central government has promoted an expressly nationalist ideology, according to which the citizens of the country belong to one nation regardless of caste, tribe, or faith. While Islam is held to be the dominant faith, social equality is not often addressed. Methos, Beharas, Jolas, or those generally called Muchi or Rishi are among the castified minorities (see the following discussion about autonomy and minority status in Bangladesh). Williams (1972) points out that there is evidence of marginalized groups belonging to castes in the Khelna and Satkhira districts. The groups include the Bajondars, the Bhagobenees, the Dhopas, and the Patnis.

Minority–majority divisions along caste/tribe and religion exist also in India. As recently as between December 1992 and January 1993, the various attacks on Muslims in the Indian state of Maharashtra underscore the minority–majority divide that bedevils South Asian countries. Banerjee points out that Shiv Sena, a regional Hindu political party in Mumbai, launched a series of attacks on Muslims in defense of "Hindu cultural dominance" (1996: 1213). According to Banerjee (1996), the political actors wielded trishuls (the trident of Lord Shiva, the destroyer) and called on the divine power to help them defeat the insurgence of Islam. Such communal violence, Banerjee contends, was framed within the logic that "the only true India is Hindu India" (Banerjee 1996: 1213).

Internal classifications within religious groups also exist in South Asia, as discussed below.

2.3 Religious and caste/tribe divisions in India, Pakistan, and Bangladesh

Divisions between South Asians along majority–minority and citizen–refugee dichotomies are not limited to the results of the partition. Internal rankings within religions based on their own classificatory systems also foster divisions between people in South Asia.

While in Islam, piety before God is considered more important than birth, some Muslims are, nevertheless, ranked differently from others in their societies. As in Hinduism, both Srinivas (1996) and Cameron (1995) contend that there are multiple hierarchies in Islam and Christianity.

For example, generally speaking, those who trace their genealogy to the Prophet Muhammed are considered part of the nobility. In Islamic law, those with wealth and learning, and families in which the Islamic law has been practiced for a long time, are believed to have a higher status than new converts (Ali 2011). There are also sheikhs (chiefs) who have higher status than other Muslims because they are regarded as descendants of those among whom Islam first spread.

Caste in Hinduism, however, entails an ideology of birth. Here one is born into a family and, mainly, into an occupationally specific community. The rank, birth, and occupations have ritual purity. Studies have found that both Pakistani and Bangladeshi citizens who live in rural areas are often governed by castified categorizations. It is for this reason that when wealthy landowning Muslims lose their property, they are seen as falling into the sweeper caste in Pakistan, and in Bangladesh, it is "untouchables" who serve as household servants, pig breeders, street vendors, and so on (Streefland 1979). Many large groups of people, on becoming members of the newly formed Pakistan and Bangladesh, occupied minority status.

In the period following partition, India, Pakistan, and Bangladesh have followed different paths toward political, economic, and social development. Though all three countries seem to be making progress improving the material and social conditions of their citizens, they continue to face challenges and are beset by poverty, illiteracy, social hierarchies, and forms of communal and religious violence.

India, for example, is not free from most of the challenges that face Bangladesh and Pakistan. India is considered the country that has made dramatic improvements in its economy. In fact, it is regarded as one of the fastest growing economies in the world. India boasts of its advances in information technology, telecommunications, and pharmaceuticals. Nevertheless, India still has millions of citizens who live in socially and economically deprived communities.

2.4 Scheduled tribes and scheduled castes in India

The Hindu system divides people into four major social classes, or *varnas*: the priestly class and intellectuals are the *Brahmins*; the *Kshatriyas* are the rulers and warriors; the *Vaishiyas* are agriculturalists, salespeople, and merchants; and the *Shudras* are servants and laborers. The *varnas* have specific rules about jobs, diet, and marriage partners. Outside of these social classes are the "untouchables," who are called *Harijans* ("God's children") or *Dalits* (the broken or oppressed). *Dalit*, as popularized by Jyotirao Pule, has come to stand for social groups including some Christians as a label of assertion against their oppression at the hands of the economically and politically dominant caste. There are many *jati*, or subcastes, within each Hindu social class.

Caste is a form of social ranking determined by the four *varnas* and their subcastes (Dumont 1980). It is the economically and socially deprived people at the bottom of the caste hierarchy who have been recategorized as SCs (Scheduled Castes), STs (Scheduled Tribes), and OBCs (Other Backward Castes).

STs are communities that fall outside the Hindu caste categorization. They are Indians who like SCs (under the Hindu caste framework) suffer economic, social, and political deprivation. Since both communities lack political, social, and economic facilities to allow them to participate fully as citizens, the Indian Constitution has made provisions to safeguard and facilitate the socioeconomic and political development of castes and tribes. Also, enshrined in the Indian Constitution is the protection of lower castes from educational, social, and economic injustice and exploitation by the economically, religiously, and politically dominant castes (Srinivas 1996).

Previously, caste-based profession was the basis of the rural local economy and this reinforced social and ideological hierarchy. At present some low-caste women resist being considered inferior and do not live and perform the caste roles that were assigned to them by the dominant castes (Cameron 1995: 230). Cameron (1995) and Srinivas (1977) argue that for the past hundred years, tribal and caste women's artisan-related professions have been replaced with other job opportunities. As a result, when women begin to increase their economic power, the intercaste patron–client relationships start to breakdown and the women assert their independence. As the women gain economic power by engaging in income-generating work, they also change the gender inequities and social hierarchies that have marked South Asian societies.

Srinivas (1977) points out that rural women or caste and tribal women began to advance themselves before present-day social and economic reforms in South Asia. He argues that when tribal and caste people begin to shed dietary practices and other ritual behavior associated with their perceived subordinate status, they take on cultural behavior hitherto considered the preserve of Brahminical families. Lower-caste people that engage in Brahminical rituals and cultural practices are described as being involved in Sanskritization (Srinivas 1977: 221). However, at both public and private levels, attitudes toward lower castes still remain in India. While Srinivas' Sanskritization is a valuable way to describe the emancipatory efforts of lower castes, this book also shows that marginalized women are now serving as rural accredited social work/healthcare activists, homeguards, dairy inspectors, and teachers that did not require that they shed some of their perceived lower-caste practices in order to take up these new roles. Also, Srinivas (1977) contends that recent urban migration, education, women's participation in politics, and government and NGO programs have fostered the upward mobility of women, even if they are few. The above scholars underscore the relevance of gender and caste in South Asia.

Gender relations, caste, and geographic location are interrelated in how this discussion explores women's power against the backdrop of patriarchal ideology in South Asia. The analysis focuses on Hindu and non-Hindu women to show how they have struggled on multiple fronts to improve their socioeconomic lives and assert their rights. The analysis will also show

how marginalized communities in order to emancipate themselves have at times migrated to different locations.

Castes and tribal people in South Asia who might have migrated to their present locations tend to use their social memory to change some of their practices, reinforce old ideas, or leave behind important practices and those practices' meanings embedded in the prestige of the past. The communities use their distinct cultural geography to benefit and contribute to the cultural practices of their larger society. The people in those communities are, in some instances, born into castes and tribal communities. In India, castes and tribal categorization tend to be assigned by the government. There are groups of people who have been reclassified as SCs or STs in order to become eligible for government assistance.

Lambanis, Koravars, Vaddars, Gowlis, and Harijans are among other rural Indian groups that have been classified as STs (e.g., African Indians or Siddis), SCs, and OBCs. Indian society defines the people, both men and women, who belong to these communities as possessing habits, behavior patterns, beliefs, dress codes, and practices that mark them as different from the normative, dominant society. Their "ascriptive characteristics" (Cohen 1999: 38) are used to objectify such communities as others.

The Criminal Tribes Act of 1871, enacted by the British, categorized around 150 nomadic and artisan tribal communities as "born criminals." During the Independence Movement, Indian Nationalists called for the repeal of this legislation, and in post-Independence, these tribes were legally "denotified" (Pandian 2008). The lasting stigma of this nomenclature was finally addressed by the central government of India in October 2003. Their present categorizations entitle these groups to some governmental support and amenities, such as rural street electrification, toilet facilities, and ration cards to buy food at subsidized prices. The resolution (given later in this chapter) clarifies some of the official perceptions about Siddi, Lambani, Vaddar, Gowli, and other OBC communities as objectified others.

There were, and still are, personal and collective reasons for the migratory customs and traditions of the above groups. For centuries, until the British imposed their laws on the nomads in the late 1800s, nomadic and seminomadic migratory life became critical for survival among Siddis, Gowlis, Lambanis, and other communities in the Indian subcontinent. Able-bodied members of these groups searched for jobs, land for farms, and partners. As "encroachers" (i.e., people living on or farming land to which they have no legal right), they were sometimes forced to move by the state or by individuals who had power to remove them from the lands they were using. In India's communities, there are castes and tribes, as discussed below, that were and are still landless; they resided temporarily in different places and then moved on. Their values thus reflected a people living nomadic lives.

A distinguishing mark about present-day Gowlis, other OBCs, Vaddars, Koravars, Lambanis, and Karnataka Siddis is that all of their forebears migrated from different parts of the Indian subcontinent to their present locations, and all of these groups are categorized according to specific habits, settlements, and government benefits purported to be available to them. Naik (2000) and Lobo (1983) argue that Lambanis originated in Rajasthan. Gowlis came from parts of Maharashtra; according to Harsha et al. (2003), their ethnobotanical practices attest to this. Koravars, according to Singh (2004), might have arrived in Northern Karnataka from places such as Maharashtra, Andhra Pradesh, and parts of Tamil Nadu. Contemporary Siddis (African Indians) are descendants of various dispersed Africans who arrived in India as part of the ancient trading patterns across the Arabian Sea, the Red Sea, and the Indian Ocean.

Karnataka Habshis/Siddis (Africans), Vaddars, Koravars, Gowlis, Dalits, and Lambanis live in parts of the Western Ghats or the Deccan of India. I discuss the Lambanis in the following section, first addressing, briefly, the Lambani sociopolitical system and cultural practices before focusing on gender relations in their traditional society.

2.4.1 Lambanis (Banjaras)

Lambani/Banjara denotes the profession of transporting, specifically of food grains (Lobo 1983: 40). The hereditary occupation of this group was the carrying of merchandise—including food, salt, dates, coconuts, dried fish, and wood—from location to location on the backs of bullocks. They were also called "'Laman'—a word derived from the Sanskrit word 'Lavan,' meaning salt" (Naik 2008: 2).

Banjaras or Lambanis originated in northern India as nomads who traveled and settled in different parts of India. For a greater part of their history, Banjaras have been nomads (Lobo 1983: 41). According to Naik, the difference in their names depends on their place of settlement (Naik 2008: 2). Some were traders for the indigenous chiefs and people of the northwest, especially during the Muslim invasions from the northwest of India (Lobo 1983: 42). Traditionally, they also specialized in being bards and genealogists.

Some community leaders among the Uttara Kannada Lambanis assert that the Koppal Holi (as they celebrate it now) was their first observance of Holi (a Hindu spring festival of colors that celebrates a good harvest), and that they later began to celebrate it in their own *tandas* (local settlements) and villages (Naik 2000) in Karnataka, in South India. According to Naik, the Lambanis "seemed to have adopted the festival and been influenced by the local Hindus, the majority community surrounding them" (Naik 2000: 43). Naik (2000: 42–43) argues that we have no proof the Lambanis/Banjaras of Karnataka celebrated Holi centuries ago, when they lived in Rajasthan, a state in the north.

Naik also states that some Lambanis might have settled in Sindh and Baluchistan in Pakistan before they migrated to Karnataka (2008: 10).

2.4.1.1 *Family structure*

The Lambani family structure points to the significance of the power structure at both the household and community levels. Lambanis tend to have a joint family system in the *tanda*, though nuclear families are also common among them.

Widow remarriage is allowed in all of the *tandas*. Marrying the wife of a deceased brother used to be practiced among them, though this has now been prohibited by the Dharma Parishat (Indian Social Reform Law).

2.4.1.2 *Sociopolitical structure*

The Lambani community has its own social and political structure. Every *tanda* has its own administrative setup. The Lambanis' setup is called a *goar panchayat* (also *samaj*). It is headed by a *nayak* (also *naik*), who works with the *kabhari* (secretary) and *davsan* (senior men). Other members form the *panch* (Naik 2008: 96). The *goar panchayat* members settle criminal cases (*nasab*), property disputes (*hasab*), and inter-*tanda* conflicts (*malao*).

The *goar panchayat,* in the traditional *tanda* context, is the seat of justice. The "members of the *panchayat* committee are recognized as infallible," according to 63-year-old Shantavva Venkappa Lambani (personal communication, 17 June 2010).

Formerly in the *goar panchayat,* there were distinctions between the leader (the *naik*) and the led (the rest of both the council and the *tanda*). The *naik*'s "role was more that of coordinating the activities of the group for which he was rewarded. But this did not lead to concentration of wealth in one person or household" (Lobo 1983: 49). This role of the *naik* is evidenced even from the present position he occupies in the *tanda*. He is still the one who coordinates and directs, but is no longer the one who may have absolute power to exploit other members of the *tanda* (Lobo 1983: 50).

In the past, the *naik* was considered a symbol of group solidarity. The *naik* and the *pancharu* (the elders) settled all disputes and decided the course of action to be taken on particular issues. In the past, the *naik* provided leadership in economic, political, and social matters. Now, some Lambani issues are taken outside the *tanda*—for example, to the local police station—for settlement.

2.4.1.3 *Importance of senior women*

In a Lambani legend, during the great Durga Devi famine of 1396–1407, when millions of people and animals died of starvation in the Indian subcontinent (the famine was named after Durga, the mother goddess and mother of Ganesh, represented by the elephant), it was through the benevolence of a Lambani senior woman who had amassed great wealth and owned a million bullocks that her people were saved. Since she saved many people, the Lambani woman earned the title "mother of the world" (Gazetteer of the Bombay Presidency 1991).

According to Shivabhai Marikamba, a 62-year-old Lambani oral historian from Kamal Nagar, Lambani elderly women are treated with reverence (personal communication, 16 June 2009). Shivabhai continued to point out that Lambani elderly women are like gods—the care that is given to divinity is extended to them. Piety is thus actualized not only through rituals performed by male religious specialists, she added, but also through how Lambanis revere senior women. When Lambani adults care for their young and old, they increase their sacred resources, which in turn guarantees their well-being in their old age, according to Shivabhai (personal communication, 16 June 2009).

In Arishnageri, senior women continue to be birth attendants for their society. When a woman gives birth, "elderly women present rice to the mother and new clothes to the child" and offer to the local deities a prayer song known as Volang (Naik 2000: 25). According to Shivabhai, elderly women are respected also because of their good behavior and their important ritual role as singers at community shrines in the *tanda*. Shivabhai's statement shows that a sound moral life is an important part of the Lambanis' notion of power in their community.

2.4.1.4 *Status of women*

Naik contends that the status of Lambani women is as high as that of men (2008: 17). He gives examples of how women and men occupy the same status in Lambani society. During marriage ceremonies, Naik argues, a special amount of money is put aside to be given as a present to senior women in the community. Senior women may be revered by Lambanis, but they were excluded from the village council or *samaj/goar panchayat* in all of the *tandas* where I conducted my research. Despite legends that show that senior women are important, they do not share political power with the all-male *goar panchayat*.

Naik continues that, in marriage ceremonies, great respect is given to the bride. Such public acknowledgement of the importance of the bride "is most visible in the Lambani society" (2008: 17).

According to Naik, the Lambanis' devotion to goddesses highlights the role and status of motherhood and womanhood. Such sacred status, according to Naik, is furthered by the Lambani legend about a senior female's magical prowess and her generosity toward her people.

While it may be true that Lambanis worship goddesses, it is not necessarily true that such worship translates into a conceptual framework in which women's status is equal to that of men. The series of legends in which ideal versions of women at times sacrificed all they had to help their community cannot aid us in understanding the complex structural and ideological forces against which women work for personal advancement.

Further, in every one of the Lambani *tandas* (about 12 communities) that I visited, I did not find a single place where women served on the *goar panchayat*. All of the men and women I interviewed provided various reasons for women's lack of participation, but all had religious or ideological underpinnings to their reasons.

I will comment next on a female member of a *panchayat* (the traditional form of local self government in most of South Asia) to illustrate how women face obstacles as they try to assert their newly gained power. Lambani women who serve on *panchayats* perform roles that differ significantly from the traditional activities that other Lambani women are known to perform in Uttara Kannada (North Karnataka).

Chennama Lambani is a 28-year-old woman, educated up to the seventh standard, who, though she has government backing for her political activity and position because of the legally required female quota for *panchayats*, is, nevertheless, not allowed to play a significant role on her village council (the *goar panchayat* or *samaj*). There are about 1,150 people in the village of Arishinageri, where she lives.

Chennama was one of 11 *panchayat* members—five men and six women—and was elected to the *panchayat* as a result of her good relationships with people in her community. In her interactions with members on her *panchayat*, Chennama said that, when she spoke, the men on the *panchayat* listened to her because of her educational background. According to her, it was through her intervention that a nursery school was established in her community by the state government of Karnataka.

However, although she was important in the community and considered herself equal to the men, she could not sit on the *samaj* because it is a traditional village council constituted exclusively by men. The *samaj* is like a court; the women sit outside while the men hold meetings in the temple of Marikamba/Maryiamma. The men in the *tanda* use legends to explain the reason why women neither go into the temple nor belong to the *goar panchayat*. According to a legend, a Marikamba priest Sevabhai (also called Sevalal) once entered the temple to offer *puja* (worship or prayers). That day he had warned the temple's devotees, including his family, that he was going to heaven at the invitation of Marikamba, the goddess. Thus, when he entered the temple, he would lie down as a lifeless body, and during that time, nobody should cry or touch his body. After his mother had waited for him to emerge from the temple, as he always did, she entered the temple and, on seeing the lifeless body of her son, she touched it. Sevalal's soul did not return to his body, and he remained in heaven. In light of this ancient story, women were banned from entering the inner sanctuary of Marikamba's temple, and the temple space was reserved for men. It is there that they hold court to discuss matters that affect their *tandas*. (Despite the fact that Chennama once helped to secure five *lakhs* [about $11,000] for refurbishing the temple, she and other women are barred from entering).

The *tanda* village council is similar to other village councils across rural South Asia that are constituted by men. The council members and their communities use religious and social ideologies to justify the exclusion of women from the council. Those views underpin how their societies have structured men and women's roles. The ideology of sexual division is used to explain and legitimize differential participation of men and women in the governing bodies and access to critical resources (Bourque and Warren 1981: 162).

Occasionally the village council explained the reasons for its decisions to Chennama. For instance, when she applied for a development project for her village and other communities, the *samaj* had to give its approval before the government projects could be implemented. There have been times when the council members told her that a drainage system approved by the Karnataka state government would be delayed because the *samaj* needed more time to assess the significance of the work.

Although Chennama does not participate in the *samaj* deliberations, she indicated that she had challenged some of the men's decisions when she thought they were wrong about an issue. For example: On 7 July 2012, Chennama narrated an incident about a woman in her village whose husband had abandoned her and their children. When the wife had not heard from her husband for 12 years, she was advised to file papers to report that her husband had died so she could qualify for government assistance for widows. Before she filed the papers, however, a male official informed her *tanda* elders about her plan. The village council summoned her and found her guilty of dishonoring her husband, so it fined her about 3,000 rupees. To Chennama, that was a great injustice. She rallied other women protestors against the village council, but the council did not change its decision against the woman who had wanted to file a complaint against the husband who had abandoned her.

The *goar panchayat* continues to wield immense power in the *tanda*. In an interview on 16 June 2012, a *naik* from the Arishinageri *tanda* stressed that members of the village council abide by very strict rules and that those who break the rules can be ostracized from the community. Such severe penalties, he maintained, will not be imposed on women because they are not members of the village council. For instance, he said if a Lambani stole crops from someone's farm, the thief would be made to pay a heavy fine. If the person fails to pay the fine, the *samaj* could impose other punishments on the person; for instance, on orders from the village council, no one in the community will visit to sympathize with the person if a relative dies or help if that person gets into a serious accident and needs assistance, for example, to go to a hospital.

Despite the village council's power, Chennama maintained that her role as a *panchayat* member has accorded her new, if still limited, opportunities to interact with government officials and other professionals outside her community.

Shanta Prabhu Burgi is another example of an educated Lambani woman who has been trained as a social worker, but appears to be ineffectual in her own *tanda* because of patriarchal norms.

Shanta Prabhu Burgi, a 38-year-old social worker in India, is also the coordinator (*sahayogini*) of a cluster of villages that have *sanghas*. She is a widow who lives in the Lambani *tanda* in Mundgod. After training as a social worker, she became a supervisor for a group of *sanghas* for the Jesuit institution, Loyola Vikas Kendra, in Mundgod. Shanta started as a nursery school (*balwadi*) teacher and later was promoted to coordinator for SHGs. Her SHG training entailed the development of leadership skills to set up *sanghas* in rural communities and empower people to engage in ongoing projects. According to Shanta, she also received legal training, letter-writing training in administration and legal correspondence, health and hygiene education, and children's healthcare education from Child Fund in India, the Indian NGO. She studied up to the tenth standard.

Shanta helps her community by encouraging parents to send their children to school. She puts poor children in schools that are run by Jesuit priests and Catholic sisters. At times, she helps the sick by taking them to a doctor.

Due to the lack of an adequate public transportation system in the remote areas where she works, Shanta and some of the other *sahayogini* walk many miles to discharge their duties. She said that the sheer distance they have to travel makes their work very tedious. Shanta, like other women who seek to help people in rural South Asia, may be determined and strong to discharge her duties, but she and women like her always face transportation difficulties. Also, Shanta said, "although I have the authority to counsel or report abusive husbands and drunkards to the police, I cannot do the same in my own community" because of her lack of influence on the decisions of the *goar panchayat* of her *tanda* in Mundgod.

Despite her power and influence as a Lambani *sahayogini*, there have been times when she disagreed with policies of the community council, but she could not challenge them because the council consists entirely of men. For instance, some time ago she reported an abusive husband to the police, and most of her *tanda*'s community leaders reprimanded her for her actions. According to the leaders, it was the responsibility of the traditional leaders—not women—to deal with anyone who contravened their community's laws.

Shanta said that, unlike the attitude toward her of people in her own community, she is respected in other areas where she serves as a social worker and a coordinator of *sangha* groups. The dilemma she faces is similar to that of Chennama (the *panchayat* leader in a predominantly Lambani community, addressed earlier). As a woman who wields new power, Shanta continues to face entrenched patriarchal obstructions when she wants to enforce women's rights among Lambanis.

In clarifying the disparity of power in her *tanda*, Chennama and Shanta said that their position on a *panchayat* or *sangha* allowed them to sit with politicians and other government officials of Karnataka, but they did not have the same political clout in their own communities. For instance, Chennama said that she was able to invite engineers and government officials to attend meetings, and they responded to her invitations. Chennama said that the "broader sphere of interaction comes with more prestige than that of the village council led by old men" (personal communication, 3 July 2011). In Chennama's case, we see a woman who has used the opportunities she had to create roles and influence beyond the traditional women's roles in a Lambani *tanda* even though she could not participate in critical decision-making processes in her village council.

2.4.2 Gowlis

The Gowli community is another caste group in Karnataka. Gowlis also have their own sociopolitical system, though one that at times elects women, such as Savakka Bin Yappa, 47, and Janubai Kokre, 50, to their village councils.

Gowlis (who are OBCs in Category 1) generally live in the forest areas of Uttara Kannada (North Karnataka) with their cattle and buffaloes. Traditional Gowlis produce and use milk, buttermilk, ghee, and honey. Some of them are small-scale farmers who produce cotton, paddy rice, and vegetables. Most Gowli men wear *lungi*, shirts, head turbans, and beaded necklaces. Rural Gowli women wear saris in a *shepoti* style (close-fitting) that allows them free movement to graze their animals. The women wear rings around their legs and wrists, and on their ear and necks, big, beaded ornaments. Some of the men also have their ears pierced. Children tend to wear big copper rings in their ears and beads around their necks.

There are about 30 households of Gowlis in Mainalli. They live on a local street called Gowli lane with their livestock, alongside Siddis and Bijapuri (Muslims and Hindus that migrated from Bijapur), Vaddars, and other communities. Other Gowlis live in their own villages, such as Joggeshwarall, Battigeri, Godnal, Basnal, Ashrigeri, Ativeri, Nyasargri, and Karkikeri. Where they live by themselves, they number between 100 and about 600.

Gowlis speak the Marathi language, which is spoken in Maharashtra state; this is because they originally migrated from Maharashtra and other parts of North India, according to such oral historians as 72-year-old Bagubai Bikku Kokre, in Battigeri, and 80-year-old Nagubai Yidege of Basnal.

2.4.2.1 Political system

Like the Lambanis, Gowlis have their own village councils. Their *samaj* leaders are called *jantos* (wise men). A Gowli village *samaj* comprises five *jantos,* responsible for settling issues that affect their communities. They enforce community laws about marriage and ensure there is peace in their villages. Recently, some of their women leaders became members of the *gram* (village) or *taluk* (subdistrict) *panchayat*. The *panchayat* women may be in charge of about twenty neighboring communities. The women's newly expanded area of influence is being used by them to perform different roles. Between 2005 and 2010, Naklubai from Basnal was a *janto* and president of her village *samaj*; later she became a member of the government-backed *panchayat*, which made her responsible for a cluster of 20 villages. At present she is the president of the *panchayat* for four additional villages comprising Gowlis, Lambanis, Siddis, and Vaddars.

2.4.2.2 Dasara

Gowlis celebrate Dasara, Holi, and Ganesh Chaturthi. Dasara is the grandest of their festivals, celebrated for ten days in Gowli communities. Men and women perform customary dances wearing traditional attire. During the dances, the performers invoke the name of Lord Vittoba, a community deity. It is a time when large crowds make public sacrifices to their deities, said Dondobhai, a Gowli from Mainalli. Over the past 20 years, Northern Karnataka Gowlis have rotated the venue of the festival. The host community organizes the public events and meals. Such rotation, Gowli leaders in Mainalli argue, allows the larger Karnataka state to know about Gowlis (personal communication, Dondobhai, 28 June 2009).

It is customary on this feast for Gowlis to distribute the leaves of the banyan/bani/shami tree to one another and go around greeting other Gowlis and their non-Gowli neighbors, wishing them happiness and success.

Also, during Dasara, the married women, the *sumangali* (Sanskrit for an auspicious person or a married woman), donate the milk that is mixed with ritually cooked rice to be distributed to all of the festival's participants. Preparation of the ritual food and other items is done by women, and men only play a public ritual role. Dondobhai further stated that the married women's ritual power is deployed during Dasara because the women's contribution is critical to the festival's success (personal communication, 28 June 2009). Gowli women can also garland and feed the deities and perform the fire sacrifice (*arati*, a rotation of flame in front of the god or goddess). Female religious specialists thus play a critical role during Dasara. The following incident illustrates women's participation in the festival.

2.4.2.2.1 Contested terrain: During the 2009 Dasara festival, when the deity Vittoba possessed the male *pujaris*, or celebrants, two women from Mainalli were possessed by Yellama (Yellama is a southern Indian goddess independent of the Brahminical Hindu deities).

The sacred space on that occasion was occupied by the male religious specialists, who were speaking to some of the participants about Lord Vittoba's wishes for them, while, contemporaneously, the goddess Yellama was communicating through the two Gowli women to other people at the ceremony. The female religious specialists' roles were significant because women provided an alternative to the predominantly male ritual roles in Gowli religious rituals. Within the same sacred space, men and women religious specialists were performing in parallel domains of spiritual power for their worshippers. Such a moment of simultaneous and parallel spiritual possession enabled Gowlis and non-Gowlis to tap multiple sources of spiritual power for themselves. The festival provided an expanded terrain for both women and men to deploy spiritual power to benefit those present.

This is an example of how Gowli women who are religious specialists asserted their version of sacred power in a context that would otherwise be dominated by men. In Pitkin's (1972) perspective on power, the women mediums were able to accomplish something for themselves and others during the celebration as they used their power to express what they believed was important for the community.

Dasara is a festival that, some Hindus argue, is aimed at celebrating the power of women, and the celebration for the Gowlis of Battigeri, Godnal, Mainalli, and Basnal emphasizes the courage, strength, and wisdom of elderly women. The reverence toward women during this festival is based on the belief that it is the woman who can bless or share all the qualities of courage and power with the rest of the family. The celebration also underscores the fact that women are the transmitters and guardians of the integrity and values of the society.

During Dasara, Gowlis collect about 500 rupees from each family and distribute the money to elderly women. Unlike Lambani senior women, who distribute food and other items to people during their religious festivals, it is senior Gowli women who receive gifts from other Gowlis. Eighty-year-old Bagubai of Godnal said that elderly women are respected and cared for among Gowlis because their cultural hero Shivaji received all of his military and political talents from his mother, Jijabai (personal communication, 2 August 2008). Thus, in some of their legends, Gowlis stress the importance of their senior women within their communities. Besides the focus on the importance and power of senior women during Dasara, Gowlis reinsert themselves in a heroic and royal past narrative about Shivaji.

2.4.2.3 Cows and buffaloes

Gowlis also have a special relationship with their cows and buffaloes, their reverence for cows in particular underscores the religiously symbolic and practical usefulness of the animals to humans.

In rural Karnataka, Gowlis use the front of their sleeping area as a cattle and buffalo pen. While, for practical purposes, Gowlis are thus able to keep watch over the animals sleeping next to them, cows (according to Takumbai Janum, a 65-year-old woman of Ativeri) intervene in human affairs by warding off misfortunes and insuring the health of their owners. The animals also provide financial security and status for Gowlis (personal communication, 20 June 2009).

Gowlis contend that their animals are as important as humans. Animals are given the front rooms in each family's house because they are thus able to signal the arrival of strangers or visitors at night. According to Takumbai, besides the animals alerting the households that a stranger or, at times, a thief has entered the house, cows give milk that their owners can then sell; so if Gowlis have enough cattle, they will not need to work in the fields, as Gowlis who have no cattle must do.

Most importantly, their cattle and buffaloes bring blessings to their household and so are like deities to them. Takumbai said that such deities deserve to share physical and symbolic space with humans. Their cows are life givers because they participate in divinity and provide channels of communication between humans and their deities.

The stories and legends Gowlis weave about their livestock point to the importance to them of their animals and, at the same time, stress the role of the women who care for their livestock. The following is an example: A woman named Gagamma took 50 cows and 20 buffaloes for grazing. The buffaloes went into a pool of water to swim while the cows stood by the edge of the pool. At that moment a tiger tried to attack the cows. Suddenly, a bull, using its horn, butted the tiger. The tiger got frightened and ran away. Gowlis have variants of the above legend.

Despite the heroic stature of women in their legends, Gowli society is patrilineal and patrilocal and, in Karnataka, women are excluded from their village community councils except in Basnal and Joggershwarall. Also, similar to other societies, Gowlis regard a menstruating woman as ritually unclean.

According to Sakubhai Biru Yidege, a 45-year-old woman from Jainmuri, men may be religious leaders and spiritual specialists as *pujaris*, but it is the women who keep the family money, disburse it, and perform domestic rituals (*puja*). Sakubhai contended that it is the work of the women that provides steady sustenance for the family and society.

The life ways of Gowlis and other communities in rural Karnataka have been affected by new government policies regarding the use of Karnataka forest produce. Gowlis especially have been affected adversely by the forest laws since they have for hundreds of years been nomadic pastoralists. In recent years they have been forced into settled agriculture. Although Gowlis previously grazed their animals over vast areas of forestlands, the Karnataka government has declared large parts of the forest off-limits to grazing. For instance, large sections of forestland between Mundgod and Hubli are now designated as wildlife sanctuaries, including a bird sanctuary.

Under new laws, lands that Gowlis claimed belonged to them have been taken, leading to landlessness and disempowerment (Paul 1992: 9). Some wealthy and powerful non-Gowli landowners have at times dispossessed Gowlis of their parcels of land. Some of the wealthy landowners employ rural Gowlis to work on their lands as daily wage earners; thus, there are cases of families working for a new landowner on farmland that was previously theirs (Paul 1992: 9).

Such limitations on grazing lands have forced some Gowlis to look for other sources to support themselves. Between the late 1990s and the present, Gowli women in particular have been taking microcredit loans to grow crops such as maize and vegetables, while others have small shops.

The new challenges faced by Gowlis are the same for other communities in Karnataka, India, such as the Vaddar/Bhovi. While the two words are synonymous, Bhovi is also used to refer to a Vaddar community leader.

2.4.3 Vaddars/Bhovis

The *bhovi* is the male leader or headman in Vaddar communities (where they are at times isolated from other groups and live in their own society). The *bhovi* rules with a council of men, though not necessarily elderly. The council consists of people who are presumed to be fair, wise, and levelheaded. They arbitrate in domestic disputes and in intercaste and land disputes. The village council does not bar women from attending their meetings and deliberations, but council membership is open only to men. According to Lalita Krishna Bhovi Vaddar, a Vaddar and president of a *gram panchayat* in Uttara Kannada (Lalita is profiled in Chapter 4), Vaddars allow both men and women to sit in the same area to discuss matters affecting the welfare of their communities. She said this to differentiate Vaddars from Lambani village councils, which bar women from meetings in their *tandas* (personal communication, 16 July 2011).

The Vaddar people claim to have originated in places such as Orissa. Some of their oral historians contend that Vaddars migrated from Andhra Pradesh and other southern Indian states. Among Vaddars are stone workers, earth workers, and agricultural laborers. Some members of the Vaddar/Bhovi community speak the Vaddar language, Telugu (a language mainly spoken in Andhra Pradesh), and Kannada (the regional language spoken in Karnataka). The Vaddars were once nomadic, traveling from place to place, involved in occupations like land leveling for cultivation for farmers, digging earth and canals, road-making, and cutting rocks and stones for the construction of water tanks, houses, and roads (Singh 2004). Vaddars often work on stones, slabs, and in quarries and in Mundgod, Yellapur, and Hubli, Vaddar artisans make grinding stones and other household articles.

2.4.4 Harijans and Dalits

Harijans and Dalits are part of a community that has received much attention. According to the Hindu caste system, they are perceived and treated as ritually unclean and thus are expected to perform menial jobs. Harijan, a term that translates to "Children of God," was adopted and popularized by Mahatma Gandhi to refer to those who were formerly deemed "untouchable." The term Dalit, whose root word "dal" means "broken," "split," or "cracked" in Sanskrit, was popularized by Jyotirao Phule to refer to people who were previously considered "untouchables." Various social groups (including some sections of Christians) have adopted the term as their assertion against their oppression. Harijans are discriminated against because of the presumed social and ritual pollution they transmit, especially to people from an upper or forward caste.

The Indian Dalit movement has protested against the persistence of untouchability (despite its abolition in the Indian Constitution). In northern India the term "bahujan" is also used, which literally means "the majority of people."

Since settlement systems in most Karnataka villages and towns tend to be organized by caste and religion, households can be identified based on their caste/tribe or religion. Harijans often lived in separate colonies so their pollution potential could be contained to prevent contamination of the larger society (Moffatt 1979b). Hence, as stated above, though "untouchability" has been abolished in the Indian Constitution, Harijan households are located in sections of communities called *harijankere* (Subramaniam 2006: 20). The larger rural Karnataka society still interacts with them as untouchables whether they are traveling or at home in their immediate community. When they live alongside other castes and tribes, they often settle in Harijan or Dalit colonies, such as Karkali near Malagi, in Uttara Kannada.

Their traditional occupations include sweeping, clothes washing, leatherworking, and butchering, in addition to other menial and unclean tasks. The Indian government has reclassified them as SC because of the depressed conditions in which they live.

Gupta (2005) asserts that Dalits are not a homogeneous group because there are some among them who present themselves as superior to other Dalits while "marginal and landless [Dalit] laborers are more concerned about economic exploitation" (2005: 418). Gupta's point has broad significance because, within each of the castes and tribes, there are members who perceive themselves as superior to others within their own caste.

Despite these self-elected differentiations, the Indian government deals with them as a single group that needs social and economic improvement. Their new status enables them, like other STs, SCs, and OBCs, to have increased access to health facilities, education, and participation in local politics (Henningham 1981).

Though the Indian Constitution has abolished "untouchability," implying that Harijans/Dalits would no longer be compelled to perform "polluting" jobs because of their caste, they still tend to be sweepers, agricultural laborers, leatherworkers, and so on (Madan et al. 1971). Owing to the low status they occupy in the caste system, there are places they do not visit on their own, and they are often not allowed to worship alongside non-Harijans. In such contexts it is the social and religious hierarchy that excludes Harijans/Dalits. In other instances, they and other Indians have been allowed to worship together (Moffatt 1979b).

There are still countervailing forces that challenge the efforts of Dalit rural women to emancipate themselves. For instance, when a Dalit woman named Radha Hulikatti was trained by an NGO to become a seamstress, the goal was to enable her to teach other rural women how to sew. During the second week into her appointment as a teacher, a group of male village elders informed Radha that they did not want her to teach in the village. The reason they gave was that the village council had learned that Radha was a Dalit. They also learned that she was the daughter of a *devadasi* (a woman who from childhood had been dedicated to a goddess or god as a temple prostitute). Radha was perceived as a woman who would bring misfortune to their community. Thus, caste beliefs remained as obstacles to how Radha could exercise her influence and talent.

Radha's story is an example of sociocultural forces that create and reproduce power inequities in South Asia. Radha, upon learning about the objections some people had about her, contacted the NGO that appointed her to the village. The NGO took the matter to the subdistrict (*taluk*) court, and, after the court's intervention, Radha was able to continue her work.

Radha's power stemmed from her own educational background, the skill set she brought to the village to teach other women, and her ability to appeal to higher authorities outside the village (Few 2002). Her *shakti* was manifest in her working with an NGO, which also drew on the legal authority of the court to resolve the matter. Radha's strength and courage sustained her as she was able to work with others to assert power against cultural prejudice. Through the exercise of her abilities, she fought, successfully, for her right as a citizen of India despite the opposition she encountered.

2.4.5 Koravars

Koravars live in the forest areas of North Karnataka. Traditionally, they were basket weavers, musicians, and farmers. Koravars played the *shehanni* (a traditional clarinet or pipe) and drums at marriage ceremonies and at ritual events. The various bamboo, cane, and grass-twine products (Kothari and Manor 1995) made by them are sold at local markets, and the men carry products not sold locally to distant markets.

Their traditional craft has been weaving baskets and ropes made from wild grass. As in the past, the men tend to travel long distances to fetch raw materials such as bamboo sticks and other resources for their crafts. The women tend to have important roles in the manufacturing of broomsticks, baskets, and ropes, and usually stay at home to weave these items. The sexual division of labor seems to be strong and normative among them. It is not surprising that, because the men travel to sell their products, get raw materials, and make deals with customers and sellers, they consider themselves more powerful than their women. Their ability and freedom to travel while the women stay at home has been understood to give the men more control over production and, thus, over household incomes and decision making.

Despite resources that, under the Integrated Tribal Development Programmes, the central Indian government has made available to Koravars, most buy their own raw materials and find their own markets for purchase when raw materials become scarce. These days, most of the men and women are forced to migrate or look for other daily wage jobs as coolies. At times, a few of them, such as women in Ambedkarhoni in Mundgod, open small shops.

The Koravars are now SCs. Though women traditionally did not inherit property, the Hindu Succession (Karnataka Amendment) Act of 1990 allows for daughters to have equal property rights as sons. Other Indian states have also enacted such laws to ensure that women have equal rights in this domain.

Basket weaving is a caste-based occupation that involves both men and women. The economic activities of the women reflect and connect with notions of male and female roles within their culture. The women enjoy basket weaving because they know their craft had been an important source of sustenance for their families and community. There are, however, cultural restrictions on women as to which aspects of the production and sale they can perform. Though village community councils are male-controlled, and thus tend to enhance men's status in Koravar society, some of their women are beginning to contend that the contribution they, the women, make to basket production, for example, is integral to the basket-weaving process as a whole. Thus, the women I interviewed in Mundgod on 23 January 2012 argued that their incomes are essential in supporting their families. According to them, their husbands' incomes were not adequate to support their families.

The sexual division of labor is influenced by the perceptions and values that underpin how and why the labor is divided in the first place. Thus there are economic, political, social, and symbolic events that shape patterns of social interactions and production (Bourque and Warren 1981: 123) in communities that continue working a traditional craft.

The following story provides an example of how a Koravar woman, despite some challenges, is using her hitherto unacknowledged influence to help her family.

Forty-eight-year-old Shobana Koravar and her family live in Ambedkarhoni, Mundgod, where she and other Koravars weave baskets. She belongs to a women's SHG, from which she took a loan to buy bamboo and tools for her trade. Because she weaves in Mundgod, the *taluk* headquarters, she is able to sell her wares in Mundgod, especially on market days. Her husband also carries baskets to distant markets to sell. According to her, the men fetch the bamboo and sell the baskets, while the women weave and stay at home.

In our discussions, it was obvious that though both husband and wife are involved in the same basket weaving, they have different roles in the purchasing and sale of the final product. While Shobana regards her role as being different but equal, her husband sees their relationship as marked by rank difference because he is a man and head of the family. Thus, to him there is a difference in degree of authority, and he wields the higher authority when it comes to matters that affect the family.

Aside from her work in basket weaving, Shobana often traveled with her children in search of jobs, applied for scholarships for them, and, when the children needed medical care, accompanied them to the hospital. She also made time to access resources to enhance the living conditions of the family, especially the children's.

When Shobana's daughter, Yellama, received a hearing aid in 2011, she was able to look for a job outside her parents' home. However, when Yellama started looking for work, her mother Shobana was supportive, but her father opposed his daughter's working away from home. Despite her father's disapproval, Yellama, as of December 2012, was able to find a job on her own as a domestic worker at a lawyer's house outside the community where she lives with her parents.

This description of the dynamics of one Koravar family raises issues of material and ideological conceptions of power such as those in this basket-weaving community in rural India. The father's perspective and behavior were shaped by standards in the Koravar community, wherein the final authority or power resides in the man's sphere. Both husband and wife contribute to the production and maintenance of the family, but the man's privileged ideological position tends to flow from the sociocultural systems (Ortner 1974: 69) that stress rank difference.

When the NGO representative (a woman) who assisted Yellama in getting a hearing aid visited Yellama's family to verify if she was now working, the mother brought up the disagreement regarding Yellama's offer of a job. Shobana asked her husband to tell the NGO personnel why their daughter was still at home, and the NGO representative discovered that the father did not approve of his daughter leaving the house. Shobana's action in the presence of a female authority figure from the NGO, especially one whose organization had provided an opportunity for their daughter, made the husband rescind his opposition. Their daughter was then taken to the location of her new job.

Shobana, like other rural women, has "extended her control, influence, and authority to negotiable and disputed areas of daily life" (Bourque and Warren 1981: 510) among communities where men and women are engaged in joint family production. The above incident is different from examples of women who use manipulation behind the scenes to achieve an objective because that is their only weapon for self-assertion. Rather, it points to a challenge or opposition located and deployed from new arenas of power and influence against a sociocultural ideology that underpins a sexual hierarchy. Shobana's *shakti* is crafted and exercised in the prestige of the Koravar past and of contemporary South Asia.

Shobana also said that she and other women in her *sangha* are gaining more awareness about their rights.

Koravar traditional village councils have always been male-led and constituted. The village council head is called a *hiriyaru*. The *hiriyaru* and his council members settle disputes, give counsel, impose fines on offenders, and, at times, reprimand people who commit antisocial acts. Today, however, especially for the citizens of Ambedkarhoni in Mundgod, *panchayats* and *sangha* leaders have assumed more powers, and thus they are able to help members settle disputes.

Since they are not far from the Mundgod police station, members of the Koravar community find it more judicious and legally binding to report or lodge complaints at the police station. While the residents of Ambedkarhoni can turn to the police, NGOs, and courts to settle domestic disputes if their *hiriyaru* proves ineffectual or prejudiced toward women, other Koravars in remote villages continue to depend on their all-male village councils to adjudicate cases.

2.4.6 Racial minorities: Sheedis (Pakistan) and Siddis (India)

While other rural people deal with caste, tribe, gender, and other class-category matters, Sheedis or Siddis, who are racially constructed and perceived as South Asians of African descent, face this additional identity marker. These African descendants, who are called by different names depending on where they reside, are another community of minority people in South Asia. Siddis are found in Andhra Pradesh, Gujarat, and Karnataka of Southwest India, while Sheedis live in Pakistan; the minority status of Sheedis is inflected with their racial identity in all the societies where they live, just like that of the Siddis of India.

2.4.7 Pakistan: Sheedis

Sheedis are descendants of Africans who live in the Baluchistan and Sindh provinces of Pakistan (Nizamani 2006). Other Afro-Pakistani people live in Lyari Town in Karachi, Pakistan. The forebears of these Africans arrived at different times in present-day Pakistan as soldiers or enslaved people. Most Sheedis may have originated in Zanzibar, Somalia, Ethiopia, and other eastern African nations (Edlefsen 1960). During the Arab rule of Baluchistan and Sindh, between 1200 and 1900, soldiers, sailors, merchants, and enslaved Africans were brought from East Africa. Still other Sheedis, in southern Pakistan on the coast of Baluchistan in Turbat, Pasni, and Makran, trace their ancestry to people from Tanzania, Kenya, and Zanzibar who were brought by the Omani Arabs. When the word *sheedis* was given to residents of Sindh, the word came to mean black people. In Sindh, the word for *sheedi* can be used as a derogatory term used for the poor and for people with darker skin. Such connotations are also found in India.

Like their counterparts in India, Sheedis have adopted local languages and cultural practices but have still retained aspects of their premigration practices. Some Sheedis live on the outskirts of Karachi, in Manghopir, where there is the celebrated *dargah* (Sufi shrine) of Pir Mangho. The annual *urs* celebration at the *dargah,* known as Pir Mangho Urs, is famous for featuring traditions thought to have East African origins.

Sheedis also have social structures into which they organize their lives. They trace their ancestry to Hazrat Bilal Habshi, who was Ethiopian and the first muezzin of the Prophet. Some Siddis are khalifas, considered to be spiritual successors of Sufi saints. Sheedis have Sufi saints, such as Shah Abdul Latif, Saman Sarkar, and Qalandar Lal Shahbaz, who serve as "the staircase" between god and the Sheedis (Nizamani 2006: 32).

2.4.7.1 *Sociopolitical structure*

According to Nizamani (2006), Sheedis have a *wadero* or *patel* as the leader of the community who makes major decisions for his people. The *wadero* was also called the *khalifo, kotar, qazi, jamadar, wazir,* or *charedar*. The Sheedis have a *paro* (settlement) in the village of Rajo Nizamani in the *taluk* and District Tando of Muhammad Khan, in the Sindh province. There are two *firkhas* (sects) among Sheedis: Sunni and Shi'a (Nizamani 2006). Many Sheedis also belong to the Al Habesh Welfare organization, established in 1954 to promote the group's social and material well-being; it organizes seminars and programs on education and health issues for Sheedis (Nizamani 2006: 37–38).

The Sheedi community has a patrilineal descent system. Property and the social role of the father are transmitted to the sons. Although Sheedis have an established sociopolitical structure, it is the NGO Al Habesh Welfare organization that helps to solve issues of tension within the Sheedi community. However, at the family level, it is the *wadero* who still mediates.

The village head of some Sheedi communities is called a *gouda,* who is supposed to be wise and powerful. In other places he is called a *mukhtar.*

2.4.7.2 *Sheedi Jaat*

In addition to practicing their Islamic faith as other Muslims do, Sheedis have a festival that is specific to them, celebrated each year and called Sheedi Jaat. According to Tunio (2010), the community gathers to pay tribute to Mor Sahib, the most sacred crocodile. The Lasi, Hyderabadi, Kharadari, and Las Bela communities gather at the Manghopir area for the festival, which involves ritual activities with spirit possession and cultural dances and the feeding of crocodiles that live at the shrine. The crocodiles were believed to have been given to the Sheedis by their African sufi saint Mor Mubarak (also called Manghopir). The celebrants also sing sacred songs, often led by elderly women or, at times, men. The singing and dancing is often called Dhamal, and the music is a blend of Balochi, Urdu, Gujarati, and Swahili phrases or motifs. In their ritual songs, they use the refrain *Sheedi Bhasha*, which in Urdu means "the black king."

Participants may pledge at the shrine by offering fresh meat, incense, and fruits to the crocodiles. Sheedi devotees sometimes get very close to the crocodiles, believing that, because they are followers of the saint Manghopir, they will never be harmed. During the festival, one person may garland the biggest or chief of the crocodiles, Mor Sahib. Further, the participants may sprinkle color and serve food such as *halwa* into the pond where the shrine's crocodiles live.

Sheedis, as they participate in the festival, are able to renew alliances among themselves and to reaffirm their connection with Africa and Africans, despite the beliefs of some Sheedis, a minority, who believe they came from Oman and other Middle Eastern countries. Since all of the shrine crocodiles live in or near sulfur springs, such places have become healing centers that people with skin diseases visit to receive a cure.

According to the Sheedis, all crocodiles, whether living within or outside the shrine, are regarded as disciples of the Sufi saint Baba Mangho Pir, and, at the death of a crocodile, the Sheedis accord it as much respect and formality as they do to a human being.

2.4.7.3 Economic activities

Some Sheedis are seasonal agricultural laborers. Others, according to Nizamani (2006), do not take money for their daily work; they receive commodities such as food or gifts from their employers. Some Sheedis are shopkeepers; some are cooks (*bowerchis*). Some of the women make traditional clothes and are involved in *Bharat Bharan* (embroidery) (Nizamani 2006: 56). The traditional embroidery is called *gaj*. The women who produce *gaj* earn income to support themselves and their families by sending their products to other villages and big towns. Some Sheedi women prepare and sell different kinds of pickles made from chillis, onions, carrots, and mangoes. Some of the women are involved in singing and dancing (to be discussed later).

2.4.7.4 India: Siddis (Habshis/Abyssinians)

From the seventh century to the early twentieth century, Africans (in India, Africans are called, variously, Abyssinians, Ethiopians, Habshis, and Siddis; descendants of Africans are called Siddis/Sidis/Habshis or Abyssinians) were transported to South Asia as part of the early Muslim Omani Arab and, later, Portuguese, Dutch, English, French, and American slave trade. Commodities on the same trading circuit included ivory, spices, hides, and beads (Alpers 1967; Harris 1971).

Habshis/Siddis (Africans) freed themselves or were freed during different imperial eras under kingdoms and empires in parts of the Western Ghats or the Deccan of India. Although they were brought to different parts of South Asia, many factors contributed to their moving or being moved from place to place. Some Karnataka Siddis are descendants of African forebears who migrated from different parts of the Indian subcontinent to their present locations, while others have moved recently to where they now live. During such migrations (forced and voluntary), religious practices and beliefs, languages, and cultures, as well as general cultural historical knowledge, have been forged and lost as people fashioned their identities (Obeng 2007: 1).

Although some of their forebears achieved fame as merchants, politicians, soldiers, artisans, and musicians, the majority of the Karnataka Siddis are not aware of most of those ancestors. The few who have been brought to their attention include Malik Amber (a military statesman in the eighteenth century); Bava Gor, who became a Sufi saint; Siddi Rehman; and Adam Desai, in whose honor *dargahs* have been erected (Obeng 2007: 20–21).

Siddi racial identity is, in some contexts, a social stigma in India, and Siddis are treated as a homogeneous people who are historically, culturally, and socially an "outgroup." Siddi identity constructions are part of how they see and represent themselves, as well as how the larger society, sociocultural, and historical factors affect their self-construction and self-representation.

Eligibility for government grants and other facilities can be a factor for some people who assume a Siddi identity under STs.

Imam Siddi, General Secretary of the Siddi Development Society, asserted, "About 70–80% of Siddis appear to identify themselves as Siddis first, before their religious affiliation" (personal communication, 15 June 2004). This seems to be a new phenomenon among Siddis, since for years the government dealt with them based on their religious affiliations. Indian society, as well as scholars, has also tended to describe them with reference to their religion.

Siddis, like other tribes and castes, have village councils of elders that have always governed their respective communities. Siddis have a *budavanta* (wise man) who heads the council; the *budavanta* is usually male.

In the next section I will discuss gender relations within Islam as practiced among Siddis in Gunjavatti, and how some women are redrawing the contours of gender and piety.

2.4.8 *Mane Devaru* (Kannada for household shrines or devotional acts for saints/*pirs*)

According to *mulla* Kareem Siddi of Gunjavatti, "Islam does not allow women to enter the main mosque (*jumma masjid*) because it considers them ritually unclean and a cause of distraction to the men" (personal communication, 20 April 2005). Nor does Islam allow women to say *namaz* (prayers) during their menstrual cycle (Kareem Siddi continued), though, on other days, they can perform *namaz* in their own homes.

Women pray for certain favors and may also pledge goats, chickens, handmade articles, and other such items. Jubeda Siddi of Gunjavatti contended that she and her family make their supplications directly at their own household *dargah* without going through an intermediary (personal communication, 25 April 2005). Jubeda and other women from Kendelgari thus circumvent the politics of the mosque to express their Islamic faith at household shrines.

Women play a major role in household worship. To build a *jumma masjid*, which is a very expensive endeavor, many people have to contribute money, time, and effort. However, the building of a household shrine for a saint, such as the African Sufi saint Bava Gor (who has many public shrines in Gujarat and Mumbai), costs less and takes much less labor.

This economic reality points out one way in which necessity produces, or is "the mother of," virtue, as well as providing an example of how Siddis shape their religious practices. If an elaborate and public form of practice, such as building a *jumma masjid*, proves to be too expensive, then people turn to a more economic and more personal, family form of practice, such as building a shrine. Although contributing to a public effort to build a mosque or *dargah* for communal devotion may draw a person closer to the larger community of the faithful, devotion to a household *dargah* may strengthen the household's practice of faith. The creation of a household *dargah* also affords women, men, and children the opportunity to worship as a family without inhibition.

Mahbub Subhani is an example of a Sufi saint's *dargah* (in this case, it is the tomb of the founder of the Qadri Sufi order, Abd-al-Qadir Jilani [d.1166] of Baghdad) in Gunjavatti and Kendelgari. The shrine is a community *dargah* that grants favors to women when they pray to him, but they have to pray from a distance, without entering the mosque or even touching the wall of the mosque. "Many childless women bear children after praying to him," asserted *mulla* Kareem Sab Siddi (personal communication, 20 June 2005).

Though Muslim men and women make sacrifices at the *dargah*, menstruating women must prepare their offerings and give them to men to take to the *dargah*. Muslims consider women impure and forbid them to come into direct contact with the *dargah*. Dube (2001) contends that although women may assert some power when they prepare food and distribute it at home and during ritual ceremonies, they still carry the stigma of purity or pollution taboos associated with food. Hence, such taboos are a reminder of how women's roles are constructed in South Asian notions of ritual purity. Thus, within the Islamic and South Asian constructs of purity and gendered prohibitions, Siddi Muslim women, through the use of household shrines, have created their own sacred places to express their piety.

These women face the same global issues and conditions that all Muslim women face. The particular Siddi Muslim women's response to Islamic discourse on gendered prohibitions helps us to appreciate the dynamic and complex gendered responses that religious people adopt in South Asia and in other parts of the world.

The Muslim women in Gunjavatti have been socialized to internalize dispositions and meanings called *habitus* to act in ways shaped by relations of male domination (Bourdieu 1977). However, and other Muslim women deploy the discourse within Islam to create space (Gaventa 2006) to worship God (*Allah*) at home.

Although household shrines are found in some Muslim households, Hindus tend to have more household deities, called *mane devaru* in Kannada (Obeng 2007).

Jubeda and other women's efforts to create spaces for their self-assertion within religious practices in postcolonial times have had antecedent examples of lower castes that have challenged the assumed superiority of the rural elites and male religious leaders (Srinivas 1977). While the rural women are asserting their rights, they simultaneously create elasticity within South Asian social hierarchies (Gupta 2005: 416). Also, during the British colonial rule especially from the 1930s, the British made some efforts to provide opportunities for lower castes to improve their lives. The British passed laws aimed at removing untouchability associated with the various lower castes (Gupta 2005). After India's independence, there have been many times when lower castes fought against caste hierarchies because the Constitution has introduced measures to promote equal rights for its citizens. Srinivas (1996: 237) argues that since India became independent in 1947, SCs and STs and religious minorities have been making upward mobility socially and politically, although not many women have succeeded in this endeavor.

The above discussion helps to elucidate how social ideologies, cultural symbols, and legends of groups of South Asia shape the lived experiences of men and women to produce power dynamics that marginalize some citizens in rural South Asia. The discussion of the different consequences on various groups of people, especially women and other minorities, opens up new areas of interest in our study of women in South Asia.

Having discussed the ways in which gender power relations are structured and replicated among minorities, tribal groups, and castes, I will now explore the governmental and nongovernmental efforts to reform some of the sociohistorical ideologies that have disempowered women and other communities in rural South Asia.

3
Policies and Interventions

This chapter seeks to elucidate recent and historical policies, discourses, and interventions that have shaped the lives of rural women in Pakistan, India, and Bangladesh, and to identify the unequal impacts of all three nations' interventions on women of different faiths and geographies. I examine relevant processes and programs, including governmental quotas and NGO activities, by focusing on policies affecting, and interventions in, rural communities. In particular, I focus on the local government level, where *panchayats*, or union *parishads*, and *sanghas* serve as the basis for local governance in which women are elected to serve their local communities.

It is also here that I address the impact of the British colonial "notified laws" policy, which classified nomadic people as prone to criminal activity, and how the Indian government is reversing the adverse impact of those laws. I address the different inheritance laws and laws regarding joint management of natural resources that have been put in place to empower rural communities, and the quota system as implemented in Pakistan, India, and Bangladesh to benefit women.

3.1 The politics of quotas

The incorporation of women at all levels of decision making has become one of the South Asian governments' goals of equality and development for all of their citizens. Pakistan, India, and Bangladesh have set up quotas for women in government. The quotas are intended to allow the women to (1) gain access to decision making, (2) empower them, and (3) enable them to contribute to the development of their societies (Kabeer 2005; Subramaniam 2009; Sharma 2011). In Pakistan, 18 percent of the seats in the national assembly are reserved for women (Farzana 2002). Since the passing of the Fifteenth Amendment Act in 2011 in Bangladesh, 50 of the 350 seats in Parliament are reserved for women. In India, depending on the state, 33–50 percent of the seats in *panchayats* are reserved for women, but seats are not reserved for them at the state or national level.

Scholars have repeatedly indicated that women who hold or have held national political office in South Asia tend to fall into one or more of several categories, which Chowdhury (2002: 3) calls (1) women who have a close relationship with a current male leader, (2) women who are a wife or daughter of a deceased leader, and (3) women whose political opportunities have come from many years of party association. Chowdury's conclusions can be applied to Pakistan, India, and Bangladesh.

Not all women political leaders of South Asia, however, have relationships with male politicians. Many rural women make use of the new possibilities to empower themselves, even though others fail to do so. *Panchayats* and *sanghas*, which require that at least one-third of all seats be held by women, provide an opportunity for at least some women to participate in politics at the local level, and thereby assert their influence in the three countries.

3.2 India: The *Panchayat* as a parastatal institution

In 1958, India embraced and promulgated the 1957 International Labour Organisations Convention on Indigenous and Tribal Populations. After 1958, STs/SCs were accorded special status with targeted opportunities and amenities because of their centuries of deprivation. Thus the reclassification of such people was for purposes of both redistribution (sharing of benefits) and recognition (Shaheed 2010: 113).

Not only have such people lived in geographically and socially isolated areas, they have also been historically and economically neglected and at times exploited. They have also been underrepresented in governmental and paragovernmental institutions. The Indian government's efforts have been aimed at reserving seats for SCs/STs and OBCs in political structures of governance at the national, state, district, and local levels. Thus the central government has made provision for representation from tribal and caste communities in political structures, including Parliament and *panchayats* and jobs in the civil service and in educational institutions.

Tribal groups, SCs, and OBCs are being given political and social opportunities through governmental and nongovernmental programs, such as schools in villages; free tuition, uniforms, and bicycles for school children; and discounted hospital fees for retirees, widows, and widowers. For instance, senior citizens who manage to acquire Bhagyalakshmi Insurance, for females of Below Poverty Line cards, are entitled to special benefits, such as free ambulance rescue in medical emergencies, under the government of Karnataka's Department of Welfare of Disabled and Senior Citizens.

Also, SCs/STs and OBCs are issued ration cards to enable the poor to buy food at reduced prices. The Government of India has instituted legislation to promote the education and the economic and political participation of women since the early 1990s (Collier 1998). The 1990s saw an increase in the activities of NGOs in India to enhance women's roles in economic and social institutions. However, though the Ministry of Labor, Government of India, has introduced a program (called the Unorganized Sector Workers Social Security Scheme) to provide old age pensions, accident insurance, and health benefits for all workers, most women workers or retirees are yet to benefit from the program.

The Government of India has also undertaken legislative and policy steps, including the *Panchayat* Extension and Scheduled Areas Act and the draft National Policy on Tribal and Castes (Recognition of Forest Rights) Bill, whose purpose is to enhance the status and lives of minority groups in India. The Scheduled Tribes Act and the Policy for Scheduled Tribes and Recognisation of Forest Rights, administered by the Ministry of Tribal Affairs, propose to right injustices committed against tribal people by restoring their rights to their traditional ways of living.

Mullen (2012) examines 30 years of India's decentralization, which has been aimed at empowering rural people to participate in local politics. The following discussion builds on the analyses of Pal (2004), Mullen (2012), and Subramaniam (2009) by focusing on *panchayats* and *sanghas*. *Sanghas,* as described earlier, are SHGs for both men and women. *Panchayats* are parastatal institutions that have been established by the Government of India as part of its program to decentralize political power and to implement the goal of creating equality for all its citizens, especially women in rural India.

I explore how different women of various ages use female power to build friendships as they advance their causes; I also detail how some women embrace the new opportunities offered by the central government of India and by NGOs.

I also discuss how some women do not make use of such resources. Depending on the communities in which the women live, some are not aware of the opportunities or how to access them. There are also women whose socialization, especially in some Muslim communities, makes them stay at home and allows men to be actively involved in politics. Chhibber (2002) contends that women who are successful at negotiating space and influence at home tend to take an active part in local politics. There are also women who are aware of the intimidation their women friends have encountered on *panchayats* at the hands of male members and thus have chosen not to serve in such organizations.

The 1992 Indian Government Central Act (73rd Amendment) was aimed at providing planning and governing space within the central government at the local and village levels for women and marginalized groups (Pal 2004: 137). The 73rd and 74th amendments to the Indian Constitution demand that, at all state levels, provisions be made that one-third of all seat reservations be given to women in the local governance structure through *panchayats*.

While some women are not formally educated, their abilities to speak in public and unite others for common civic activities are criteria used to elect them to serve on *panchayats*. Through additional training, some of the women have learned how to sign documents. Uneducated and minimally educated women increase their confidence as they participate in meetings and organize others for both civic and political action. Such "decentralized democracy" (Pal 2004: 137) allows *panchayats* that have been thus empowered to "safeguard and preserve the traditions and customs of the people, their cultural identity, community resources and customary mode of dispute resolution" (Pal 2004: 137). Such provisions undergird the respect the government has for the traditions of India's marginalized peoples.

Pal asserts that "the constitution (73rd Amendment) and the Extension Act was aimed at according powers and authority to women and marginalized Indians so that they form (i) *gram sabha* at the village level, (ii) a uniform 3-tier system at the village, block, and the district levels with the exemption for intermediate level in states with a population of less than two million; (iii) direct election to all seats for all members at all levels; (iv) indirect elections of chairpersons at intermediate and apex levels; (v) reservation on the rotational basis for SCs and STs in proportion to their population both for membership as well as chairpersonship of *panchayats* at all levels; (vi) reservation of not less than one-third of the seats and offices for women; (vii) five year term; (viii) fresh elections within six months in case of suppressions or dissolution" (2004: 134). According to Pal, the "seventy-fourth Amendment to the Constitution is part of the Central Act which stipulates that the respective state governments may endow the *panchayats* with powers and authority to function as self-governing bodies" (Pal 2004: 137).

As Pal argues, "power sharing with *panchayats* depends on the political leadership at the state level" (Pal 2004: 140). In the 1990s, several states, including Karnataka, formed the Panchayat Act, under which a financial commission was set up to help *gram panchayats* (village *panchayats*) receive financial support. The Indian government and NGOs' efforts to empower people have, to some extent, encouraged some women and other marginalized people to take up leadership positions. This enables them to be actively involved in the planning and implementation of social and economic development projects at their local and district levels. As a result, it is estimated that between 40 and 60 percent of women and other minorities who have been involved in politics and social improvements have seen a positive change in their visibility and status in their families and communities. In 2000, about 40 percent of Indian women were planning to run for local political office (Panchayati Raj Institutions—A Balance Sheet 2000).

Pal admits, however, that despite the lofty goals of the central and state governments regarding *panchayats*, *panchayat* members, especially women, are often helpless when asking for the power to become involved in decision-making processes as well as when asking for financial benefits that people in their communities demand from them. For instance, in Mavinkoppa, some people did not get pensions because they could not tell their exact ages; for example, an approximately 80-year-old woman did not get pension benefits although her son, at 60, who lives in Haliyal, a bigger town, does collect such benefits. This is an example of how the issuance of pension benefits is at times done arbitrarily in rural India. Census data collectors seemed to have overlooked the woman's age. Also, as of 2010, the Siddis in Mavinkoppa village had not as yet been granted ST status because no government official from the Dharvard District had issued them with documentation or certificates that would have made them eligible for ST status. ST status has been acquired by other Siddis outside of the Dharvard District since 2003.

Indian national law requires *panchayats* to reserve places for SC/ST women at the local and district levels. Seat reservation for STs/SCs allows women to be elected to *panchayats*; however, without adequate political training and effective implementation of government policies, some of the women may sit on *panchayats* as disempowered representatives. Nevertheless, some *panchayat* women, who for the first time have become decision makers in affairs affecting their families and communities, do their job with enthusiasm and optimism.

Systems of patriarchy, caste politics, and local customs at times impede the *panchayats'* work. Suzanne Dovi has argued that increased "descriptive representation of women has to be matched by their increased substantive representation" (2010: 184), and she opts for "preferable group representatives." The preferable group consists of women with a strong relationship with groups of people who have been historically disadvantaged because of race, gender, caste, religion, and so on (Dovi 2010: 215–224).

However, although the efforts made by the Indian government and NGOs are new bids for power distribution and empowerment, unless these organizations translate the relevant documents into local languages, there may not be many qualified women who have adequate levels of formal education, are articulate, have political awareness, and are capable of disseminating critical information to other women in rural India. Thus, other qualities are used as criteria for electing articulate, courageous, respectable, and selfless women as political representatives. Some of these women have become role models for others who have formal education because of their increased presence in local politics.

Despite the Indian central government's and Karnataka state government's policies that encourage the inclusion of women in local and regional *panchayats* and other local political groups, not all citizens have benefited from these policies. Village council quota systems for women, lower castes, and tribes seem to promote gender equality in the village social and political realms (Iversen and Rosenbluth 2010: 130). However, as Kagitcibasi (1986: 485) points out, "legal and formal institutional reforms provide the formal structures and mechanisms for changes in life-styles if such changes are initiated or demanded." The formal structures and policies per se do not prevent old cultural and ideological attitudes from impeding women's efforts to empower themselves. Also, because of how some women have been socialized and resistance from men who have dominated these groups for a long time, the women are not able to govern with the necessary political clout that the men often wield.

Current values, attitudes, and men's perceptions of women, as well as women's self-perception, create ideological barriers that such women contend with. Women face such challenges as they try to change attitudes to allow their contributions, new status, and influence to be appreciated. As a result of long traditions of male domination and privilege, women leaders who take up women's abuse, dowry requirements, girl-child neglect, and inheritance laws are often vilified and restricted. At times, however, law enforcers and local and state government officials organize training programs, share policy statements, and enforce laws that enable women to create possibilities beyond the status quo, which tends to be based in patriarchy.

3.3 Rural women's political representation on *panchayats*

In India, most women's lives and status tend to be prescribed, inherited, and on some occasions ascribed; that is, their status is earned. The discussion below focuses on women political representatives who are good agents of social and economic change in their respective communities. As they transform their communities, they too are changed as concrete examples of how power unfolds. Individual women's *shakti* is discussed below. In addition, the way a group of women literally chased corrupt government officials from a village provides an example of collective female power (*grumpu shakti* in Konkani) in rural communities.

Some of the women discussed here, who enter local politics, are courageous, have *vajen* (weight) or authority, *shakti* (strength, power), and are resourceful in educating the young, training others in such things as tailoring and animal husbandry programs, village drainage, and road construction. After winning a seat on a local *panchayat*, 40-year-old Bagubai Kokre, a Gowli from Ativeri, said, "I wanted to use my position to impact policies and projects to benefit my community. As I served my people, I gained some confidence because I had bargaining power because I was known by many people outside Ativeri and I had an important role in the new political realm in Karnataka" (personal communication, 15 August 2010). Bagubai further asserted that she and other women have achieved social power.

There are many women like Bagubai who create or claim centers of power for themselves and others. Their social and political experience begins to shape their social realities. Omvedt (1993) points out that women are creating new alternatives by reformulating issues of gender, class, caste, and their livelihoods as they focus on *shiva–shakti* (women's power). These women use their status, determination, and different grades of strength, courage, and honor to take control of and shape their conditions in ways not open to them in the past.

I begin by providing an example of how some rural women in India who had no formal education but were armed with the knowledge that they were being misled confronted their exploiters. Access to information has been one hallmark the Indian government has promoted as part of its efforts to bring equality to Indians.

3.4 The power of information

In 2005, the national government of India passed the Right to Information Act. The objective of the Act is to ensure that any citizen of India who requires crucial information from government officials has a right to receive the information within 30 days. The Act also stresses the recognition of the citizen's legal right to government information that will help them improve themselves, or to take legal action if their rights are violated. This Act was to encourage civic engagement and community participation in local and national discourses. It is against the backdrop of the above Act that the following discussion helps us to understand some of the challenges rural Indian women face and the steps some women took to challenge abuses of power.

Eight Siddi women, whose ages at the time ranged from 27 to 50, live in Tavalkata, near Honshettikoppa. The village has about 200 residents. The women have formed a *sangha* and often travel as a group to subdistrict (*taluk*) government offices. As good citizens, the women pay taxes for electricity, water, and library facilities, yet they lack all of those amenities. During my visit to Tavalkata, they became aware that they were also being taxed for library services, though none of them ever used a library in Yellapur, which is the nearest community that has a library. They made this discovery because my friend Pramod and I had asked them to show us records of the benefits they have been receiving, as they are now STs.

They admitted to us that what they need is information that will enable them to improve their community, but they had no one to give them such information. They explained that a month prior to our visit, a non-Siddi male *panchayat* member once visited Tavalkata in the company of his senior officer and claimed he had helped build modern houses for the villagers. In reality, with the exception of two houses belonging to non-Siddis, all the other houses had been built by the Siddis themselves. The women informed us that they got angry and chased the officials out of the village. They did so, they said, because they had just learned from a Siddi *gram panchayat* member outside their village that the government had sanctioned housing schemes for villages, including Tavalkata. The women realized they had been denied the information that would have helped them pursue the building project. The male *panchayat* member had lied about what he had done for the Siddi community.

After that incident, the women said, their local *panchayat* started building houses for some of the families. According to the women, it came to their attention that, although they were entitled to modern houses, the government official and others had mismanaged the funds.

Later, when the women wanted some of their people to serve on the *panchayat*, they were told there were no vacancies for Siddis because other castes and tribal groups on the *panchayat* would take care of Siddi needs and concerns. This explanation also reveals the corrupt measures some officials use to undermine the laudable goals behind the *panchayat* system.

The government makes available a number of seats for women and tribes and castes on *panchayats*. However, not all qualified people get the opportunity to serve their people, because the interpreters of the policy who implement the laws tend to deny people access to information that would have enabled them to contest in elections or serve.

At other times, when women stand elections by campaigning, they do not always win seats in the *panchayat*. Those who win may not have the support of some male local leaders if the winner was not the leaders' choice. Such instances underscore Lukes' (2005) point that, when the oppressed try to assert power by challenging their oppressors, the exploiters punish the oppressed. At the same time, what the Siddi women of Tavalkata did help us show that marginalized people may not have formal power, but they can develop the capacity (Clegg 1989) to disempower those who hold traditional influence (Bourdieu 1977).

There are many examples of women who felt they were qualified to represent their minority communities whose turn it was to fill in a *panchayat* position, but then lost in the elections. When S. Siddi lost in her bid for a *gram panchayat* presidency, she said she learned her lesson not to listen to any male politician who advised her against campaigning in her own community. In the end, the communities in which she spent time canvassing for support did not vote for her because they voted for a woman who belonged to their own caste. The lesson S. Siddi has learned may help her to be more politically astute in her future political activity. Some of these women may learn from how and why they lost and improve their chances of winning in subsequent elections.

3.5 SHGs, or *sanghas*

In addition to *panchayats,* it is through SHGs, or *sanghas*, that some women's lives are impacted directly. Most villages have at least one *sangha,* but not every woman is a member of such a group. In India, *sanghas* have become another important tool for development interventions in the lives of the women of rural India.

The majority of women who are members of *sanghas* attest to the benefits they get from membership as they simultaneously transform their lives and the lives of others. Subramaniam (2009: 10) points out that the lives of the women of rural India are shaped by "inequalities, at intersections of class, caste and gender." *Sanghas* are mainly organized by NGOs at the grassroots level and, though they usually include both men and women, they tend to be women-controlled processes of change (Subramaniam 2009: 9). Few *sanghas* comprise all men. *Sanghas* are groups within which rural women foster consciousness raising and empowerment to identify and resist forms of repression. Group membership and the loans the *sanghas* provide are only some measures that are needed for rural women to support themselves and their families. Women begin to receive steady personal income as they take small loans for house projects and grow areca nuts, mangoes, paddy rice, and vegetables.

Sangha programs are also aimed at creating awareness about the importance of education, health, and community development. Through *sanghas,* women establish saving schemes and decide how much members have to contribute on a weekly or monthly basis. They also determine how to use their savings in giving loans to members at fixed interest rates, often about two percent. When the women meet to take loans on rotation, they also discuss issues that affect them and their families. Women who did not previously interact with outsiders and never did any public speaking but are now in *sanghas* have begun to express themselves publicly and to support one another. The female network in *sanghas* has become a resource for women's self-empowerment. When the women interact with one another to exchange stories and experiences, and to look for solutions to their shared problems, they build solidarity to challenge exploitative power structures. They learn skills that give them the confidence to manifest their different forms of influence.

The *sangha* women's enterprising spirit and their desire to improve themselves and their families' conditions seem to have converged with the central and state governments' and NGOs' objectives and attendant resources. The women capitalize on resources such as microfinance and reserved seats for them in politics and to serve their people. Though some caste/tribe/OBC communities benefit from the Indian government's policy on education and job quotas, most rural people do not have access to opportunities to better their material conditions (Subramaniam 2009: 9–10), and *sanghas* help to fill that gap.

As they engage in the activities described above, the women gain a new sense of power as they participate in decision making, enforce relevant laws such as laws prohibiting violence against women, and take leadership roles. They learn skills that give them self-confidence and the ability to confront those who exploit them. At times such organizational structure of empowerment enables them to assume more leadership roles in their families and communities.

Therefore, some of the women undergo change as they change their material conditions. For the first time, women are visiting government offices unaccompanied by male family members, presenting petitions on behalf of others and themselves, and receiving the attention of both men and women in the government.

Against that background, I will examine the roles of NGOs and how women between the ages of 20 and 60 use resources to advance themselves under conditions of entrenched, countervailing cultural and ideological forces.

3.6 NGOs

Local and international NGOs are apolitical institutions that are also involved in the improvement of the material and social lives of rural communities. In Pakistan, Bangladesh, and India, in rural communities that have local *panchayats* or union *parishads* (local and village-level governance structures in Bangladesh), women leaders often work with NGOs or government officials to empower other women at the grassroots level. For instance, in the three countries, the women help organize meetings, build alliances with political leaders and government officials, and organize trainings for women that focus on health, education, and women's rights. Some of the women are involved in the improvement of sanitation in their local communities. Other women help to establish adult literacy, while some assist in raising awareness about women's rights so that women can vote on social and economic matters.

3.6.1 Pakistan

The central government of Pakistan theoretically has been looking for ways to empower women socially and economically and to create employment opportunities and income-generating programs for them. But the Pakistani government's efforts to bring equality between men and women highlight the obstacles its female citizen entrepreneurs face in environments of predominant gender inequalities.

Pakistani women live in an environment of social, cultural, traditional, and religious forces that have shaped citizens for many centuries. Women have always lived in subordinated or lower status to that of men. The central government, therefore, in an attempt to rectify the imbalance in the power dynamic between men and women has made efforts at the constitutional level, producing policy documents and institutional systems to promote equity. For example, Pakistan established the Devolution of Power Plan (a local government plan) in March 2000, which reserves seats for women in legislative councils at the local *tehsil* (a local political administrative unit). The Pakistani government, NGOs, and organizations such as the Pakistan Poverty Alleviation Fund, the National Rural Support Programme, and Rural

Support Programmes provide microfinancing to women as a means of promoting woman's entrepreneurship.

3.6.2 Bangladesh

The central government of Bangladesh is also making strides to bring about gender equity in its country. I will begin with how some Bangladeshi women seek to exercise their rights while they serve on the union *parishads* (the lowest tier of the local government system in Bangladesh).

In Bangladesh, the government has reserved seats for women in union *parishads* so that the women elected can have political influence in their communities.

The Bangladeshi government has embarked on decentralizing governance structures in order to allow local communities to fully participate at the local level (Das and Maru 2011). Bangladeshi *gram sarkar,* which is the village government system, is gaining prominence because it involves a fusion between traditional and formal local institutions. On the *gram sarkar* level are the *shalish,* the village or local court, where land and marital disputes are settled. At times, the *shalish,* which is headed by men, sentences flogging as well as death penalties for offenses that may not merit such harsh measures. In those instances, while NGOs and human rights activists argue that the village courts have overstepped their legal bounds, the village courts tend to argue that they have been set up to enforce justice and harmony at the village level. What happens in such cases is that the *gram sarkar* that is supposed to allow women to have a voice is sometimes undermined by entrenched patriarchal laws enforced by the *shalish.*

At the *gram sarkar* level, Lewis and Kanji (2009) argue that, when NGOs mobilize against exploiters, some of the village landowners, Muslim religious leaders, and the rich and powerful begin to resent those NGOs and accuse them of interfering in Bangladeshi law. In April 2013, Hefajat-e-Islam Bangladesh, which is an Islamic group, held demonstrations to demand, among other things, that the Bangladeshi government prevent women from attaining equal rights with men, stop NGOs blaspheming against Islam and the Quran, and the repeal of all non-Islamic laws. They also threatened that, if the national government did not abide by their demands, its members would be thrown out of office.

Women face other patriarchal impediments in Bangladesh. The challenges that most of the women on the local *panchayats* and union *parishads* face include what Panday (2008) has described as "representation without participation." For example, some of the women who have males sponsoring them to serve on *panchayats* are without formal education and lack self-confidence and therefore are not able to mobilize others. In other instances, the women *panchayat* leaders have to travel long distances in order to attend meetings, or even run programs for other rural citizens. A case in point is what Panday addresses as the "mobility obstacle." In that case, women are prevented from taking part in decision making or attending emergency meetings when they are called deliberately at inconvenient times (Panday 2008: 502). Panday also indicates that some of the women leaders do not have access to transportation. For instance, in rural areas, women are not allowed to ride bicycles because women who use bicycles are considered to be acting inappropriately. Such women are seen as violating social customs and being unfit for marriage (Panday 2008: 502). Unlike Shanta Burgi, a Hindu coordinator of *sanghas* in India who could ride a motorcycle if she could afford it, women who ride motorcycles would not be looked on kindly by the Bangladeshi Muslim conservative communities.

The above cultural impediments are compounded by the ticklish relationship between NGOs and the government of Bangladesh. Rahman (1993) contends that the Bangladeshi government and a few NGOs have made attempts to bring development interventions to minority groups. However, those efforts are yet to gain traction or have a significant impact. The NGOs, by default according to Rahman, have become the institutions to which some Bangladeshis turn when they seek redress or equality in their social relations. Thus, in Bangladesh, there have been times when an NGO seems to have usurped the powers of the central government. NGOs that are often regarded as apolitical can by default assume powers that may undermine national and state governments. Rahman's argument helps us to understand ways in which the de facto usurpation of government power may hurt as well as help the furtherance of women's rights; for instance, if an NGO becomes a for-profit organization, this might impede its efforts toward social justice.

As an example, Haque lists organizations, including the Grameen Bank, which has now become a "full-fledged bank for rural credit institution" (2002: 416) and the Bangladesh Rural Advancement Committee, which started as a relief organization in 1972 to assist the rural poor through education and entrepreneurship development and has now become a profit-making commercial institution engaged in "printing presses, cold storage, poultry farms, retail outlets, and garment manufacturing" (2002: 416).

Haque further argues that foreign donor agencies seem to consider NGOs to be more reliable channels for providing aid to Bangladeshis than the central government, thus marginalizing the government. Since the government appears marginalized, national development programs may be fragmented (Haque 2002: 426–427).

NGOs, despite their pervasive influence, are not able to enforce laws that were promulgated by the state or central government; for example, NGOs may work in communities where women suffer from acid attack violence, but since they lack the legal authority of the government to enforce antiacid attack laws, at best such NGOs can create awareness in the women about their human and legal rights. Violence against women persists even though some women are able to set up businesses or use microcredit to earn income.

Economic independence alone does not guarantee freedom for women (Kabeer 2001; Batliwala 2011).

Despite entrenched cultural obstacles, some rural Bangladeshi women form networks of pressure groups to challenge local leaders and militant groups that try to restrict women. The few women who are able to challenge the patriarchal abuse of power gain respect in their communities. Rural Bangladeshi women activists often form networks that receive training from women's rights organizations based in Dhaka, the capital of Bangladesh. It is through such ongoing interactions that rural women become aware of how they can assert their rights in their respective societies. Since urban women tend to have more education and more access to resources, their collaborations with rural women end up strengthening their bonds and their sharing of ideas with one another.

However, there is still some resistance to these collaborations by local village leaders, known as *matbars*. The Bangladeshi example also underscores the fact that a one-size-fits-all government intervention does not necessarily accomplish the government's or NGOs' goals. It is therefore important to pay attention to the intertwining relationships between formal and informal networks, local notions of community, the power of religion, and the power of the women who function within the networks.

3.6.3 Women's Organizations in Bangladesh

Bangladeshi women's organizations, like other all-female groups in South Asia, are critical in the empowerment of women. They create spaces for women to increase capacity for one another, and they create awareness across networks of women. These networks provide support as they provide self-confidence and the strength to demand rights and gain recognition in their societies (Kabeer 2001). Although some women have set up their own businesses, such as the village payphone programs, which are supported by Grameen Telecom, it is when women act collectively that they are able to change aspects of patriarchal culture.

Women's agency is highlighted by Khattak, who points out that NGO involvement in the improvement of the conditions of women's lives can be, at times, exaggerated, because NGOs often come with agendas to promote the legitimacy of their own work; however, a comprehensive understanding of the effectiveness of governmental and nongovernmental interventions should always include the active participation of women and women's organizations (Khattak 2010: 6).

Kabeer and Huq (2010) contend that the Saptagram NGO in Bangladesh provided a context and other resources that fostered social mobilization systems that have enabled women to form relationships to empower one another. Such relationships, the authors argue, enabled the women to gain knowledge of their rights and courage to stand up for their beliefs and to develop leadership skills (Kabeer and Huq 2010: 1). Their analysis moves beyond institutions of intervention to the agency of women engaged in self-advancement. An emphasis on women's expanding social relationships and the ways in which women build solidarity among themselves while increasing their capacity for collective action has been noted by Batliwala (1993) and Agarwal (1994).

The above scholars' positions stress women's relationships beyond predictable family, kinship, and client–patron networks to address women's capacity for agency (Kabeer and Huq 2010: 80). Further, they contend that women use their social mobilizing *shakti* also to transform social structures that have subordinated women. Further, unlike *sanghas* and NGOs that support local programs that only promote the economic well-being of women, Saptagram (they argue) had its successes because of women's social relationships. The women were able to create their own private and public spaces and, in the process, redefined their identities and relationships. The enduring aspect of such organizations was based on a loyalty and solidarity on which the women could always count (Kabeer and Huq 2010: 86).

Other intervention programs involve the reversal of British colonial labels for rural nomadic communities, particularly in India.

3.7 British colonial classifications

The lived experiences of rural women are situated within the sociohistorical contexts of gender, class, and denotified and SC/ST status. In this section I address how local notions of women's power, status, and influence are embedded and shaped in the larger historical framework of South Asia. Women and their families who lived in certain rural communities were under suspicion and often accused of committing crimes because the British authorities could not control the movements of these rural people.

India, Pakistan, and Bangladesh all inherited British colonial laws that have impeded their democratizing programs. In addition to cultural and patriarchal impediments that rural women face, the subcontinent continues to reel from the British colonial classificatory system that labeled rural communities as prone to criminal activities. Such communities were called Notified Tribes by the British (discussed below). Between 1871, when the British issued the Criminal Act designating these tribes, and 1948, communities that were nomadic or seminomadic were regarded as unruly because the British authorities were unable to control them. Ironically, according to Metry (2007), the British used some of these nomadic and seminomadic people to construct railway lines and roads across the subcontinent.

By 1950 an amendment to the Indian Constitution was promulgated to provide opportunities for groups of people who were socially and economically deprived as STs/SCs. "By the 1950s classificatory systems were used so state governments would give reports to the central government for census purposes and about the number of tribes and castes and ways in which such communities could be assisted to improve their conditions," said Metry (personal communication, 12 July 2009).

Pandian (2008) and Metry (2007; personal communication 12 July 2009) assert that until the current (as of 2003) reclassification of nomadic and seminomadic communities, the designations Notified Castes/Tribes were used to describe segments of Indians as possessing "impulsive, habitual and instinctual criminality" (Pandian 2008: 88). According to Pandian, the label goes back to the British official designation under the Indian Criminal Tribes Act of 1871. Denotified Tribes (DNTs) were the Indian rural communities originally listed under this Act as Criminal Tribes, who the Act claimed were "addicted to the systematic commission of non-bailable offences."

Once a group of people became "notified" as criminal, all its members were required to register with the local magistrate, and those who failed would be charged with a crime under the Indian Penal Code. The Criminal Tribes Act of 1952 repealed the notification; that is, it "denotified" the tribal communities. This Act, however, was replaced by a series of Habitual Offenders Acts, which asked police to investigate a suspect's criminal tendencies and whether his occupation was "conducive to a settled way of life." The DNTs were reclassified as habitual offenders in 1959 (Bokil 2002; Pandian 2008; Metry 2007; personal communication, 12 July 2009).

The above categories should be seen in the context of colonialism. It was the British authorities who listed them separately by creating a category of castes or tribes labeled as criminal, the name "Criminal Tribes" itself being a misnomer as no definition of a tribe denotes an occupation. The first census of the Indian subcontinent was in 1871, and at that time there was neither a consensus on nor any definition of "tribe." The terms tribe and caste were used interchangeably by the British for these communities. In the colonial context, the term tribe connoted primitiveness and backwardness and hence an assumption that these people needed to be civilized or transformed (Bokil 2002). Since the Criminal Tribes Act assumed that itinerant traders, forest dwellers, and nomadic and seminomadic herders had criminal propensities, such groups were to be governed with what Pandian (2008) calls "pastoral power." Thus, the "Criminal Act" treated nomadic and seminomadic people as humans with criminalist tendencies that are passed on from generation to generation.

After the Criminal Tribes Act was passed, most rural people were subjected to suspicion, and, consequently, officials kept, and still keep, a tight rein on them. For instance, it is not surprising that, before 2003, when Siddis were reclassified as STs, some non-Siddis treated Siddis with suspicion. The label "*Siddi ka bara budhhi*—a Siddi is not trustworthy" (Lobo 1983: 34) could be understood in this general construct and objectification of groups of people as being prone to criminality.

At present, most of the seminomadic people seek to build permanent settlements where they can cultivate land, in some cases encroached on by them. The few who own pieces of land may possess two to six acres, with a small number of animals they raise. Some contend that their lack of education and their nomadic lifestyle were among the reasons for their lack of development.

The following Indian government reoslution in 2008 that was brought by the Indian National Commission for Denotified, Nomadic and Semi-Nomadic Tribes of Ministry of Social Justice and Empowerment provides an illustration of what the subcontinent inherited from the British colonial period:

Notified and Denotified Tribes

1. RESOLUTION 7.1 MINISTRY OF SOCIAL JUSTICE AND EMPOWERMENT (SCHEDULED CASTE DEVELOPMENT DIVISION)

New Delhi, 23 October 2003 scd (R. L. Cell) ... Whereas the Government of India has been seized of the development needs of the Denotified tribes, nomadic and semi nomadic "tribes," which are spread amongst the scheduled castes, scheduled tribes and other backward castes and others.

It further stipulates:

2. the denotified "tribes" have been wrongly stigmatized as crime prone and subject to high handed treatment as well as exploitation by the representatives of law and order as well as by the general society, it has inter-alia recommended that the Ministry of Tribal Affairs should strengthen the programmes for the socio-economic development, generation of employment opportunities, social liberation and full rehabilitation of Denotified Tribes, Nomadic and semi-Nomadic tribes/Communities.
3. Now, therefore, the government of India has resolved to constitute a national commission for one year to study the development aspect of the Denotified Tribes, Nomadic and Semi Nomadic "tribes."
4. The terms of reference of the commission are given below:
   a. To identify Denotified, Nomadic and Semi-Nomadic; tribes and prepare a State/Union Territory–wise list of those who have been categorized as Scheduled Castes, Scheduled tribes and other Backward Classes.
   b. To study socio-economic and educational needs of Denotified Nomadic and Semi Nomadic "Tribes." To recommend to the Government of India the Specific intervention required for their overall development aspects, and
   c. Make any other recommendations connected therewith or incidental thereto which the commission considers necessary.

5. The commission may obtain such information as considered necessary or expedient for its purposes from the Central Government and any other authority, organization or individual.
6. The commission shall consist of a Chairperson and four other members with suitable expertise; one of them will function as the Member Secretary.
7. The commission will adopt its own procedures of working and may visit any part of India it considers necessary.
8. The commission shall submit its report within one year from the date of this resolution.

In addition to changing the notified status, the Indian government has reclassified some communities so that such people benefit from government support.

Another aspect of the Indian government's effort to destigmatize rural people was the reclassification of these groups into STs and SCs. The following is an example of a certificate that allows a person to claim to SC or ST status:

Certificate

> This is to certify that ...son / daughter ... of village / town ... in District / Division ... of the State / Union / Territory ... belong to the Caste / Tribe which is recognized as a Scheduled Caste / Tribe under the constitution (Scheduled Caste) Order 1950.
>
> Scheduled Caste / Tribe under the constitution (Scheduled Caste) Order 1950 was amended by The Scheduled Caste and Scheduled Tribes List (Modification) Order 1956, The Bombay Recognisation Act 1960, and the Punjab Recognisation Act 1966, the State of Himachal Pradesh Act 1970 and the North Eastern Areas (Recognisation Act 1971).
>
> Scheduled Caste / Tribe Order / Amendment Act 2002 (No 10 / 2003)
>
> Shri / Smt / Kumari ... and / or his / her family ordinarily reside(s) in village / town ... of District / Division ... of State / Union/ Territory of ...
>
> Source: Indian Ministry of Social Justice and Empowerment

Besides the stigmatized statuses and roles associated with the above communities, which are being repealed, India, Pakistan, and Bangladesh are taking other steps to foster social, economic, and political equity for women in the inheritance system and women's right to property.

3.8 Inheritance

Inheritance has been a thorny issue for rural and urban women in South Asia. In South Asia, land is valued immensely because it provides economic, political, social, and symbolic security for both urban and rural women. Yet, while some educated women have fathers whose wills include their female children as legal heirs eligible to inherit property at the father's death, many rural South Asian women do not inherit their fathers' or family property. The Indian (Hindu) Succession Act of 1956 (amended in 1985 and later in 2005) aimed at correcting this injustice against females in India. The disparity about property has been addressed by Agarwal (1994) in her seminal work on gender and land ownership.

In India, tribal women living in communities ruled by patriarchal laws and customs are subject to gender discrimination in land inheritance. The Indian central government has used amendments to the inheritance system to exemplify reform efforts to bring about equality or parity for both women and men.

According to Agarwal (2004), the Hindu Succession (Amendment) Act originally deleted the gender discriminatory clause on agricultural land. However, only Hindu women were to benefit from the Act, leaving Muslim and tribal women open to all forms of gender injustice. Muslim women's rights fall under the Muslim Personal Law (Shariat) Application Act of 1937. The Muslim Personal Law applies to Muslims in India, Pakistan, and Bangladesh. According to Agarwal, Pakistani and Bangladeshi women appear to be better off because their law takes care of women's welfare. In India, the Muslim Personal Law (Shariat) Application Act of 1937 did not include women's rights to ownership of agricultural land. Later on, a few states (Tamil Nadu, Karnataka, Andhra Pradesh, and Kerala) extended the act to include women's rights to ownership and inheritance of agricultural land (Agarwal 1994). In other states, however, the Act has not been amended to ensure gender equality. She further argues that Pakistani and Bangladeshi women may have played a key role in a reform that included agricultural land inheritance in their countries.

The Hindu Succession Act about intestate succession (inheritance in the absence of a will) was adopted by the state of Andhra Pradesh. The Act, which is generally called the NTR Act (Lakshmi 2007: 23–27), gave daughters and sons equal rights to the property of their father. Karnataka joined Andhra Pradesh, Tamil Nadu, and Maharashtra to extend equal intestate inheritance rights to women. Thus daughters in the four states were to enjoy co-parcenery rights.

While the NTR Act made daughters co-parcenars, not all daughters in India benefit from the Act (Lakshmi 2007: 26–27). According to the Awaz Foundation Center for Development Services in Pakistan in 2010, though Muslim inheritance laws may guarantee equality for women, it is not easy for Muslim women to acquire land and other property even when government laws require it. According to this study, there are Muslim women who do not demand their rights to inherit property even when they are legally so entitled, because they are not assertive. There are also women who are not educated enough to be aware of their legal rights. The study points to other women who relinquish their rights in order to please their parents and their male family members. The above factors therefore prevent women from gaining equal access to land as men do.

According to a 2009 report by the Rural Development Institute concerning women's inheritance rights to land and property in South Asia, there are some groups in Bangladesh who have suffered immensely regarding the inheritance system in the country. Although there seems to be no caste system in Bangladesh, there still exist certain marginalized groups, such as the Bawalies, Mawalies, Methor, Dalich, Mymal, Muchis, Magarchis, and Kulies, living a segregated life in conditions of extreme poverty. Bangladesh also faces the pressure of losing one percent of its arable land annually due to land erosion from extreme floods (Rural Development Institute 2009: 31), making land a scarce, valuable resource.

The intestacy rights of Muslims in India are enshrined in the Muslim Personal Law (Shariat) Application Act of 1937. The Act states:

> Daughter's share is (1/2) half if there is no son, two-thirds (2/3) together if there is more than one daughter and if there is a son, daughter takes in such a way that each daughter takes half of what each son takes.

Christians fashion their intestate succession laws based on the Hindu Succession Act. This Act, stipulated in Article 25 of the Constitution of India, declares that a

> man's widow and children, male and female, inherit equally. However, a man may, by will bequeath his property to any one, totally disinheriting his own children and widow.

Individual families and communities tend to bequeath property as they choose. In the rural Indian communities of Komptikoppa and Tatvanaggi, most Muslim men do not think their daughters should inherit any land. They argue that the female child will carry the property to her husband's family, thus impoverishing her natal family.

In some cases where senior women inherited land, they have leased it to be cultivated or they cultivate it themselves, as in Nageshettikoppa and Ugingeri in India.

Women's access to property gives them economic security and status. Besides the material and economic security, women become *kartas*. *Karta* is the Hindi word for a "doer" or one who has the right to make major decisions for his or her family. Traditionally, adult males automatically become *kartas*. Recently, however, the central government of India has revised that tradition so that females can become *kartas*. A *karta* is the caretaker of the family and watches over the welfare of all the members of the family. The *karta*'s relationship with other members is based on trust and confidence. According to the amended 2005 Hindu Succession Act, a woman can be a *karta* when the father dies and she has no brother. Thus a daughter or a mother can be the *karta* of the family's property, signaling that women and men are equal in the eyes of the law. Thus there are cases in which both sexes, whether married or not, can support themselves on inherited resources.

There are, however, other instances, in which both men and women are not be able to augment their status, power, self, and social worth to enable them to create or find resources to support themselves (Lakshmi 2007: 25). Some daughters inherited their mother's property and also had a right to the patrimony (i.e., to a share of their father's property). In inheritance among some communities, the women and men enjoy similar status and rights, but, despite the above rights enshrined in the Indian government's acts, in some of the villages listed earlier, men do not conform to the government's stipulations.

3.9 Forest, land, and water resources

Other steps South Asian countries have taken to empower local communities include joint management rights to land, water, and forest resources. Omvedt (2005) argues that, in Pakistan, local communities traditionally have had control over their natural resources. But with the emergence of different nation states (India, Pakistan, and Bangladesh), the respective countries have now promoted joint forest management (JFM) programs with a goal to empower local communities to have oversight over local natural resources. Though individual JFPM programs may differ in their specific aims and agreements, they are generally programs in which village residents assist in the protection and management of forest resources in exchange for limited use of forest products and revenue from the sale of timber.

The use of forest, land, and water resources for economic activities has been important for all rural citizens of South Asia. Besides gathering fruits, collecting firewood, and hunting and fishing, the traditional prominent members of their respective communities either owned the natural resources or obtained contracts from government officials before using them. However, with recent attempts by South Asian governments to empower people at the local level, and to rectify injustices under the inheritance laws, Bangladesh, India, and Pakistan have instituted new natural resource laws.

3.10 Joint management and natural resources

3.10.1 Bangladesh

Community management of land, water, and forest resources at the local level has been promoted by South Asian countries. However, Omvedt (2005) points out that community management of land, water, and forest resources does not directly benefit women. Though such joint management programs were intended to empower all rural citizens, men and government officials in charge of the programs tend to marginalize women. Sultana and Thompson (2007) show that fishery in Bangladesh and India is an area where discriminatory activities are pronounced; they further contend that *jalmohals* (water estates) are leased to the highest bidders rather than to poor people, for whose benefit the fishery's management programs were instituted to start with (Sultana and Thompson 2007: 5–8).

The women do not often have control or decision-making rights or access to forest products. In contrast, Janubai (a Gowli woman from Jainmuri, whose profile I provide later), was able to win the right to build houses in a JFM area in Karnataka, India. Recently, there has been consensus on the intersection between women's empowerment, rights to land and health care, education, and decision-making roles.

Women's land rights may be agreed upon in Pakistan, India, and Bangladesh in principle; however, very often women still do not share in the properties that men pass on from generation to generation. Most men in South Asia argue that if women were given land rights, the social relationships where men are perceived as providers and women as dependants would be dramatically changed. This patriarchal perspective undermines the respect, honor, dignity, and economic power that women's rights could confer on them.

3.10.2 India

In 1993, the Government of Karnataka instituted a JFM program for all rural caste and tribal groups in the state. Though passed to give Lambanis, Gowlis, and other rural communities control over their local forest resources, most of the people affected are not aware of their rights under the policy. Gowlis, as described earlier, had always freely grazed their livestock until the new forest laws, through which the state government took over control of all forestlands, were passed. As a result of these laws, Gowlis are among those who have suffered immensely. The JFM programs were meant to partly amend such effects of the forest laws.

In other contexts, the JFM program is referred to as JFPM (Joint Forest Planning and Management) and is supposed to help villages, largely with support from British DFID (Department for International Development) grants. About 25 percent of the villages are covered under the JFPM program. The JFPM has been mostly assigned highly degraded parts of the forests for management.

All village households are deemed members of the JFPM General Body. The General Body appoints a Managing Committee, which, per statutory requirement, should have a minimum of two women members. The JFPM General Management Body's responsibilities include developing microplans for fodder development and use of energy-saving devices, raising of nontimber forest products and fuel wood–yielding plantations, encroachment (squatting) problems, and various other location-specific issues.

3.10.2.1 *Sharecropping* (koru palu)

When village community leaders had more control of land, some practiced sharecropping (*koru palu* in Kannada, the state language of Karnataka). Lobo (1983: 49–50) asserts that workers were usually gathered together by a contractor from a single *tanda* (a Lambani settlement). At times about six overseers assembled a hundred or so workers. The Lambanis had their own workforce to perform jobs that benefited their communities:

> In *koru palu,* the owner pays the land tax; the tenant contributes labour and draught animals; except threshing, which is seen to by the tenant, all other activities and expenses are equally shared by the tenant and the owner. The tenant has usufruct right over the land which is inheritable. (Lobo 1983: 50)

Gowlis, Siddis, and Vaddars were and some are still engaged in sharecropping. According to the Karnataka Land Reforms Act of 1974, this tenancy is exploitative and hence illegal; therefore, sharecropping agreements are entered into orally by the concerned parties. In *yettala palu,* or bullock-labor share, a tenant contributes labor and bullocks. (Some senior Lambani, Gowli, Dalit, and Siddi women give their bullocks for hire these days.) All other inputs are borne by the owner. The yield is not shared equally. In a *khandu,* or an annual lump-sum payment, the owner pays the land tax. All the expenses of cultivation are borne by the tenant. The tenant gives a certain portion of the harvest in a lump sum soon after the harvest.

> In *lavani,* or annual lease payment, the owner gives taxes. All inputs are made by the tenant. The tenant has inheritable usufruct rights. The tenant takes the land on lease for a specified number of years for an agreed amount of payment in cash, which must be paid soon after the agreement. It is usually six times the land tax or one fifth of gross produce. (Lobo 1983: 55)

According to Lobo, when the Karnataka state government began to clear forestlands, some Lambani leaders began to employ their own people to work for the government. The leaders employed Lambanis on the basis of wage labor, creating the start of unequal distribution of resources (Agarwal 1994). According to Lobo, limited land resources fostered conditions in which some Lambani leaders seized the opportunity to amass lands for themselves and evolve new structures in which the leader took advantage of other Lambanis. Some Lambanis acquired land, which they cultivated to grow paddy rice, beans, cotton, and vegetables, while others practiced tenant cultivation (Lobo 1983: 55). This observation helps us understand class and privilege differences within the same caste in rural Karnataka in India.

When the lands of the various caste and tribal communities were incorporated into the town municipalities, all residents had to follow the rules about building permanent houses (Lobo 1983: 45) and abiding by the forest regulations that forbid the use of forest produce without a permit.

3.10.3 Pakistan

Pakistan has also passed joint management laws, but the laws are not implemented to benefit women. Also, women's access to critical resources has been restricted by traditional structures from which they have been excluded and by the belief that women are not capable of owning property.

Omvedt (2005) argues that in Pakistan, local communities traditionally had control over natural resources. But with the emergence of the different nation states (India, Pakistan, and Bangladesh), Pakistan began promoting JFM programs. According to Mumtaz and Noshirwami (2007), customary practices and religious traditions restrict women's mobility and their control of resources: the women may lay claim to property rights, but Pakistan does not have or does not enforce structures and mechanisms that allow the women to achieve their rights. Mumtaz and Noshirwami (2007) further state that family pressure, fear of ostracism, and dependence on male relatives when dealing with the outside world and controlling property may inhibit women from affirming their rights to land, water, and forest resources.

Against the above background, I next turn my attention to women between the ages of 20 and 60 to show the ways in which some of them use resources to advance themselves while others do not.

4

Governments, NGOs, *Sanghas*, and Female Entrepreneurs (20 to 60 Years of Age)

In this chapter, I explore ways in which women are not just recipients of change but active agents in different forms of change (Malhotra et al. 2002). I also explore women's unequal responses to the resources available to them as they acquire new roles to expand their arenas of self-determination in the burgeoning public and private spheres of their respective countries. Also, I focus on the processes and institutional structures that influence the ways in which women craft and assert power.

As the women of rural South Asia attempt to deploy different forms of power, their efforts put into sharp focus the deep-pocketed and privileged few who wield social, religious, and political power that aims to conserve and maintain control over the marginalized. This chapter examines religious and other social forces that influence women's attitudes toward resources offered by their central governments, the state, district, and local political institutions, and NGOs.

The rural women in this section manifest formal and informal modes of power in context-specific systems that are underpinned by expectations regarding women's and men's behavior. It is when women exercise strategic choices in situations where they were previously prevented (Kabeer 2001) from playing roles as agents of change (except, at best, as recipients of development) that their female influence is both embodied and made manifest.

The central governments of India, Pakistan, and Bangladesh have been engaged in efforts to empower women and other minorities. Such measures have led to the formation of statal and parastatal institutions such as *panchayats*/union *parishads* and *sanghas* to equalize social and gender disparities. The programs include enterprise creation through income-generating projects.

I will now explore the variety and range of lived experiences of rural women who are using their newly won opportunities and the resistance they face as they seek personal advancement.

In rural communities, men are the heads of the village councils, and rulings from such councils tend to be male-biased. Such rulings, coupled with corruption, cronyism, and misappropriation of public resources, make it imperative that at least some women assume responsibilities in their communities. Among the female actors in new roles and jobs are *panchayat* members who are making a significant difference in their communities and use or create spheres of influence to assert their *shakti* within the context of social cultural attitudes, perceptions, and sexual hierarchies.

4.1 Members of *Panchayats*

I begin by profiling women who have been elected to serve on *panchayats*. For instance, Lalita Krishna Bhovi Vaddar is a 30-year-old *gram panchayat* president (*sarpanch*). Lalita, who belongs to the SC of Vaddars (as is made clear by her name), has three children—two girls and a boy. Because Lalita has had no formal education, at times her children, who have completed their primary education, read and interpret for her documents on how to run *panchayat* meetings. She showed us some of the government pamphlets she brought home for her children to help her understand—documents put in simple sentences and having illustrations, so that, with the pictorial help, she is able to imagine what the written documents purport to communicate.

According to her, "When men put impediments in my way, I circumvent them, and I work directly with women who support and appreciate my efforts."

Lalita's husband is a stone worker who occasionally helps her at her shop to sell wares. Her husband continues to cut stones and engage in construction; sometimes he works as an agricultural laborer. She and her husband are from the traditionally stoneworker Vaddar caste, so she does construction work as well as coolie work during the rainy season. She learned construction work from her parents. At the moment, she said, her *panchayat* duties prevent her from helping her husband in constructing houses. Lalita used to work with her husband in road construction and stone work, and in agricultural labor. When she became the leader of the Roshni *sangha* in Mainalli, she said, "People saw me as articulate and fair in how I treat people. I think that's why both my family and people in Mainalli area asked me to consider running for the position of *panchayat* member. I'm happy that they encouraged me to do it because I was nervous about doing it because I only saw men serve on the *panchayat*."

She campaigned to become a member of the *gram panchayat* and later became president. The village leaders, especially women, had encouraged her to run for election; otherwise, she said she would not have. She said that now she wants to see that government schemes for the poor reach the poor in her village and that, though she did not receive any formal education, she has the wisdom, intelligence, and courage to succeed on the *panchayat*.

Lalita contended that male service providers often neglected some of the critical needs of children and women in their communities. She compared such service providers to the upper-caste Brahmins and political elites who often ignored the needs of lower-caste people (personal communication, 17 July 2011). In contrast, Lalita said, female-led village and community councils tend to promote family, individual, and community development in education, health, and general infrastructure.

Lalita enumerated some of the services she has helped others receive since she became a *panchayat* leader. For instance, as *sarpanch*, Lalita is responsible for acquiring project contracts for people under her jurisdiction, and she has given government-sanctioned contracts to workers, ranging from masons, electricians, and water-servicers to house builders. Asked how she awarded contracts, she said she looked up people's telephone numbers or asked for the numbers from other people. Once she had contact information for electricians and road contractors (for example), she called them to negotiate pay before assigning a job. She said she always vetted potential workers before giving them an assignment. For her *panchayat* work, she is paid 600 rupees per month.

She said, "Since I'm diligent when people call me to report shortage of water supply or electric power failure, and land disputes, I act promptly."

As part of their on-the-job training, she and other women *panchayat* leaders were taught how to handle people's conflicts in order to maintain peace and order, including different conflict-resolution approaches, by officials from the national and state governments.

Despite her lack of formal education, Lalita is perceived as a woman with status and determination in her society (Dovi 2010). When she was elected, she said she wanted education for her children and all of the children in the communities where she serves as *panchayat* president; she, therefore, has taken an interest in the selection of teachers for the villages. She also relies on the advice of the Sisters of the Holy Cross in Mainalli, where she lives, on how to serve her area's educational needs. For instance, she said that "the Sisters often advise me about some of the qualities and adequate facilities that a teacher for rural India needs to have." With that information, Lalita and other *panchayat* leaders help to find housing for teachers hired from outside the community. Lalita is thus able to ensure that the teachers get good and attractive accommodations that will make them want to live and work in the villages.

Lalita discusses political issues that come up when she and other leaders hold meetings with government officials. For instance, she said that when Mainalli needed electrification for its streets, she learned that another *panchayat* leader wanted to divert the electrification project to his area. Her husband advised her to go the headquarters of their *panchayat* to contest the matter. She did, and Mainalli got the amenities. (On other matters, she said she does not as a rule consult her husband.)

Lalita indicated that whenever some man commits violence against women, she and other female *panchayat* members collectively challenge the man and reprimand him when necessary.

She has representatives in the *gram panchayat* that she leads from all 14 villages under her jurisdiction. The members (seven women and seven men) hold meetings in the *gram panchayat* meeting center in Gunjavatti. Initially, she was nervous about how she was going to perform her duties as president. At the moment, however, she has built enough confidence as she has attended meetings, learned how to speak in public, and helped people settle disputes.

Lalita is also the president of the Roshni *sangha*, where she was elected to the post because she is knowledgeable and articulate. While she feels that the group has collective ownership of the *sangha,* the *panchayat* is a job for the government, so there will be a time when she is no longer the leader of the *panchayat*.

Since she lacks formal education, it has come to light that she is often sidetracked or that those taking contracts on her behalf do not give her the commissions that are expected in such cases. For instance, if she applies for a drainage contract for a village, and the government approves it, she is expected to get some monetary benefit; she realized recently that she had not been receiving commissions on such contracts because certain politicians had been pocketing the money meant for her. Her effectiveness and what is due to her are thus undermined by forms of corruption and by disregard for her interests. These entrenched attitudes still rear up in the face of the Indian government's democratizing efforts to bring about equality for all castes, tribes, and women.

During my interview with Lalita, several men and women from Mainalli expressed their views about her. According to a 30-year-old male Siddi community leader named Prakash Siddi, since Lalita is now a government-elected political leader, she has both legal and political backing to perform her duties. Prakash, though elected by his community members in a village of 3,000 people living in Mainalli, has the support only of Siddis, who make up only about 14 percent of the village. He said, further, that his own influence is felt only among Siddis in Mainalli, but Lalita is known and has *vajen* (Marathi for weight or administrative authority) over more than 8 (in fact, 14) villages.

Another person present at the interview was Shanta Jorge Siddi, a kindergarten teacher and, like Lalita, a *sangha* leader. Shanta compared her role to that of Lalita and said, "As *sangha* president, I am leader of a volunteer group of men and women who form a social network to support one another. While *sangha* members may come to me for financial help in microcredit loans, Lalita is often approached in matters regarding community development, education, health and water or electricity" (personal communication, 16 July 2011). Shanta also said that it was through the efforts of Lalita that a kindergarten was established in Mainalli.

According to Sushila, who is a member of the *sangha* Lalita has headed for the past eight years, "Lalita has provided leadership by articulating the needs of other women, and taken initiative to bring political authorities' attention to the needs of Mainalli people" (personal communication, 16 July 2011).

As a professional stonecutter, Lalita's father-in-law joined the discussion and said that stone cutting is specific while *panchayat* leadership involves dealing with many people and issues. He said, "Vaddar people know what and how the stones have to be cut, but I've seen my daughter-in-law who is not educated being asked to be president over villages of people of different traditions, and that may be more challenging than cutting stones" (personal communication, 16 July 2011).

Lalita's effectiveness as a leader is a result of more than her ability to articulate to state and government officials the needs of her constituents. She delegates to those who are educated when she needs their help to perform her duties. Through such delegating, she shows she respects those who have abilities she does not have; thus, they empower one another (Few 2002) to sustain the work they do.

Matters affecting the villages she is charge of that Lalita has addressed include bad roads, boreholes, and crops that have been damaged by extensive rains during the monsoon season. Farmers and others come to see her for ideas or help. According to Lalita, she collects a list of people who bring complaints, and goes to the Mundgod *panchayat* office to forward the informations she has been given to the *taluk* (subdistrict) office, and then she goes to Bangalore (the capital of Karnataka) for government help for farmers and small-shop keepers. In Bangalore she gets to speak with agricultural officers and invites them to consult with the farmers who need advice about (for example) damaged crops.

As Lalita tapped expert ideas to help her meet the needs of her people, she says people's confidence in her increased. "I also felt confident that I'm becoming a good leader for my people," she said (personal communication, 16 July 2011).

At every *panchayat* meeting that Lalita presides over, she is asked to share some advice. She often spoke about how women are responsible, caring for the house and children, while men tend to squander money. She said men have muscle power, but women are people with *budhi* (wisdom). And some women are beaten by their husbands, she said. At times she did not have time to eat because she was always busy. According to Lalita, in the past, some men did not respect her position in the community; those who had jobs and power tended not to recognize her influence.

During our interview, two men from Mundgod looking for her husband spoke with her without respect: they asked, "Where is your husband? He's supposed to be at work." She responded that he was at work elsewhere and that, when he finished that job, he would come to them. The men were surprised to hear her respond that way because they thought she would call the husband immediately.

Lalita later explained that she had learned from her new position that "no one should treat another as if he owned another person" (personal communication, 16 July 2011). She gained this awareness from trainings that government officers responsible for *panchayats* gave to *panchayat* leaders.

Lalita's *shakti* has been manifested in her role as an advocate for her constituents. She has expressed her anger at injustice as the female diety who uses her energy to ensure that justice is done. For example, recently two Vaddar workers died in a quarry near Hubli, and Lalita was informed about the incident. She took up the matter with the Karnataka state police, where she lodged a complaint on behalf of the deceased. In March 2012, the families of the deceased were compensated by the owners of the quarries.

Previously and at times also presently, in rural communities injustices against minority people occur and continue to go unchecked. However, Lalita's new role has enabled her to fight for the bereaved families, a role that up until recently only men with recognition and money could play.

At times, Lalita has sought advice from her husband; for instance, in Mainalli when the construction of a street gutter for good drainage was approved by the *panchayat*, she asked her husband, who is also involved in road construction, for his views about where and how the work could be done.

When asked how she considered her role as a *panchayat* leader in light of what she used to do, she said, "I know some people see me as a Vaddar president, but I am a leader for all castes and tribes in the villages. Cutting stones under the sun is taxing, but now as a shopkeeper and *panchayat* president, my work brings me respect and dignity that is not based on the traditional expectation of my caste" (personal communication, 16 July 2011).

In January 2011, Lalita had requested that some streets in Mainalli be provided with electric lights. She wanted to have "children and women in particular to walk at night without fear," she said (personal communication, 20 June 2011). She had asked an electrician to begin the electrification of a street near the local Catholic convent because "they are all women living there and they help our community and other people," she said (personal communication, 20 June 2011).

According to some people in Mainalli, including the Catholic nuns, when the electricians were at work, Lalita frequented the site to inspect it. At some point she visited the workers and reprimanded them because they were too slow in installing the lights. She visited all the sites, Lalita said, to ensure that, if the workers were short of materials, more could be purchased so the work could be completed on time. Lalita had become a decision maker and a supervisor of public works, a job that was until recently done only by men.

Though at home she defers to her husband on some matters, Lalita's public performance shows that she displays competence as a public leader despite her caste and the fact she is a woman.

Thus, despite the cultural, caste, economic, and sexual hierarchies used to exclude and exploit women, *panchayats* are becoming avenues to elevate rural women, making them visible as role models for others. Lalita's membership in both *panchayat* and *sangha* in Mainalli accords her access to resources that she translates into decision-making power in her household and in her constituency. Besides having control over critical resources, Latlita is a government representative who gives road construction and rural electrification jobs to workers; Lalita also hires workers and pays them. She said she feels empowered by making decisions beyond her family. There are other women who have not had the opportunity to be involved in decision making, even within their own households.

She maintained that, at the moment, she knows she has respect and recognition in her communities and at government offices. In my 13 July 2011 interview, Lalita underscored the fact that she and other women are better at handling financial matters than men since they have been efficient at accounting for all that was entrusted to them, while most of the men in and around Mainalli tended to squander their meager family resources.

While Lalita lives in Mainalli, a village settled by different castes and tribes, Savakka's community is settled by Gowlis. Savakka Yappa, a 45-year-old Gowli and a *panchayat* member, living in the village of Jogeshwarhalla, is one of two female members who sit on the traditional village council, or *hiriyaru*, where local decisions are made and government programs are agreed to before any work can happen at the village level. Savakka said, "For over 50 years, since our parents settled here, the men have not done much to better the lives of people here, so I credit the people for including Janubai [another Gowli woman, profiled later in this book] and me on the village council."

Savakka became a *hiriyaru* member before being elected to the *gram panchayat*, where she represents eight villages. Her responsibilities include helping *panchayat* members get government houses built for them and working on the development of infrastructure, such as getting good drinking water and electrification of the streets. She said that, whenever she needed to complete government documents, she checked with those more knowledgeable to explain them to her.

According to Savakka, it was through her efforts that the people in Karginkoppa and Anjali received nursery schools and daycare centers from the government. She described herself as someone able to visit government offices to advocate for her *panchayat* constituents. She said, "This advocacy role was previously either performed by men, or no one cared about the welfare of the people in those villages" (personal communication, 13 July 2011).

When asked to comment on her understanding of power, of *shakti*, she said that "God is the only powerful being. After God, the knowledgeable person is powerful" (personal communication, 13 July 2011). Later she said, "One who thinks about the village people and its improvement is powerful because the rich keep their money in their pocket. Such rich people are not powerful." Savakka further stated, "Rich people do not have *vajen* [Marathi for power or 'weight']" (personal communication, 13 July 2011). She regarded herself as a person "with *vajen* because I'm able to help improve the conditions or the lives of my family, my community, and myself" (personal communication, 13 July 2011).

She said she goes around her community encouraging children to go to school. As she encouraged people to improve their lives, she argued that she was increasing her own *vajen*.

Savakka is a Gowli whose family still raises livestock, including cows and buffaloes. During the planting season, the family leases some of their land to farmers. Her husband grazes animals and milks cows and buffaloes. Savakka said that her husband goes outside to work but she makes "the decisions that affect their household. I keep the family income, and my husband and I decide how to spend money since we both know how much income we have. Men may contribute to the family income, but I make all decisions as to what the children will eat and how often they eat" (personal communication, 13 July 2011).

She continued, "The *ghar* [Hindi for house] falls or stands on the woman. *Nai, nai* ['no, no' in Marathi and Hindi], men are not powerful; women have more power than men. The reason we banned alcohol sale or drugs here is that some men only get strength from the glass or bottle," she concluded.

According to Savakka, women engage in domestic work all the time in addition to what they do outside. She maintained that women and their contributions have been the firm foundation of Gowli societies. For instance, she said that before she and Janubai became *panchayat* and *hiriyaru* members, the men did nothing about improving the social and material life of the villagers. At the moment, the two women's efforts have brought about clean drinking water for their villages and include their ongoing fight to secure lands for farmers in their community.

She further said that her village faces an eviction threat from the forest department after Jogeshwarhalla residents received a notice from the department that they were living on encroached land. This happened about two months before my visit.

After a *panchayat* meeting in which Savakka learned that anyone who has lived on a piece of land for ten years can lay claim to the land after procuring a deed to it, she said she was emboldened to fight against the forest department official, taking an active role in her village's land dispute: in response to the notice, Savakka and other *panchayat* members went to the Karwar District Office to fight for the right to live in their village. She told the officials that if they try to evict the villagers, "we will go to Sirsi, Bangalore, or Delhi until we have been heard and our needs are met" (personal communication, 13 July 2011). On 20 July 2013, the Jogeshwarhalla residents were informed by the Karwar District Office that they were no longer going to be evicted.

Savakka said that since she began to serve on the *panchayat*, she has increased her social power. To her, power (*vajen*) or influence means that she is able to travel outside her immediate community to meet and advocate for more people and to help her people. The feminization of public space, especially at the local level, has created gender-equitable cultural norms as she and other women are seen as performing roles previously reserved for men. Also, as Savakka and other women leaders perform their duties, men and women are challenged to review their own notions of women's appropriate behavior as it was traditionally understood, even though some of the women in her village, Savakka said, "still think a woman should not be seen traveling to all the places I have been going because I have to take care of the children." Also, some of the women were not concerned about being actively involved in changing the social and economic conditions of their communities.

As a *panchayat* member, Savakka has been a trailblazer for other women in rural India. I was first led to Savakka's village because I had heard about her and her influence from a newly elected woman *panchayat* member in another village. Women such as Savakka thus are becoming agents of change as they compel society to change their understandings about female agency.

Men used to be the ones who made critical decisions among Gowlis and other rural communities. Today, however, Savakka and other female leaders are seen as making valuable contributions to their communities. They have created or used opportunities to participate in local politics for multiple purposes. Though most of these women have limited or no formal education, they participate in nonformal and institutionalized processes of decision making and development (Bourque and Warren 1981: 177) to help create new opportunities for both men and women to advance themselves and their societies.

Today in India, Savakka and other *panchayat* women are often cited as examples of influential *panchayat* women. Such role models may not themselves know of the impact of their political activities and social influence. As Savakka and the likes of Chennama, Janubai, and Lalita increase their administrative and political skills, they have become pressure groups in their communities, choosing issues relevant to their communities to galvanize men and women into action.

The women's responses to the new opportunities and their understandings of the impact of resources are shaped by the social values and political contexts in which they live and work. For instance, when the government formulates policies about such matters as road construction, education, health, or ration cards, the implementation of these policies is now filtered through the lived experiences of local women.

Savakka pointed out that she stood in a long line of women in India's history who have expressed creativity, self-reliance, and autonomy. She was alluding to Gowli folk stories that stress the power of women to rescue whole communities during times of famine and war. As examples, she mentioned Jijabai, who was the mother of the powerful national hero, warrior, and King Chhatraprati Shivaji, and the heroine Gangamma, who was a cow herder who used her courage and strength to protect her livestock.

Savakka's example demonstrates, in concrete ways, how she and other women manifest influence that is self-empowering and transforms the lives of others, advancing their causes, beyond just invoking a mythical heroic past, by challenging social hierarchies.

Lalita and Savakka are Hindu; some women *panchayat* members are Muslim. The Muslim Urdu education has been found to limit some women's ability to take on social and political roles in their communities. However, there are Indian Muslim women who have used their personal force and determination to assert their influence. Such is Hayatabi Allabhakha (Allabaksh) Patil Siddi, 28, a Muslim *gram panchayat* member living in Gurlehalli, in Karnataka.

While her influence is not derived from overt political activities like those of Savakka, Hayatabi argues that the help she has given women in her jurisdiction as a *panchayat* member makes her feel that she has *gaurava* (Sanskrit for strength, power, pride). Hayatabi said, "My Urdu education prevents me from reading and understanding documents written in Kannada, so now that I seek help to understand *panchayat* records, my power in the community is increasing."

Hayatabi defines power in the following way: "I see power as the opportunity to mingle with people on the *panchayat* administration. With this opportunity, I become confident." She admitted she is not fully powerful because the *panchayat* office has many records that, because of her limited education, she cannot read or understand; she was educated in an Urdu medium school, and all *panchayat* records are in English and Kannada, neither of which she understands. Despite this limitation, she said she had been able to draw inspiration from many people as she discharged her duties.

As an example of such inspiration, Hayatabi described a young Member of the Karnataka Legislative Assembly, from Haliyal in the Joida constituency, an MLA (Member of Legislative Assembly) named Hegde, who stood against the prominent politician called R. V. Deshpande, former president of the Karnataka Pradesh Congress Committee, and defeated the latter in an election by a huge majority. Hayatabi said, "Now Hegde has power in his hands and is serving the people very well. This young MLA inspired me to contest in the election, and today I am a *panchayat* member."

She argued that her power on the *panchayat* increases when she is effective in delivering government schemes to the people. In our interview, Hayatabi said,

> Power is not felt at once. I grow as I do more things for people. I change my present condition with the new experiences I gain through my service. Earlier, I had less respect and appreciation from people. The men

> in society always prevented women from becoming influential. Many of them are corrupt. Men don't want to give equal status to the women. So I work hard to set an example by being honest, and I get *izzath* [Urdu for respect]. I have *izzath* and it makes me happier. I will not lose hope. (Hayatabi, 19 July 2012)

According to Hayatabi, the state government has started a new program, called Bhagyalakshmi Insurance, for female children of Below Poverty Line (BPL) families. The insurance also has a widow payment program, which it is also extending throughout Karnataka.

Hayatabi said, "As a *panchayat* member, I am getting more information to improve myself because people have elected me to serve the villages. Here, I claim and insist on my rights and the rights of others to improve women's lives."

The *panchayat* president (*sarpanch*) holds various meetings to introduce *panchayat* members to the government's new forms of opportunities and resources for women. The president provides information about various facilities, including house or toilet construction.

> The government-given power is different from other powers. Because, we, the members of the *panchayat,* always work with our *panchayat* officers, they bring and introduce facilities to us, and we convince them about the appropriations of the aid to the villagers. We get this new form of power through our membership. In our village, women are forming *sanghas* to create awareness among the women. Through the *sangha* structure, the women are learning how to save money. Some have started opening bank accounts. This kind of change has improved our village women's lives. The women have also taken political action, she concluded. (Hayatabi, 19 July 2012)

Hayatabi also said that she led a group of women to stop the sale of alcohol in their village; so, at the moment, no alcohol shops are funded in their community.

Hayatabi is an example of a Muslim woman who, though she is without formal education, yet engages in politics to make a difference because of the respect (*izzath*) and trust she gives and, in turn, receives from her community. Her *shakti* is the self-empowering type that enables her to encourage women to take control of their financial resources by opening their own savings accounts, and to fight for their rights (Few 2002; Gaventa 2006). She has also helped women in her village to join local *sanghas*.

Hayatabi does not comprehend all the information used by her *panchayat*, and her limited level of education makes it difficult for her to understand the functions and rules of the *panchayat* administration. But, she said, "I'm like a blossoming flower on the *panchayat* administration."

Hayatabi defines power as consisting of *dairadith* (Konkani for courage, respect) that the people give her for her hard work. "Each day's hard work on my part leads me towards success and community improvement." She described luck and hard work as two faces of the same coin (Lukes and Haglund 2000). Hayatabi's ideas help to clarify what Lukes and Haglund (2000) argued about how power works. According to them, luck is a crucial part of power. Some who hold power do not always succeed at what they plan to achieve; on the other hand, there are others who attain their objectives despite the fact they did not try harder than those who failed. Similarly, Hayatabi said,

> Power does not come to people easily; we must strive to gain it. The way of obtaining power is based on one's relentless effort, ability to monitor what has been done, and sheer hard work. Power is a kind of bubble of water we don't know when it breaks. People who do not know how to hold it lose it. The public always observes the work and the behavior of its leaders. If we, the leaders, fail in the public's estimation, our power base erodes, and we may end up really losing in future elections. If it is possible, I plan to contest for the *taluk panchayat* election. I am interested in having power like that of the politicians. I told you earlier that I am a bud of a flower in the *panchayat* administration. Increasing my knowledge base during my three years will help me to use my power in the development of people.

Hayatabi continued,

> In India we have a number of great leaders who became famous because they served their people. For example, Mahatma Gandhiji led a life of dedication and determination [Konkani: *Gandhijile sevakarche gunha tenka shakthishali karle*; Hindi: *Gandhiji ka sevamanobava unako shakthishali kiya*]. He utilized his *vajen* power to overthrow the Britishers in India. Thus Gandhiji was self-disciplined, and he used the same skill to galvanize others and guided them to become united as Indians. (Hayatabi, 19 July 2012)

According to her, the central government of India has begun a new program of house construction especially for women—the Indira Avar scheme. The Karnataka state government has also introduced other programs, such as the Ashraya and Ambedkar housing schemes, for rural women.

Women in Hayatabi's village are beginning to form support networks. For example, in January 2012, the Anganwadi (nursery school) teachers, who are all women, united to fight for better working conditions and salaries. They protested for two weeks, and their struggle paid off: eventually, they received salary increases and were offered teaching assistants so their workload would be lessened. Hayatabi's ability to organize and lead the protest expresses an example of women's *shakti*, formed through networking, to make the government provide resources the teachers had a right to demand.

> Today [Hayatabi continued], most women are sending their daughters to school because they are beginning to value education after realizing that education enables people to know about and insist on their rights. One of the major results of my activism was when Siddi people struggled hard to receive ST status. For the past seven years, Siddis have been enjoying the benefits of their new status as a Scheduled Tribe because they worked together and fought for their rights. When the women realized that they could stand election for real political offices, Siddi women encouraged me to compete with other castes/tribes in the society for government resources and political participation. (Hayatabi, 19 July 2012)

Hayatabi said she has helped to secure environmentally improved iron stoves, and houses sanctioned by the state government for the rural poor. The stoves, which are said to cut toxic emissions and reduce cooking time, are part of the Indian government's effort to provide appropriate cooking facilities for rural Indians.

She also sought permission for basket weavers who live in her *panchayat* area to cut bamboo trees to use for their trade. The authorization she sought was significant because, unlike previous times, when basket weavers could easily obtain raw materials from the forest for their trade, they could no longer do so without a permit from the Karnataka forest department. Now, through the intervention of a new governmental structure, the weavers are able to continue with their traditional caste-specific profession.

This right is not automatic because the forest department officials who enforce the forest laws tend to issue permits based on cronyism. Most businessmen and politicians are often allowed access to forest produce and land while marginalized communities are forbidden.

In response to my question about how she knew about the forest permit, she said, "The *panchayat* secretary and *panchayat* development officer (PDO) gave the *panchayat* members the information about the government's facilities." According to Hayatabi, furnished with the relevant information, she and others were able to get the appropriate permit and thus improve the lives of the basket weavers in her community.

Her personal example and the stories she shared indicate how, as women gain more knowledge, they increase their status and power. Specifically, when women gain more awareness, they are able to unite around issues that matter to them; an example is the success of Hayatabi and the women she mobilized in banning liquor shops from the Gurlehalli community.

Hayatabi has used her *panchayat* membership as a means to develop her skills and gifts and gain a reputation among both men and women in her community. Despite her lack of a formal education, Hayatabi understands much about the politics of service to the poor and the power that accrues from service to others. She has used her positional power to enlist help and material resources for her community (Clegg 1989; Dowding 1991). She also makes important decisions to transform her life as she pays attention to the needs of other people. That is an improvement over the past when women did not have the strategies and government backing to deal with social evils.

Twenty years ago, it would have been inconceivable to see Harijans/Dalits serve as local *panchayat* leaders. Today, Mamata ma Chandra Shekar Harijan has made use of the new opportunities in India to become a vice-president of a local *panchayat*.

Mamata ma Chandra Shekar Harijan, 30, lives at Ajjihalli, near Chigalli. She is a Harijan/Dalit (SC) and was educated up to the eighth standard. Mamata is among Harijan/Dalit women who have begun to increase their power as they tap the new possibilities available to them in India. She grows rice and takes care of animals, including buffaloes and cows.

Before India's current democratizing efforts, Harijans/Dalits generally did not have opportunities to hold political office. Now, however, Mamata ma Harijan, as a *panchayat* vice president, uses her new power to benefit others and herself in rural India. Mamata's new role is the result of the ways that the government of India, through legislation, has relocated or transferred some of its authority and power to rural Indians. The rural people are now being asked to perform tasks that used to be in the hands of male government officials.

Asked to talk about power in my interview with her, Mamata said,

> More people go to the rich to borrow money, and they end up being in debt to the rich men. Since rich people are seen as powerful, people are afraid of them. The person who has power sends his or her children to private and English medium schools, but not to municipal or government schools. The rich people are always getting the best education so their children will get government jobs. (10 June 2012)

Mamata, going on to identify conventional notions of power in her society, included the rich, who have economic power over the poor in her community, and people who have been educated and therefore have a government job.

She said that when any of the children in her village received a college education, the parents felt their dreams were fulfilled, and that made them powerful. According to Mamata, the children's education was a key factor in guaranteeing that their people, especially the Harijans/Dalits, would have a better future. Mamata said that before *panchayat* seats opened up for her, her community relied on and became used to only male government officials informing her and other people about amenities the government was planning to provide for her community. At present, however, she and other women have become critical channels of information about government facilities for their people.

She said the information she and the other *panchayat* women give to their communities did not have political motives. An example of this (according to her) was that, when she and other women leaders learned that the Karnataka government was going to build modern homes for the people of Ajjihalli, they did not take bribes before sharing the information. For years, Mamata said, for any assistance her community received, the men who brought the news asked for the beneficiaries to pay a bribe. The corruption of the men made it difficult for the very poor to receive their due share of government support.

She said that whenever she is asked to inform her community about government programs for the poor, "I get information through the village *panchayat* members, and I pass it on to others so they can better their lives." As she works hard on the *panchayat*, she realizes that her power and influence emanate from the state government and the *panchayat.*

As a *panchayat* vice president, she admitted that she has experienced incremental power because she has helped people get government services; for example, under her supervision, the community cleaned the surroundings of the village pre-primary school, refurbished water tanks, and distributed plants to the schools for teachers and students to plant as part of Karnataka's reforestation program. She is now helping to get the roads and gutters of the village repaired. After that, she wants to tackle unemployment for the young people in her village.

Under her leadership, women are raising awareness in families to unite to prevent the supply of liquor in the village. Alcoholism seems to have an adverse impact on families and communities in rural India. Thus, she and some *panchayat* women see their roles as focusing on efforts to eradicate that social evil.

With the expanded power of some women, the local women have become a formidable pressure group aimed at reversing the chronic problem of alcoholism among men, since alcoholic husbands often spend money on drink and neglect their families, and some drunken men commit violence against their wives and children.

Thus Mamata's (as a female) expanded legal rights and political representation at various levels of society have enabled her to organize other women to take collective action for altering policies to enhance people's lives.

The changes Mamata and other women are introducing were not priorities for the men who were in charge of community development before the women joined the *panchayats*. Also, although the women have always felt a need to improve their own education and the education of girls, cultural attitudes impeded women's education. Moreover, the skill set that *panchayat* members are being given today was not in the past available to women. Women's previous lack of influence was also due to prejudice against women. Those who wielded entrenched patriarchal norms underestimated women's capabilities.

Mamata listed some of her accomplishments, saying,

> through the *panchayat*, I have been granted 10 thousand rupees for the handicapped people, a 30 thousand rupee loan has been granted to Shree Shakti *sangha*, and Udyoga Katri [employment insurance that enables cardholding workers to verify that their incomes are deposited into their personal savings accounts] work has been instituted in some of the villages. I got all of this done for the people during my five months of leadership. (10 June 2012)

She said she is gaining more knowledge about how the *panchayat* works. According to Mamata, before she became a *panchayat* leader, "I was living within the four walls of my home, and I did not know the world outside my community. Now I understand how the world is bigger than my village. I know how to walk in this new world."

When her life was limited to her home, Mamata was powerless in the face of conditions she wished she could change for the better. She felt that men and the rich had power over her. Now that she has been elected to political office, she exercises power with others to effect change.

However, Mamata said that, although she is respected in her village, not all of the communities within the *panchayat*'s jurisdiction acknowledge her newly gained power. She narrated an incident at a village where the village elders did not give her a seat with their community leaders. According to her, because she is a Harijan/Dalit, the community's male elders considered Mamata to be ritually unacceptable. She told the elders she had come to the community because a number of women had invited her to assess needs they had to improve the village's health and sanitation conditions. On that occasion, she said she mustered her courage and drew on her power within to address the gathering while she remained standing, and assured them she would do everything in her power to send workers to study the conditions in that village.

Mamata later reported to the *panchayat* head office in Mundgod how she had been treated badly. As expected, officials went to the village to educate the elders about the new laws outlawing discrimination based on caste, religion, or gender. Mamata said that, when she went back to the village, she was received without any of the initial unwelcome attitude.

As Mamata expands her knowledge about the wider world, she contends that she finds more possibilities to advance herself and to assist others. Her transformative power (Batliwala 2011: 65) enables her to perform new roles in rural India as she engages patriarchy and other social hierarchies.

"People will give you respect if you become a member of the *panchayat*, even as a Harijan," she said. "In the past, I was only going outdoors to work in the field as a coolie. Now I mingle with everybody. I have no fear to interact with all people, as I previously did." Mamata's transformative power (Giddens 1984) enables her to break down barriers that Harijans/ Dalits often face.

According to her, she hopes to encourage other women to form informal networks that will empower them to learn about women's rights. Though activism is not a part of a *panchayat* leader's responsibilities, Mamata, a Harijan/Dalit, is reconfiguring her role to raise consciousness among rural women about their rights as citizens of India.

The villagers respect and honor her. As some of the village people say, "Mamata ma is a small idol with a big heart and great fame" (in Kannada: *Mamata yavara vishalahridaya avarannu thumba dada vyakthiyannagi maadithu. Moorthi chikkadaadree keerthe doddadu,* in Konkani: *Mamata ka khoob hod hrudaya asa, thhekka sati thhe hamka dev asilethas*, in Hindi: *Mamata bada dilwali hai, isliye vo devataswarup hai*).

Panchayats have been used by some women in rural India to create opportunities for their own development and the social and economic improvement of their families and communities. While not all elected women leaders are effective members, village communities and the *panchayat* women attest to the fact that, since some women became *panchayat* members, their communities are beginning to directly receive benefits from the state and central governments. Moreover, all the *panchayat* members are perceived as government representatives who work with the government's legal authority. When they receive their pay from government offices, some of them contend that their income, even if meager, is preferable to working in the fields as coolies.

Another *gram panchayat* president is Janubai Janu Gowli, 30, of Jainmuri, which has a population of 400; she is also a dairy inspector for a milk company.

Since becoming president of her *gram panchayat,* she has also served on the village *samaj* in her all-Gowli settlement. She has succeeded in acquiring a Karnataka government land permit called a *patta,* which allows the residents of Jainmuri to build houses on *gautana* (Kannada for vacant nonagricultural land deemed suitable for housing). As Pitkin (1972) asserts, Janubai has the power to accomplish goals—*shakti* that is not power *over* others but rather the ability to achieve something for oneself and others.

Janubai and her family raise cows. In addition, she is employed by a milk company, ShriKrishna Milks Private Limited, as their inspection agent for Jainmuri and other communities. The company supplies milk and milk products to manufacturing companies, restaurants, and hotels in Karnataka. For about an hour every day, Janubai inspects milk brought from local suppliers before it is sent on for processing and distribution by the company.

Her new role as a dairy inspector is built on a preexisting village practice in which people collect milk to deliver to customers' homes in their community. Janubai and her family have been working in the milk business since her childhood; now, however, she is not working with or for her family but instead for a company that has its own work ethics.

She received only two days of training, and she has no formal education, but she uses her "knowledge" (*budhi,* the word for wisdom in Hindi) based on her previous dairy work with her family producing and selling milk in her present occupation. She said that her children, because of their schooling, taught her how to write in Kannada, the state language of Karnataka (her own language is Marathi); as she is able to write and keep accounts for the dairy work, the company has employed her as their agent in the villages.

She has four children—two boys and two girls. She kept her children in school, so, she said, one benefit she has received from her children's education is that she can now speak and write in Kannada.

For the dairy inspection work she gets 100 rupees per week. She is the only woman in a radius of about 20 miles who does milk inspection, and that makes her feel she has status and power beyond her village. In other localities dairy inspectors are men.

She explained that she is strict about the quality of milk she gives to the milk company and is pleased to have been hired by them. Janubai said that some of her village people who often dilute their milk prefer to sell to agents who do not use a lactometer (as Janubai does) to check the butter quality or for dilution. Nevertheless, Janubai said she was sympathetic toward villagers who choose to sell to other agents in order to avoid her stringent rules about quality.

She was elected to the *panchayat* and, in the eyes of her community, had *vajen* because of her work for the dairy company. According to Janubai, enforcing her company's strict rules has given her credibility as well as making some people in her community resentful. Despite this resentment, she was elected to serve on a *panchayat* and is now *panchayat* president.

The community people find her to be fair and hardworking. Even those who sell diluted milk through other agents acknowledge that, because she works for a big company and receives a steady income, she has power and influence. For instance, at her milk inspection office, Janubai prevented a man from bullying his wife. During our interview, the man was yelling at his wife and ordering her to go home since, according to him, she was to stay home and not be with Janubai and strangers. Janubai asked the husband to leave the site and made the woman stay. Janubai later explained that she had told the man that he had no right to humiliate his wife in public. In this way Janubai used her newly gained awareness about women's rights to advocate for another woman at her place of business.

Janubai explained later that some Gowli men drink heavily and verbally or physically abuse their family members. She also explained that the man had left on her orders because Janubai works for a big milk company and is a *panchayat* president: to the village people, Janubai, who grew up among them, is seen, at present, as the representative of both the government and a powerful private company.

In addition, Janubai said she had learned from the *panchayat* meetings that women should stand up for their rights and not allow anyone to intimidate them. Some women would have obeyed the husband and gone home as he wanted. Janubai's intervention pointed to a new reality in which a relatively youthful woman in her 30s, as Janubai said, "could stand up to a married man whose culture taught him that his wife should be treated as property."

Another source of her power is the honesty with which she does business. While senior members of her village were diluting their milk to increase the quantity to sell to outsiders, Janubai used a lactometer to measure the purity and the butter content, thus doing her work with honesty and fairness. She enters the lactometer measurements in her books, provides proper accounting for the milk going to ShriKrishna Milks, and pays the villagers who sell their milk to her. She exemplifies the *sarnana* (Kannada for courage and respect) and *izzath* (Hindi/Urdu for honor, respect) dimensions of power.

Since she uses the company's money to pay the milk producers, she says she has achieved important social status despite her lack of formal schooling. Janubai's job gives her economic independence. She also brokers the price of milk for her clients in her village and surrounding villages. According to her, she is sympathetic when the milk suppliers complain that, due to cow diseases and lack of rain, it is getting difficult for them to get enough milk to sell. She often negotiates with ShriKrishna Milks to increase their buying price of milk from the producers. Janubai's influence thus is shown in how she champions the interests of her people.

Janubai has sought government assistance for drainage, toilet facilities, and electricity for her village. She also wants to improve village roads, help people in her community purchase modern houses, and refurbish the village temple.

She asserts that whoever is educated and is knowledgeable has power. Since she does not have a formal education but does have power, she explained that "any person who has intimate understanding of the needs of the poor and knows how to address those needs has *budhi* [knowledge or wisdom]" (in Kannada: *oodi thildukon diruvadkkinth mukyevagi. Yavada vyakthi badjanara samasseyannu aritu avarige sahaya maduvadari nda avarige samajadali gaurava hechenguttada*).

According to Janubai, it has been about a year since she succeeded in getting approval to construct houses for Jainmuri. As of 4 January 2012, no work had taken place since the forest department of Karnataka had put an injunction on the building project because of encroachment. The case was in court. Then, in May 2012, after Janubai had made numerous trips to the court, the government granted the Gowli community a permit to live in Jainmuri.

Janubai is an example of marginalized women who now have a chance to participate in India's decentralized governance, capacity-building, and decision-making practices in their local communities.

Janubai is powerful in some areas but, since the forest department prevents her from implementing some of the projects for which she has sought government permission, she feels she is not able to do as much as she hopes. As mentioned above, Janubai's personal force and the spirit of the Indian government's reform goals are thwarted by the forest department, a branch of government that exerts unfair influence on local-level people who may not know how to circumvent or challenge the department's uneven application of the new forestry laws.

It was only on 17 June 2012 that Janubai was informed that seven houses had been approved by the municipal government to be built under her jurisdiction. Her task was to select families that would benefit from the government-housing scheme.

Whereas her *panchayat* job faces roadblocks, her dairy inspection job is doing well, and she says that, after being successful at milk inspection and serving on the *panchayat*, she wants to become a contractor. She plans to persuade the *panchayat* members to allow her to take development contracts in the villages. As a contractor, she will be responsible for choosing workers to build schools, village drainage systems, and electrification. She also said she would then have the power to pay workers at government-regulated rates. As she hires workers and pays them their salaries, she will make more money for herself and her family. The opportunity will give her the power to inspect the work as a local citizen so she can provide firsthand progress reports on the development projects to the *panchayat* or government. To Janubai, this anticipated new role will accord her more power and prestige in her community. She said she had heard about women contractors in Mangalore and other big cities but did not know of any woman contractor in the Mundgod area.

She, like other rural Indian women, is fostering or directly creating new opportunities to earn more income and change her social and political conditions as she improves herself and her community. She argued that she would have time for her family and community because she does not wish to travel far from home.

Married women like Janubai who have public responsibilities as well balance family life with their public duties. Janubai, like all the other women with public responsibilities, straddles different spheres of influence. She hopes to balance her role and status as a citizen of her local community, remaining a responsible family woman while she is engaged in new roles that increase her prestige and authority. The challenges of the public roles of women like Janubai have become a basis for debates in conservative communities where women are not allowed to interact with nonfamily males; such attitudes cut across caste, tribe, and religion.

She uses her interactions with influential outsiders to seek educational opportunities for children in her village; for instance, on our visit on 20 June 2011, she appealed to us to help find funding for two girls who have enrolled at a local private school. Janubai also showed that she is resourceful and always looking ahead to improve the social and material conditions of her people.

4.2 A teacher

Shakuntala Saju Gowli, 26, is a teacher and warden of a nursery school hostel run by the NGO Loyola Vikas Kendra (LVK) in the village of Shregeri.

She studied at Belgaum College, where she earned her Dip.Ed. (Diploma in Education), whereas most Gowlis from her village do not get to the level of Dip.Ed. She has also received training in Mundgod, organized by the government, for farmers and livestock owners. To her, education is a source of power for herself and others. Her mother, first, and, later, her father encouraged her to continue her studies. (In some Gowli families, the parents get their daughters married at 13 or 15, at which time the daughters' education ends.)

Her parents are cowherders and also do daily wage work as coolies. She has two brothers and two sisters. One sister studied up to the tenth standard and stopped, the other sister only completed the third standard. Her brothers did not go to school. Her siblings help their parents in herding cows and milking animals. According to Shakuntala, she had a teacher who encouraged her to study hard so she could go beyond elementary school. After teaching for some time, she said she wanted to continue her education so she could become a lecturer some day.

When she was a child, she helped in grazing their family animals in the forest, but she was always determined to go to school. When she and other Gowli children went to school near Manchikeri, she remembers that "we were always late and some of the teachers made fun of us because of our lateness and the fact that we were not dressed as neatly as the other children." Since her parents did not receive a formal education, she did not receive any help with her homework. Also, because her family used kerosene lanterns in the evenings, the family had to put out the light by a certain hour; everyone had to go bed, and she was prevented from doing her homework. She said,

> I decided to use recess and lunch times at school to do my homework. Sometimes I managed to complete the work and there were times when I could not. I remember that some of the teachers did not think I could advance beyond elementary school. I became more determined when I had high grades one year and a teacher encouraged me to continue my education. (Shakuntala, 15 August 2012)

When she arrived in Shrigeri, she said, "The first thing I did was to encourage the community to clean up the village by clearing bushes and keeping their homesteads tidy." She was met with opposition because the people there did not appreciate her trying to impose on them her sense of cleanliness or sanitation. She changed her approach and decided to focus on the children who lived at the hostel. More than twice, before the students went home to visit their families over weekends, she said, "I made them take a bath, and wore clean outfits before I sent them home." She also held meetings with the parents and taught them about personal hygiene, and the parents began to understand the importance of keeping their children clean. On subsequent occasions, when the children returned from home, they were tidy and brought additional clean clothes, she realized.

Aside from teaching her pupils further about the importance of hygiene, such as taking a bath before coming to school, she has also given training to people about nutrition and good sanitation.

Having learned from her student days, Shakuntala made a timetable for the students' study, sleep, and sports schedules, and she supervised the children during the hours they were with her. She and other LVK hostel teacher-wardens had monthly meetings where they exchanged ideas and experiences. She has found those sessions important because they discussed how to discipline children. She learned that, when a student misbehaved, it was not appropriate to cane or reprimand the student before the whole class. Rather, the teacher had to pull the child aside and find out what might be causing the child to be acting up.

Since she wants to continue her education beyond her Dip.Ed., she has registered for a correspondence course for a B.Ed. (bachelor's degree in education), which she said she hoped to complete while still teaching so she could pay off much of her student loan.

Shakuntala said, "If I am a teacher, people will remember me for many years. Education has given me a say in other people's lives; whatever I'm doing with my Dip.Ed. is important. Politicians like the Karnataka state Chief Minister often tells lies by promising things he cannot give the people. But for me, when I teach children, what I share is a foundation for their future."

She said that after she had earned a graduate degree she would marry, because she did not want her husband to interrupt her educational career.

In addition to teaching, Shakuntala has written plays and said she hopes to travel to villages to stage them. Some of her plays have been staged in Mundgod, and in one contest she won second prize. Her plays focus on child marriage and violence against women and children. She drew her themes from her own experience in her community. Her other subjects include alcoholism, kidnapping of girls, and different forms of discrimination based on caste and gender.

As a teacher she saw herself as a mentor for children, a role model for Gowli women and children, and a leader for a SHG (a *sangha*) of women.

According to her, "Someone who has influence/authority is the person who alleviates suffering of the poor and works hard to bring about justice in society. The powerful person also assists poor children to receive a good education because he/she has concern for the poor people." The powerful person seeks solutions for people's problems. She further said, "*Shosheta jananga badavaregi*" (Kannada for "I provide care for exploited and poor people").

There are over 100 people in the village of Shrigeri. As a teacher and hostel warden, she was consulted about registering the births of newborns, and any document that required someone to read and interpret. Shakuntala kept track of birth, death, and marriage records for the Gowlis in the Shrigeri community. Keeping track of such records enabled her to take that responsibility from the hands of unscrupulous men, she said, "who took bribes to adjust dates and ages to show their power."

Shakuntala said she used her knowledge to benefit others rather than to exploit people. She thus had control over channels of access to governmental and nongovernmental resources.

According to Shakuntala, the village people protected and respected her; for instance, there was a particular day on which people in the community advised her not to go out because they had heard rumors that some "troublemakers were harassing women in their neighboring communities."

She argued that she has more power than the village *pancharu* (a traditional village council, constituted only by men). Even the *panch* members often deferred to her about matters affecting the village.

She asked rhetorically, "How is a man more powerful than a woman? When I, as a woman, can educate children, be in charge of important records that cover birth, death, and marriage." Also, according to her, power is not based on money.

Shakuntala's story provides an example of how the new opportunities for women have also fostered new skills as well as self-confidence and expanded roles, with attendant competence and capability building.

Her power resides in her education and her ability to extend that power to others, in particular, to the children in her charge. And she has also used her position to educate and inform the community at large about government facilities and programs.

4.3 A cook

Another arena in which rural women exercise status and influence is in the kitchen, as cooks.

Kitera Gustin Siddi, 40, is a cook for the Holy Cross Convent in Mainalli. She got a subsidized loan for 8,000 rupees from a Catholic priest, Father Anil. She also borrowed 10,000 rupees from the Sisters of the Holy Cross and used it partly to purchase cooking vessels, she said in a personal interview on 19 June 2012.

In addition to using the loan to buy utensils, she used part of it to purchase two cows that she and her family are raising. This is not a traditional occupation of Siddis, as cowherding used to be practiced mainly by Gowlis. By taking up cowherding, Kitera and other Siddis are beginning to cross over into the traditional caste-specific profession of Gowlis. Thus, Kitera's enterprising spirit has opened new avenues for her to create, sustain, and express her influence and status by taking up livestock raising to supplement her daily job as a cook. Economic necessity has made it possible for Kitera and her family to perform a new role that was previously used to stigmatize Gowlis.

Kitera also rented the utensils she bought with her loan to individuals and groups for use at marriage functions, festivals, and other festive occasions, thus increasing her family income from the rental fees. She has three children—one boy and two girls. According to her, when the Mainalli Catholic Sisters employed her as their cook, she accepted the position because she could not find consistent coolie work.

Kitera is highly respected in her village because she is among the salaried professionals in rural Karnataka. She is paid by the Holy Cross Sisters just like other cooks who work with Jesuits and government institutions in India. Her position as a cook for the nuns also gives her an important advantage. Kitera and other cooks use their professional relationship with the priests and nuns to maximize opportunities to expand their material resources and to improve the chances their children will receive higher education in the Roman Catholic educational system. For instance, all the children of the cooks such as Baistiav, Dungi, and Josephine have been educated beyond the tenth standard in the villages; however, most of the children have not had the opportunity or the financial support to advance beyond the fifth or seventh standards in most of rural North Karnataka. Also, while many *sangha* women are not able to pay back the loans they borrowed from their *sanghas*, Kitera is one of the few women who had paid back all of her loans. She wants to expand her business by buying more cooking utensils with her current loan.

According to Kitera, "I hope to expand my business by buying more cooking utensils, learn new skills and develop ideas in order to raise awareness about the injustices suffered by people like us Siddis." She pointed out that she knew that most of the people without formal education were always at the mercy of some unscrupulous politicians and other government officials. She gave an example from the distribution of provisions such as rice and corn. She said,

> Most of our people who go and get rations, they don't take rice, mostly just kerosene and sugar, but the teller writes everything—sugar, kerosene, wheat—and he doesn't give them a receipt. He throws it away. The carbon copy remains with him and the ordinary is thrown in the garbage,

> because, if they have the receipt, they can go and complain to the food inspector. I went to get a receipt four times, so they gave me one, but most people won't do that. So much injustice is done in the distribution. Those who are very poor are supposed to get 20 kg of rice, but they don't because he can sell in the shop. (Kitera, 19 June 2012)

She now tries to ensure that government officials will be honest. Honesty is important everywhere, but much more so in parts of India where corruption is rampant. According to Kitera, her *shakti* comes from the fact that she is clear about what she wants for herself, her family, and the Siddi community. She is fearless because her power of loving, caring, and inspiring others comes from within her (Gaventa 2006). This inward or intrinsic *shakti* flows from the experiences she has gained over the years to build the capacity (Batliwala 2011: 37) to assert herself and empower others.

Kitera also understood the issues around ration cards and the fact they are not always issued to people who are legally entitled to them. She said, "People from low-income communities, where each member is entitled to 4 kgs of rice, such people are often swindled. Those who have so much property are given BPL funding, while those who have no land get nothing. The injustice of it is that those who deserve to benefit from government assistance do not have ration cards."

She said she wanted her children to receive a good education so they could support themselves; that is, with a higher education, it will be easier for them to be offered gainful employment beyond coolie work.

As a cook she receives sick pay and pensions, unlike some other rural people. All of the cooks who work for the church and their families go to clinics and hospitals run by the Catholic Church.

Kitera and other cooks, such as Dungi Siddi, who has cooked for Catholic and nuns for over ten years, have learned to form productive connections with government officials who give them and their families access to opportunities and resources of benefit to them. The cooks show their *shakti* through social competence in interactions with NGOs and other officials.

She attended evening adult literacy school in Mainalli for about two months to enable her to read and write Kannada. The sisters regard her as their "co-worker," said Sister Valentine, the Mother Superior at the Holy Cross Convent. Kitera is an important source of information because she helps the sisters in her role as a cultural expert on Siddi matters: she helps the nuns get information about Siddi births and deaths and how the sisters, none of whom is Siddi, can address these issues for the Siddis. She is often included in orientation sessions for new Sisters at the convent.

According to Kitera, she is respected in the village, and that respect and her enterprising spirit allow her to access critical resources and accord her much status and influence in her community.

In the next four sections, I will profile women whose lives have been impacted by new government employment opportunities and the ways in which they negotiate power to advance themselves while performing roles for which they have been specially trained.

4.4 A healthcare worker (Accredited Social Health Activist, or ASHA)

Girija Shankarapa Kalavai, 34, lives in Badhrapura, where she works in health care. She studied up to the seventh standard and attended a 21-day training program in Yellapur, organized by the Karnataka National Rural Health Mission (NRHM) under the Accredited Social Health Activist (ASHA) program. Before she received ASHA training, Girija was a coolie, relying on daily wages in construction and farmwork.

Since the Indian Central Government set up the ASHA program, healthcare providers have been viewed as government workers, and their role comes with prestige. When an ASHA healthcare provider can team up with nurses and doctors in villages, the provider gains respect and influence in those communities. ASHAs have direct interaction with their community members and are thereby able to identify people who are sick or otherwise in need of health care. They are also able to treat colds, coughs, dysentery, malaria, and tuberculosis.

As part of her work, Girija visits homes, and when she finds people who are sick, she may refer them to a doctor; there are also occasions when she herself takes the sick to the hospital. In addition to providing medical support, Girija also supervises government projects to build toilet facilities in people's homes. "Some of the village people come to me," she said, "asking that I help them to get government authorized facilities."

After the Ottawa Charter of 1986 for the promotion of health worldwide came the 6th Global Conference on Health Promotion in 2005 and the Bangkok Charter for Health Promotion. As a result, on local levels, village health and sanitation committees were set up in India, Pakistan, and Bangladesh. The block, village, district, and subdistrict levels as well as the state sought to link up with *panchayats* to improve health awareness. Girija and her colleagues are thus part of nationwide efforts to promote global health; the NRHM is an umbrella organization for what Girija and her teammates do in Uttara Kannada (North Karnataka).

She and other healthcare workers have identified diseases and illnesses such as HIV/AIDS, diabetes, TB, drug abuse, skin diseases, and dysentery in their areas. At times she and her team advocate for the rights of women and children to have access to health care. Rural healthcare workers such as Girija also enter into partnerships with village women and guide them to work with other women to practice good sanitation, personal hygiene, good nutrition, and preventive care.

Part of the work ASHA does involves helping parents to immunize their babies and advising young mothers about breastfeeding and the importance of exercise. Since many rural people do not have easy access to good hospitals and other health centers, Girija is now the person who teaches and brings preventive and curative health care to the people in her community. Her *shakti* is manifest in how she alleviates suffering for the sick, and her status and authority involve how she provides health care to people who tend to be neglected by the government.

On 26 June 2011, when I arrived at her village, Girija had recently taken a pregnant woman to the hospital in Malagi as part of her responsibilities as an ASHA. The mother of the expectant woman was part of the focus group I interviewed; her name is Shilpa. According to her, Girija provides immediate help, as in the case of her pregnant daughter. She also said that, because Girija helps in all health-related situations, she sees Girija as a woman whose influence is more relevant than what politicians living and working in big towns and cities can offer.

Girija's work enables her to broaden her access to critical resources that have enabled her to take a woman in labor to a hospital and administer first aid to the sick before they are seen by a doctor or nurse. She uses her expanded role to influence decisions and help people formulate new choices or options about their health needs in her community.

As a government official, she is respected because there are people who define a powerful person as someone who works for the government. Although it is not part of her job description, "some people turn to me to intervene in their marital conflicts and advis[e] the men to end violence against women and children," Girija said. As a government official and representative, she thus intervenes in marital conflicts in place of the traditional village council of men.

She said that, for a long time, it was their all-male village council (*hiriyaru* or *pancharu*) that tried to resolve marital conflicts and other social issues. In 2011, Girija mobilized a group of women to contest the election on the council. She said, "This move was considered unheard of before. I took this step because the other women and I understood role and status differently from what the all-male council perceived them to be." While the village council used its male-privileged status to seek to continue to subordinate women, the women created their own alternate domain of relevance and influence to articulate their own needs and concerns. They insisted that their needs had to be heard.

Since Badhrapura is a community of people of heterogeneous interests, views, and abilities, not all the women agreed with Girija, and the other women who wanted seats on the *hiriyaru*. In the village, there are both men and women who are not interested in serving on the village council or do not think women have the ability to challenge the entrenched patriarchal position of the village council. However, Girija uses acts strategically, with defiance and determination (Few 2002), to enroll support from other women, negotiating with others, in order to effect change in her society.

Girija is also president of the local *sangha*; consequently, she has a following among some rural women who trust and respect her. She has created alliances by convincing people that they would also benefit if they cooperated with her to effect change in her community. Thus, her *shakti* was manifest through her ability to create cleavages to challenge the conservatism of the village male-dominated council.

The larger community and the village council have for many years used their power to define social reality and social relationships. She and the other women live and operate within structures of institutions and cultural practices that are regulated to expand or restrict women's access to critical resources. Girija and her network of women's groups were thus actively engaged in decision-making processes in domains where control was contested and negotiated. At the moment, Girija and the other women exercise local political power and influence despite the ideological restrictions of their societies.

Asked if the possession of cows, land, and money can be a measure of power, she said, "How will cows, money, and land benefit people who need service to improve their lives? If you serve people, that is important. The powerful people, people of dignity, are more powerful than rich people."

Mohammad Hussein, a 30-year-old resident of the village, stated, during the interview, that a man may have muscle strength, but a woman has more responsibility. He said, "A woman will take care of the family while the husband goes out to work." He continued,

> Some men confuse cultural freedom to go out with the idea that they have power. They abuse their power by committing violence against women. If some man does wrong against a woman, that man should be punished. The punishment will deter others so that they will not commit the same crime against women. It is because of such bad people who commit crimes against women that women are not able to move freely in India. (26 June 2011)

Girija provided recent examples of how some men have committed violence against women in the big cities of India, such as Bangalore, Mumbai, and Delhi. She said,

> Recently a woman going to work in Bangalore was raped and killed. Some women have suffered the same fate in big cities of India. So it is not the women's fault, it is because of evil men. At times women do not go out for fear that some criminally minded men may attack them. This is not because men are powerful. They are criminals. (Girija, 26 June 2011)

The distinction Girija made between people who have power and people who are criminally minded cowards was supported by a 30-year-old Muslim resident in the village. Mohammad Sharif Madansab, 28, who had studied until the second PUC (pre university course), said,

> Our *Bharat mata* (president of India) is a woman. If India could have a female president, then it means that both men and women can lead their nation. When my father died, my mother took care of herself and the rest of us children. Some men always like to drink. They drink and yell at their children and beat their wives, but that is not power. It's being like an animal without thinking and feeling. What Girija does as a woman shows that she is strong and can be an effective leader when she has the opportunity. (26 June 2011)

From the above comment, it is clear that Girija's work as a rural healthcare provider is influential, and she is truly regarded as a woman with *shakti.*

Girija's courage to rally other women to challenge the all-male village council and demand that women be allowed to serve as council members and, most importantly, her caring for the sick and ensuring that women are protected are attributes that make her powerful to people in her village.

4.5 Muslim women fighting for their rights in Pakistan

Girija's courage, determination, and capacity to achieve results have parallels in Pakistan. In predominantly Muslim Pakistan, there are women activists who draw their inspiration from awareness that they have to fight for their rights because neither the government nor religious institutions are effective in fashioning gender equality. For instance, in rural Sindh, the presence of Muslim women in local governing bodies is opening doors for women's contributions and voices to be heard in political discourse. Rural women are becoming social activists; some are engaged in protests against local landlords and even government officials through such actions as blocking roads. Among other forms of protest and activism is the rise of "free-will marriages." At the moment, according to Meghan Ladly of the *New York Times*, some Muslim women in Pakistan are entering into marriages that may violate caste divisions or even challenge family preferences and social norms. Mahnaz Rahman, the director of the Aurat Foundation, an organization dedicated to women's rights issues, says, "Things are changing; the girls are becoming bolder, they are continuously taking steps, and they are not afraid to die. They know that they will be killed, but even then they are taking these steps because they can't conform to the values of their parents. They are the girls of this modern age." Although the above comment sees these Muslim girls as expressing notions of being modern, their attitude also points to an articulation of an understanding of their rights against cultural and social structures that have oppressed women.

Another example provided by Rahman about women insisting on their rights is the following story: Nusrat Mochi, 25, eloped with Abbas Bhatti, 27, against her parents' wishes. Promised since birth to her father's cousin, a man 15 years her senior, Mochi instead fell in love with Bhatti, and they secretly wed. The couple has faced constant threats and harassment from Mochi's family. In fact, they even pressed false charges of kidnapping and ransom against Bhatti; however, Mochi successfully testified in court and obtained an affidavit signed on her wedding day that contained evidence that the decision was truly her own. Though honor killings still occur in many areas of Pakistan, Mochi remained undeterred in her decision, and the couple has remained content with their decision.

The above women's articulation of their strength, courage, and defiance needs to be understood against Pakistan's efforts to foster equal rights to all its citizens while it faces internal and external challenges. As Giddens (1984) contends, power plays out in a complex social context in which human agency and social structures have intertwining relationships. In the interconnection between agency and social relations, the powerless at times may resist their exploitation or may acquiesce because they have internalized a distorted consciousness that favors the dominant (Lukes 2005). Bourdieu (1977) also contends that marginalized people may not wield formal power but have the capacity to disempower those who hold traditional power and influence.

In local newspapers and international journals, a focus has been on present-day Pakistani efforts to build prosperity, human rights, and programs to improve energy and water resources, economic and political systems, health care, and education, as well as combating Islamist extremism. As Pakistan tries to implement democratizing programs, it is caught between warding off Islamist violence against the country's minorities, including Christian, Buddhist, and Hindu women, and its efforts to foster social, religious, economic, and political equality for all Pakistanis.

Pakistan's central government since the 1970s has had an alliance between its military and Islamist militant groups. It seems that, since the country's inception, Pakistan's efforts at promoting equality have been situated within a religious ideology that has combined with military authorities aimed at challenging Western notions of democracy. This alliance between military rule and Islamic culture has set the tone for the creation of Nazim-e-Salat (Arabic for the significance of ritual prayer), a controller of prayers, the introduction of Sharia law, and an Islamic banking system in the country. Some of these ideologies are paramount in rural Pakistan (Nasr 2002). According to Kronstadt (2010), the Pakistani army's role, though less visible in recent years, has not been reduced, because it remains an unelected center of power, with its own links with foreign governments and institutions.

However, stories of Pakistani women show that some Muslim women, with the assistance of NGOs and civil societies, have been able to advance themselves. Further examples of Pakistani women's *shakti* will be addressed later.

4.6 Home Guards in India

I turn now to a government institution in India that provides short-term employment opportunities for some rural women: Home Guards; this serves as a context for India's citizens to gain employment while at the same time serving their communities.

Home Guards are paramilitary auxiliary personnel for the police force in India. Home Guards are recruited from all walks of life, including "doctors, lawyers, teachers, employees of public and private sector organizations, college and university students, agricultural and any Indian who can serve their communities" (GlobalSecurity.org 2012). All 18- to 50-year-old citizens of India are eligible for membership, and they normally serve from three to five years each. The positions are not full-time; members are called up for service when needed and paid an allowance for the time they serve.

After their first three years, all members "are eligible to be trained by the police in the maintenance of law and order, crime prevention, anti-dacoit measures [efforts to eradicate armed robbery and kidnapping for ransom], border control, disaster relief, fire prevention and firefighting, election and social welfare activities" (GlobalSecurity.org 2012). Home Guards are also deployed to maintain law and order and to help the community in emergencies (including natural disasters, national emergencies, and communal unrest) to promote communal harmony and assist the government in protecting the vulnerable. Home Guards are under the Indian Ministry of Home Affairs. The Department of Home Affairs trains and equips the Home Guards through local commanders. After the establishment of Home Guards in 1946, the concept of a voluntary citizens force has been adopted by several states.

On 25 October 2011, in Yellapur, two female Siddi Home Guards (Vidya Siddi and Ganapati Siddi) discussed with me how their job had given them status and influence that they did not have in the past. As Siddis, they used to work as coolies; also, all of the Home Guards they had known were male. Vidya said, "Since Ganapati and I joined the Home Guards, the citizens of Gullapur and other communities give us respect and honor because they always call us 'madam.' When there is a domestic dispute and some men are threatening to hurt their wives, women will threaten their husbands by saying they will call 'madams' (meaning Ganapati and me) to come and arrest their abusive husbands."

Vidya Siddi, 20, and Ganapati Siddi, 25, both from Gullapur, and both educated to the eighth standard, have been Home Guards for three years. They were trained for about ten days to become eligible to enlist in the Guards. According to them, they were given rigorous training like police officers. The chief Home Guard officer, who assigns them to places where their services are required, often calls them to the Home Guards headquarters. Vidya said. "We wear the same uniforms as police officers, but we wear a cap that is different from that of police officers. Though we received training to use a gun, we carry only the truncheon baton."

Home Guard duties, Vidya said, "give us power, *gaurava* or *shakti*, especially when we perform festival (*jattra*) duty, election and religious events, communal tasks [for potential conflict between religious groups]." They work throughout the state of Karnataka and at times are sent to other states during communal violence. Ganapati said,

> We are happy when people call us "madam" because of our public service. For instance, working in villages where Catholic Churches were being burnt and priests were attacked by some Hindu protestors, we were sent to quell the violence. At first we were afraid, but since we were deployed by the government to prevent communal violence, we put on our uniforms, and went. We had some confidence that the protestors would not intentionally hurt us because we wore uniforms. It is when we are in uniform that Siddis and non-Siddis appeal to us for protection. That makes us feel that we are using our power to help Indian citizens. (Ganapati, 25 October 2011)

Ganapati and Vidya said they are paid 150 rupees each day they are on duty. The pay is about a 100 rupees more than what people who perform coolie work receive per day for construction work or harvesting crops for farmers.

During my interview with Ganapati and Vidya, which took place at the Siddi Lamp Society Office in Yellapur, a senior woman who happened to be at the office said, "Because of education, the young women have made us proud. We old people are like forest monkeys just eating and climbing trees. In their uniforms everybody respects them even though they are Siddi young women."

In addition to their part-time profession as Home Guards, Vidya and Ganapati are members of Makambika's Siddi Mahila Vikas Sangha, which has ten members. They said that the government has given the *sangha* 100,000 rupees, from which they could take loans. It is through their membership in a SHG that they can use loans to further their education. While doing that, they also want to enlist in the police service. Vidya and Ganapati said that their present job does not give them any job security and that their Home Guard salaries are not enough to support them. Because of their limited formal education, there was no guarantee they could advance to become full-fledged police officers.

The two women's stories are similar to many stories of rural women who use government opportunities for personal advancement only up to a point.

Such a "sticky floor" or "glass ceiling" is a major obstacle in the path of rural women who desire personal advancement.

However, since Vidya and Ganapati seek to reach higher goals in their lives, they are actively looking for resources to build on their present achievements. Also, they indicated their assignments sometimes took them to different parts of India where they knew no one and did not have adequate police protection. On some of those occasions, Vidya said, "We relied on each other as two female Siddis for all the support necessary until we got back to places where we felt safe."

Their influence comes from working for the government but is amplified by the way they are using the opportunity to improve themselves. *Sangha* membership may help Vidya and Ganapati take loans to promote their interests, but there are other rural women who have achieved status and influence as *sangha* federation leaders.

4.6.1 A *sahayogini (sangha* federation president)

Surekha Paolo Siddi, 30, is a *sahayogini*, president of a federation of *sanghas*. Surekha used to be a *sangha* member before serving as treasurer; in 2011 she was elected president of a federation of *sanghas* covering Mainalli, Pala, Mundgod, and Hangal. In addition to her responsibility as *sangha* federation president, Surekha is also the leader of an informal woman workers' union (discussed later in this chapter, in the section "Women's Informal Workers Economic Sector").

Surekha has three children and lives in Mainalli. She is a coolie and at times works with other women in building houses. She and her husband also sell fish to supplement their income. According to Surekha, her husband's parents sold fish, and so her husband Paolo Siddi encouraged her to do a joint business doing the same. Paolo is also a carpenter, but recent forest department policies forbidding the collection of wood from publicly owned lands without a permit have prevented him from acquiring raw material for his trade. When he has wood, he makes tables and chairs and sells them in Mainalli, Gunjavati, Siddiligundhi, and elsewhere. Unlike Paolo, who feels unable to find new opportunities for new roles, his wife Surekha is an entrepreneur.

As federation president, Surekha sets the agenda for each monthly federation meeting of members, male and female, of the *sanghas*; the federation members rotate the venue for the monthly meetings. The federation has thirteen *sanghas*. Surekha has oversight of loans from which the *sanghas* and their members borrow money. She assists with the required documents to apply for microloans, ration cards, and so on. Whenever there is violence against *sangha* members, she helps the victims file a complaint and assists them in going to the court or police station to address the situation. She said,

> I encourage *sangha* men and women to discuss and debate matters that affect them and reflect on such issues, they in turn lay claim to their own social spaces to express their power. Now I appreciate how far I have come in terms of voicing my opinions on issues that affect women, children and men. Also I have observed how women are showing new energy and commitment to get involved in activities that enhance the welfare of their communities. (Surekha, 10 December 2011)

Surekha and other *sangha* leaders are helping women in particular to create and politicize local arenas of influence where they would determine issues that benefit them and their society. Surekha has leadership qualities; courage, eloquence, and hard work have served her well as president.

In February 2011, Surekha heard that some *sangha* members had emergency medical needs but were never given ambulance service when they needed to go to the Mundgod government hospital. Since Surekha knew that the government has made provisions that people below the poverty line are entitled to free ambulance service in cases of health emergencies, she collected petitions from a number of women and led a delegation to Karwar to report the negligent act at the District Health Office. When the Director of Health Services received the petition to reprimand those in charge of the ambulance department, Surekha said, "since that incident, when people from the villages call for an ambulance, the ambulance personnel respond promptly." A Siddi woman, whose community received citizenship as a ST in India in 2003, has become a *sangha* federation president who mobilized a pressure group to effect change in medical officials' attitudes and behavior.

Surekha and other *sangha* leaders seem to be better at enforcing rules and helping people insist on their rights than some government officials, including police officers. According to her husband, "some police officers take bribes and often do not attend to the needs of the poor people. But Surekha, deriving strength from seeking justice and being courageous, seems to succeed while government officials and law enforcement agencies have failed" (personal communication, 12 June 2010).

Surekha articulates her power in social relationships (Giddens 1984) and castified structures to create new possibilities of relief for the downtrodden in her community. As mentioned above, traditional village councils tend to have members who are all male. Siddis have a *budavanta* (wise man, in Kannada) who heads their community council. At the encouragement of the NGO LVK, the Ugingeri Siddis for the first time elected a female *budavanta* in 2008.

4.6.2 A *budavanta*

Anjali Salu Siddi, 26, of Ugingeri, is the *budavanta* of her community council and a member of a village *sangha*. According to Anjali, "People recognized me as a leader during *sangha* meetings. For instance, I asked questions and sought answers to why our village did not have a public transportation system. During that time, Ugingeri people had to walk for almost forty minutes to get to the main road before we could catch a bus to travel." She is articulate and, by drawing inspiration from her uncle, Juje Siddi (a former *budavanta*), she has learned to foster peace and harmony among people in the Siddi community in Ugingeri.

Anjali said, in a personal communication, that it was through the efforts and leadership of her predecessor and uncle that a *balwadi* (a nursery school hostel) was set up in Ugingeri. Juje Siddi, a Catholic Siddi, exercised leadership in the local Catholic community as a *budavanta* for eight years. He was involved in several activities that focused on the welfare of Siddi people, activities that were organized at the LVK (a Jesuit NGO headquartered in Mundgod). Juje helped recruit people in constructing a church in Ugingeri as well as building and maintaining the kindergarten school. He said that, even though he had no formal training, he managed to play a primary role in all those projects (personal communication, 19 July 2010).

The new *budavanta*, Anjali, felt that a community-owned flourmill enterprise had to be started. She made that recommendation because, she said, "since we don't have any business projects here, a flour or cornmill can generate some money for our village while the mill will employ some people."

When Anjali Siddi was elected *budavanta*, she was the first woman in the history of Ugingeri—in fact, in the history of *budavantas* among the Siddis—to be elected to that post. (Later, in 2009, another Siddi woman was elected *budavanta*, in Honshettykoppa.) The election took place through secret ballot supervised by Father Anil D'Mello, the director of LVK. The Siddi Catholic community thus elected Anjali as a *budavanta* for all the Siddis in Ugingeri.

Anita Ramesh Belse, a non-Siddi teacher from Ugingeri, helps us understand the people's perception of Anjali as the current *budavanta*. According to Anita, "The Siddi community was slow to accept the leadership of the first female—and a relatively young female—*budavanta*, even though our people elected her. The Siddis had a difficult time accepting a woman, as a *budavanta* was traditionally a male post. Furthermore, the elders in the community felt they could not go to her with personal issues because she was too young to consult; some considered her the same age as their own children or grandchildren" (personal communication, 19 July 2010).

When asked why she was elected, Anjali said that people wanted her although she did not have any formal education. Her experience outside of Ugingeri, however, might have been considered an asset for the post. For 15 years she worked in Mumbai as a housemaid and helped with the cooking for the family she served. Her parents asked her to come back home when it was time for her to marry. She used to send 300 rupees monthly for her family. Besides that, she had saved some 3,000 rupees in a bank in Mumbai.

When Anjali was elected, she understood her role in bringing about amicable solutions to conflicts and disagreements, calling meetings of Siddis when there was need for them.

Some of the issues the *budavanta* and her advisors dealt with included lack of community space for youth, lack of land ownership, low wages, higher education that was unaffordably expensive, and housing, including how to acquire modern houses through government assistance programs. Some of these problems, according to the *budavanta*, were and are still overwhelming.

After about six months, it seems that the younger generation and some of the elders in the community had embraced her leadership. The community found her to be a strong, articulate woman who voiced their concerns to the larger community and mediated between the village and government officials. That Anjali had lived in Mumbai, a cosmopolitan city, and worked for non-Siddis were, no doubt, perceived as assets she brought to the position. Also, that her uncle was her predecessor as a *budavanta* and had left behind a good reputation and legacy was probably another important factor enhancing Anjali's chances to be elected.

Besides acting as a spokesperson for her community, the *budavanta* is also a negotiator and mediator for marital problems. For instance, when Devdita Siddi, a former resident of Ugengeri, had issues with her husband in Gardoli, a community away from hers where she lived with him and their children, the *budavanta*s of both communities tried to resolve the conflict. Devdita Siddi escaped from her abusive husband in Gardoli, taking her children and mother back to Ugengeri, her hometown. The *budavanta* in Gardoli, police officers, the husband, and his relatives went as a delegation to meet with Anjali and her council of village leaders. When Anjali determined that Devdita's husband did not show remorse at beating his wife, she persuaded her council members to allow Devdita to stay in Ugingeri and not return to the abusive husband.

Anjali's power to intervene in an abusive relationship despite the delegation that wanted Devdita to return to her husband indicated the *budavanta* was also courageous. Anjali used what Gaventa (2006) describes as "power to" to protect a woman in an abusive marriage.

Her decision was unconventional because male-led village councils often issue verdicts favoring men. She explained later that she was not intimidated by the police officers or the other members of the delegation. Asked why she made the decision to keep Devdita in Ugingeri, she said, "What mattered in my decision was the safety and well-being of Devdita and her children. I know of cases when some male community leaders were not able to advocate for women who lived with abusive husbands."

Anjali also said that, during training sessions provided for *sangha* members, she learned that women have to stand up for themselves and others because financial empowerment alone did not give women the respect and power they deserved. Anjali Siddi's story points to how a young woman used a nonformal position as a village council leader to defend another woman who exercised her rights by escaping from an abusive husband. Her position also enabled Anjali to reverse the status quo of years of disregarding female victims of male violence in South Asia.

Having discussed the various domains of influence where women are taking charge of their lives and helping others, I will now turn to the informal labor sector where many rural women exercise influence. Despite an emphasis on formal economic sectors as arenas for economic and social development, scholars point out that the informal labor sector plays a major role in contemporary South Asian societies.

4.7 The informal labor sector in India, Pakistan, and Bangladesh

Policymakers in India, Pakistan, and Bangladesh consider it as part of their national development to create opportunities to integrate women and other minorities in their citizenry (Dixon 1982: 373). The expansion of income-generating employment for rural women and the promotion of health, education, and social advancement for majority and minority citizens tend to be hallmarks of South Asian countries (Dixon 1982: 373).

Rural women in South Asia have always been known to display initiative, organizing skills, and industry in forming savings clubs and informal economic activity groups, engaging in agriculture, shopkeeping, poultry farming, and raising milch animals. Though rural women have always operated in societies that are highly stratified by caste, class, religion, age, ethnicity, and language differences, it is important to acknowledge that these women are differentially situated within these categories. Some of them by virtue of their class within their caste are able to access cash and other resources through political affiliations, though others cannot. Some create their own conditions for promoting and achieving their economic and political goals. Such women may build support networks based on indigenous sources of solidarity whereby they form alliances of women workers. The women may share "cultural traditions and religious rites" (1982: 383). Other women form collective work groups that may at times transcend caste identity, but what really matters is the common objectives the women create for themselves.

Among the women are some who develop skills and professions outside their traditional caste professional roles. For instance, some rural women who belong to basket-weaving or fishing communities learn new income-generating skills, such as raising animals. It is at this level of women's initiative that we find examples of informal networks.

According to Dixon (1982), some Bangladeshi women mobilize to form joint economic ventures to grow vegetables and make fishnets. Informal social networks have become critical contexts in which rural women in India, Pakistan, and Bangladesh create support for one another to promote economic advancement, self-help, and the enhancement of self-esteem.

4.7.1 India

One example that has emerged in North Karnataka, India, is a women's informal group organized under the leadership of Surekha Paolo Siddi, the *sangha* federation president profiled earlier.

Surekha heads a group of women who work together on a variety of projects in their communities. Rani, Anjaline, Bustine, Sushikela, Surekha, and Mary are members of the group. In their farm work, they rotate helping one another to avoid hiring paid workers. "It's efficient that we work together so we can each attend to family duties," says Surekha (20 June 2010).

This workers' union operates on the idea of "reciprocal labor exchanges, doing tasks such as weeding" (Bourque and Warren 1981: 143), plowing, and harvesting on one another's land. Though all of the women are relatively poor, they live in Mainalli, where most families, with the assistance of the Sisters of the Holy Cross, can own pieces of land. In most cases the members of the cooperative who provide assistance are not paid for their services; the host or beneficiary for the day prepares a meal for them. Those who have no land are paid money as wages for the time they work—anywhere between 100 and 120 rupees per day. These labor exchanges are important because the women are thus able to get labor assistance with a minimum of expense.

Bourque and Warren (1981) conclude that women who belong to the agricultural cooperative work groups tend to be poor, and that their operation underscores sexual divisions. What these Siddi women in Mainalli do offers them strong bargaining power to enable them to advance their interests beyond what some men can do in their communities. There are Siddi and non-Siddi coolies who are paid daily wages of 50 to 70 rupees, and most of these workers are not able to bargain how much their employers pay them.

The women may have "limited cash income" (Bourque and Warren 1981), but they end up having greater social influence in their community because, as Rani, a union member belonging to Surekha's group, said, "my husband is surprised that I make more money in a day than what he makes."

Surekha and her union of workers are learning bricklaying, carpentry, plastering, painting, and mortar mixing and aspects of building design—where a fireplace has to be placed, for instance, or appropriate locations for a bathroom, living room, and so on. Since June 2010, they have been helping to construct houses for Siddis in Mainalli.

In 2011, some men joined the group because they saw the success and graded power base the women were acquiring. Three men who later joined in January 2013 help roof the houses the women have taken contracts to build. The new houses have modern facilities, so their building requires more labor force and technical skills than their previous homes for Mainalli residents.

Besides housing construction, the women in the union look individually and collectively for jobs. Once they have found a job, be it in the fields or in road construction, they join forces to complete the work and look for additional opportunities. As a result, the women are able to bargain with contractors about their wages.

The women's initiative to form this network of workers has also helped them create a women's infrastructure that enables them to gain new perspectives on themselves and how to advance their own aspirations. According to Rani, "We motivate and support one another and maintain our independence. In our activities we use collective enterprise of sharing resources, trusting one another and sharing power to create a sense of group power."

Though she remains influential, Surekha admitted that she, at times, consults senior women such as Dumgi Moshie, who is one of the wise women and respected persons to whom people in Mainalli go for guidance and advice. Dumgi is one of the senior women who are "power reservoirs" (Oommen 1970). Power reservoirs are community leaders and groups who shape decision-making processes but do not necessarily have formal public power or positions (Oommen 1970). Also, Surekha said that, because Dumgi has raised children and grandchildren and still cares for children, Dumgi has increased her status and influence in her community. Some of Dumgi's grandchildren are among the few Siddis who have obtained college education. For instance, Vino Violet, Dumgi's granddaughter, is an elementary school teacher who holds a Dip.Ed. from Loyola College in Mundgod.

4.7.2 Pakistan

Despite the lack of recognition for Pakistani women's contribution to the formal economy, many women are engaged in the informal labor sector. In Pakistan, as in India and Bangladesh, many social, cultural, religious, and economic factors tend to limit women's participation in the formal sector of labor. Most rural women work in the informal sector because of their limited formal education and few marketable skills. Nevertheless, some of these women are respected and have self-confidence outside the formal or public-sector employment spaces.

The informal, unorganized, sector thus has become an area where most rural women work: some of the women are domestic servants who may not even have any legal protections. Domestic servants form an important part of the informal economy. Khan et al. (2005) contend that the informal sector where most rural women work is labor intensive and often based on kinship and personal relations rather than contractual arrangements that could have ensured protection for the women. Low-earning and insecure employment benefits also mark the informal sector.

According to Sadeque and Zeenat (2009), women do not usually unionize in Pakistan, India, and Bangladesh. They argue that women do not have the means to collectively bargain for their rights because of social and cultural norms and that women are afraid of losing their jobs and are constrained by social censure.

Millions of rural South Asian women are a critical part of the economies of their countries, but their contributions tend to be underestimated or neglected. The informal structures of their economic activities "arise from a myriad of factors that range from economic conditions to sex roles, from religious beliefs to family and household structures" (Kagitcibasi 1986: 485). In some cases, women have become the caretakers of their aging parents instead of the male children who are often expected to care for their elderly parents. The women who provide security for their parents blur the cultural expectations of having male children, but their contributions, however, are undervalued (Paul 1992: 5). Other rural women have become entrepreneurs who own small shops and sell farm products or raise livestock.

There are cases in which some women may be elected to serve on local and district councils, but the women leaders, for fear of social censure, are not able to perform their roles with courage. There are some women who see themselves as integral parts of their family and so may defer to their sons, husbands, fathers, and other male relatives. Sathar and Kazi (1990) have also argued that, when women are engaged in formal employment that carries respect and status, they are able to improve their own independence, self-esteem, and social status.

In Pakistan, in the district of Pishin in Baluchistan (majority Pushtun), the citizens live by rigid codes of Islamic law. In the few cases when women are allowed to vote, they often vote for candidates their husbands or male family elders have instructed them to vote for. While India and Bangladesh have almost intractable cultural and patriarchal forces that mitigate against women's empowerment, Pakistan's years of faltering democratic regimes have undermined women's efforts to advance themselves (Nasr 2002).

Khattak (2010) contends that the presence of women in local government has played a key role in the implementation of Pakistan's efforts to democratize the nation. Local governments, according to Khattak, and their roles are better understood in the context of whether or not women are engaged in local decision-making processes. Khattak is also concerned about the continuing obstacles that central governments sometimes can have on local governing bodies.

For instance, when local government elections were held during the first term of Nawaz Sharif's government in years, elections took place throughout the country; in his second term, however, local elections were held only in Punjab and Baluchistan. Male provincial-level politicians who were opposed to the central government's provision for women to sit on local level governing bodies undermined the central government's efforts. This was because women's quotas were left to the discretion of the provincial governments (Khattak 2010: 2). According to Khattak, during the second round of elections, the government reduced the total number of seats at the council level but was forced to keep the women's quota at 33 percent in the face of protests by women council members and NGOs. In 2005, women's mobilization and women's readiness to contest the general seats compelled the local and national governments to pay attention to female power.

Although women are not prevented from participating in the formulation of policies, there are no mechanisms to allow them to be present in policy-making sessions, according to Khattak.

Despite the apparent halting of democratization in Pakistan, changes in technology and the presence of NGOs and INGOs (international nongovernmental organizations) have fostered some empowerment in the lives of a small number of rural Pakistani women.

In February 2012, the Sughar Women Program of Participatory Development Initiatives launched Sughar (which means, in English, a "skilled and confident woman"), Pakistani's first rural women's clothing and accessories brand. The Sughar Women Program, active in around 20 villages in the Sindh and Baluchistan provinces, aims to end certain customs of exchange marriages, child marriages, and honor killings and promotes socioeconomic empowerment for women in these tribal communities. For example, they have established Women Centers in each village where they offer a six-month course that focuses on teaching sewing and achieving basic literacy. They offer microloans to the women who complete the course, to help foster entrepreneurship. They even organized a fashion show to showcase these rural women's talents and advertise their products. (Each product depicts a folk tale or tradition held by one of the many tribal communities in these provinces.)

The 2010 floods that destroyed homes, possessions, lives, and livelihoods had a horrific impact on Pakistani citizens, especially those who live in the Swat Valley. Among the organizations that responded to the plight of the Pakistani people was Oxfam. In the village of Jarray, Oxfam's Cash for Work programs typically involved road and irrigation reconstruction, jobs typically taken by men. Women who received money through the program focused on the production of shawls. In total, 807 women were employed to make shawls, quilts, and sweaters, which were then distributed to 482 people in Oxfam's Winterization kits.

Sadar Jehan, a mother to five children, was a seamstress. She estimates she used to make 60 to 70 rupees on each piece of children's clothing she made. She had previously never dealt with financial matters or even been to a bank. With the help of Oxfam, she now makes 5,600 rupees for every two shawls she makes. She said she used most of the money she earned to buy food for her family. Her understanding of her influence entails the fact that she has been able to earn a higher income and so is able to provide better for her family.

Sadar is also able to go to her bank to take a loan, deposit money, or pay back a loan, without her husband accompanying her. According to Sadar, when she received the cash from Oxfam, she was able to pay doctors' bills. Not only that, she said,

> after I received the check I went to the bank in Fatipur. I gave them the check and they gave me the cash. I'd never been to a bank before and I was afraid, but when I got there I asked the security guard what to do and he showed me where to go. I felt very happy when I got the money. As soon as I got the money, I started thinking about how to spend it. (Sadar 2010)

Sadar used her earnings to pay her children's school fees and bought them warm clothes for the winter. She explains that she made the decisions on how the money she earned was spent. Her *shakti* was derived from her financial independence, as she said, "I felt that because I earned the money I was the person to spend the money. I had the right and no one could ask me how I spent it. I felt the power of my money and I was not answerable to anyone else" (Oxfam International 2010).

This bold assertion of independence and freedom by Sadar to use her income could not have been imagined before the intervention of Oxfam in that part of Pakistan.

Another woman who benefited from the Oxfam program was Haya Begum. She said,

> We are happy with the Cash for Work program. We want to earn more money because we have no other opportunities to earn money. I used the money to pay school fees and to buy a school sweater. I became a decision-maker. It was the first time. My husband is out of the country so my children are depending on me. It made me feel that I was in power. I had the right to determine how to use the money I had earned. I was not answerable to anyone. (Haya 2010)

Salma, a mother of four children, said that she made decisions about how the money she earned through Oxfam was spent. She used the money to pay off loans taken out for medical treatments, saying, "I paid off a loan of 5,000 rupees, which we'd taken due to some medical treatment. One of the children had chest infection, and I'd taken out a loan for the delivery of my baby." She was also appreciative of the fact that she was able to work in her home. Her *shakti* came from the fact that she was able to contribute financially to her family and take on responsibilities that her husband, who is unemployed, would have been expected to shoulder. Salma's judicious use of the income sets her apart from other people who do not invest their earnings.

The above examples of different articulations of female power may give the impression that other women may not necessarily benefit from such limited sources of power. For instance, Kabeer (2001) argues that individual women's success in challenging structural inequalities may have their full effect when they engage in collectively empowering other women. However, Schuler et al. (1996) contend that individual women's actions in how they deploy their *shakti* could inspire other women to engage in activities that may transform social structures and norms of inequalities. Also, they argue that as some women gain autonomy to exercise what may seem to be limited forms of power, the ideas that undergird such actions may be distributed in their social relations. As the above women make strategic choices to change their situations, they not only inspire other women, but also embody the change and *shakti* that is manifest in their lives.

Schuler et al. (1996) also show that as the women devise creative responses to structural norms that impede women's progress, such structures also change. Sadar's actions would be conceived as unacceptable according to the normative practices for Muslim women.

The women of the Swat Valley are responding to new conditions and opportunities as they see fit to improve their lives. As they use the financial support they have received from Oxfam, the women's social networks also expand as they interact with men and women outside the confines of their immediate families. Through such interactions, Sadar and the other women are directly or indirectly creating shifts in people's perception of the roles of women and transforming market, gender, and family norms.

The power exhibited by Pakistani women and the conditions under which such women operate have similarities as well as differences with those of women in India.

4.8 Invisible roles: women's position in the labor force

4.8.1 India

Indian women are engaged in many income-generating activities to enhance their power. The women's labor force contributes to India's national socio-economic development, though most of the rural women are part of the unorganized sector of the economy.

Most rural women tend to receive lower wages because they are low-skilled or unskilled and work irregularly, depending on the availability of jobs. Since most of the women work for daily wages, their employers do not provide good working conditions, social security, or employment benefits. The women though they are "active wage earners are informally employed" (Henderson and Jeydel 2007: 239).

The 1991 Indian census defined work as "participation in any economically productive activity, whether the participation is physical or mental." In this new definition, activities aimed at providing food for "self-consumption" and unpaid work for family businesses fall under work (Sankaram 2006). Unpaid nonmarket jobs are also included as work. Casual workers, artisans, ragpickers, agricultural laborers, firewood suppliers, beedi workers (a beedi is a thin, Indian cigarette), salt workers, livestock rearers, tamers, small traders, and domestic workers are all in the labor force of this unorganized sector.

Though most women work in this sector, their status is shaped by the health care they receive, their lack of job security, and the sector's often deplorable work environment. The labor-intensive jobs they do affect their backs, sight, minds, and so on; some of them develop emotional and physical illnesses that are related to their jobs. Though low-paying jobs and the stress they cause affect their self-image and self-esteem, they still remain in the labor force until they can no longer work under the unhealthy conditions. The conditions under which they work are similar to those of Bangladeshi garment factory workers, which I have alluded to in this work. (Surekha and her workers group, described earlier, have been able to negotiate for better pay because they have informally unionized to give themselves power over their productivity.)

Women's labor is also spent in the informal sector as, self-employed, they run small kiosks or stalls in markets or as they work as paid domestic employees. The women tend not to have such benefits as secure contracts with customers or employers or unemployment and disability insurance and maternity leave that are available in the formal economy.

Their daily income depends on "their ability to sell their skills, products, or other services" (Henderson and Jeydel 2007: 240) for fees they can negotiate. The women who line the streets in villages, towns, and cities as vendors selling their wares are visible; other women engage in livestock raising, sewing, embroidery, basket weaving, pottery, and incense selling. Most women try to balance many jobs and responsibilities. They do both paid and unpaid jobs, including being both heads and caretakers of their households, and they buy supplies to feed and care for their families and themselves.

At times, outsourcing that relocates jobs opens up new forms of economic and social opportunities for women. They learn about the world outside their homes, have control over their earnings, and get involved in decisions about how to spend money; they may change fixed notions of sex-specific divisions of labor.

Henderson and Jeydel (2007: 241) describe the challenges that people face in the informal sector as "sticky floor—low paying jobs, low skilled position, less job security." With the globalization of trade, goods and services get outsourced to places that have lower labor costs, no job security, and no bargaining power and benefits (Henderson and Jeydel 2007).

Some of the women develop their human capital as they gain access to good nutrition and basic and technical training that teaches them how to do such things as inseminate cows and work water pumps to irrigate farms. This in turn increases their ability to participate in local, district, and domestic decision-making processes. Some talk about how their suggestions have been sought by men toward policy formulation for village and town development projects. Some of the women serving in village or *taluk panchayats* have helped in infrastructure development, by working on such issues as adult literacy, health, good drinking water and sanitation, electrification, roads, and veterinary care.

According to traditional norms, a woman is to marry and preferably have a son to continue and enhance the family's status and wealth. Rural, poor women tend to do the bulk of the housework because they are expected to be responsible for household duties, care of the children, and, at times, care of their elderly parents and/or in-laws. Further, their health is often neglected. Their life is marked by labor-intensive jobs at all levels.

Although some women have often been cast simply as those who reproduce, produce, and work for their families and immediate communities, some women work outside their immediate surroundings.

The following discussion explores the extent to which rural women are now taking charge of their lives by engaging in informal income-generating activities to gain status and influence and inspire other women. Previously, most of the women depended on their husbands as the breadwinners of their families. Having set the stage for understanding how women contribute to the economies in which they work, I will look at specific examples to substantiate women's "invisible" roles.

4.8.1.1 A seamstress

Sangetha Chandrashekar Kokre, 40, of Vidrolli, studied up to the fourth standard. She is a seamstress and learned sewing in Halliyal at a relative's house. She belongs to Sri Shakti Sangha, which has 18 members. She described how she went about starting her sewing business, saying, "First, I borrowed from someone and paid [the loan] back. Later, I took a loan from the Kendra Bank and paid that back. The *sangha* to which I belong helps me with loans. When I borrowed from the moneylender, I paid a higher interest than that of the bank. But when I joined the *sangha*, our interest is very small."

Sangetha's comment about moneylenders is accurate because, before the creation of *sanghas* and other lending institutions, some rich men could still take interest ranging from 20 to 30 percent on loans they gave to poor people. Most borrowers ended up not being able to pay back their loans, so some people and families went into debt bondage, in which people in debt work for the creditor until their debt is paid. Debt bondage in South Asia, although has been legally abolished, is rampant in rural communities.

Sangetha said she did not want to be in servitude to any moneylender, and that is why she now takes loans from her *sangha*. She said, "I learned how to sew from my mother who was also a housewife and worked in the field as a coolie. My mother sewed a little but not on as large a scale as I'm doing." She said she has customers from her village and about eight more communities.

Sangetha said that she derives satisfaction from sewing. "If one is not focused, one may not achieve *vajen shakti*. *Shakti* is not money. It is knowledge that enables one to use money."

Foucault (1977) describes the intertwining relationship between knowledge and power by pointing to the strategies used by some people to shape or change realities for others. In this case, Sangetha applies her knowledge to accomplish goals that benefit her. Though she only finished the fourth standard, she has power because she is raising her children and supporting their college education. To Sangetha, "*shakti* is like *budhi*—knowledgeable persons may be poor but can face all obstacles. They care for themselves and support their family." According to her, "Money does not give power. *Bhagavana* [trust in God] helps me in managing the household." Since her ex-husband drinks and was beating her, she took her two sons and one daughter and left her husband, relocating to her grandmother's village.

Through her work as a seamstress, she bought a house and became independent of her abusive husband. She bought the house in 2010 for 25,000 rupees. She has paid off much of the loan except for an 8,000-rupee balance.

She laughed and said, "What shows men are more powerful than women?" She said that because she takes care of the home, raises the children on her own, had the courage to leave an abusive relationship, and bought land to build a house on, she sees herself as a powerful person.

Sangetha has regular customers in her village. The customers bring fabrics to her to sew because she has a reputation of satisfying all such customers. Her sewing, the *sangha* to which she belongs, and her self-confidence are her sources of power and influence in her community. Through the informal sector in which she works, Sangetha supports herself and her children.

4.8.1.2 Agricultural workers

Agricultural work, especially for others, is perceived as tedious by coolies; nevertheless, such work provides other domains for women to exercise and negotiate different forms of influence. Small-scale women farmers grow vegetables and rice for their household's consumption. Women also tend to work on other people's lands as agricultural laborers.

Agricultural laborers account for the majority of the workforce of women in rural Karnataka. They are coolies who live on daily wages. There are, however, a few women who are independent farmers and own their lands and agricultural implements for their farm work. Some of these women may hire laborers to work on their farms. The farmers use compost for their crops and at times produce enough compost to sell to other farmers.

Shantava Somana Valmik, 60, and Somaka Somana Balvatti, 35, are farmers in Choudalli. When they lost their husbands, the 60-year-old Shantava moved in with her sister-in-law Somaka, who was living alone in her house. When the two widows and Somaka's children began living together, the women decided to embark on joint agricultural work. Unlike the views of some scholars that rural farmers are not as enterprising as urban people (Mathai 1979), Shantava and Somaka demonstrated great entrepreneurial initiative and managerial skills to organize and manage their business (Kanitkar 1994: 25). The two women, between them, plan the kinds of crops they need to grow and where to find markets during harvest, as well as the number of personnel they will need during clearing, planting, and harvesting.

They are independent farmers who manage and maintain their farms by occasionally employing other workers. Their economic independence accords them status and power in Choudalli and neighboring communities.

Through an NGO called RUDSETI (Rural Development and Self-Employment Training Institute), the two widows have farmed seven acres of land in Choudalli, a village of about a 1,000 people. Residents of the village include Muslims, Hindus, Harijans, Marathis, and other caste groups. The village has no village council, such as a *pancharu*. As shareholders in the RUDSETI program, when the government has agricultural fairs, Shantava and Somaka are among the first to be informed about them. Program directors educate the farmers about the prospects of cashew nut production, organic farming, crop mixing and rotation, and the like.

When I visited them on 10 June 2011, Shantava had attended a meeting at which the central government encouraged farmers to be involved in growing cashew nuts. The two farmers indicated that they planned to grow about 200 cashew trees. Though they do not know how to grow cashews, they will go and learn from other farmers how to grow the nuts. At present, they grow coconut, mangoes, areca nut, rice, cotton, and bananas.

During the clearing, planting, and harvest seasons, they hire workers from their village and surrounding towns. The workers are paid about 80 rupees because there is not much opportunity in the area and the competition is high, so by paying a decent income they attract good workers. According to them they learned farming in their childhood from their parents and grandparents.

The joint-farming idea came from both of the women. Somaka's late husband inherited land from their father, so upon his death Shantava, as the sister of Somaka's late husband, decided to join forces with Somaka to farm. They see themselves as more powerful than "some *panchayat* members who just get elected and drink tea and take bribes instead of spending government money to improve our communities," said Somaka.

Somaka's husband planted about 100 mango trees. When RUDSETI officials encouraged the two to plant more crops besides the mangoes, they planted rice, cotton, and so on.

The farmers use a variety of laborers, and, at times, Shantava's son helps with the farm work. They sell their produce in Mundgod, or customers come to their home to purchase the produce. They have regular customers for their rice, cotton, and mangoes who often come to their home to make purchases. At times, they sign contracts with agents to harvest and sell the mangoes. The contractor then pays the women an amount of money based on sales.

The women also raise milch cows. They bought the cows using some of the income generated from the sale of their farm products.

Shantava can read and write, so she maintains the accounts, keeping records of expenditures and payments. The two women said they are respected in their community because of their hard work. Men and women recognize them as powerful because they are women to whom some people come for loans. That they work for themselves and educate the children in their household are indications that they have power. They always pay off loans they take from RUDSETI.

They have *shakti* and nobody can cheat them, they maintained. They realize that to grow 200 cashew nut trees does not mean they can expect to see all of the trees bear fruit in their lifetime, but Shantava said they hope the children in the family will "carry on the tradition of farming so the land does not go outside the family." From the resources they have gotten from farming, they have been able to marry two girls off.

Their *shakti* comes from their decision, when their husbands died, to team up and farm. They use their collaborative action (Giddens 1984) in light of their understanding that power is an important component of social relationships to provide for themselves and care for the young people in their family (Foucault 1977). It was after they diversified their farming that they began to make more profits than when their husbands were alive.

To Shantava and Somaka, men were traditionally considered powerful, but the two now exemplify women who have triumphed in the face of the loss of their husbands. Their success is building on itself to increase their self-confidence as they change their circumstances. Shantava and Somaka's incremental *shakti* provides an example of Gaventa's (1982) theory of power whereby their success helps expose the various forms of inequality and social powerlessness in rural Asia.

The two women also know that the Indian government has been promoting the status and influence of women. According to the two women, both men and women have equal *budhi*—wisdom. Men may think they "have more *shakti* or *budhi* than women," but these two women know that, for instance, the men in their household who take no interest in farming prove that the women are more sensible and powerful.

Shantava was educated only up to the fourth standard. Somaka has six children and all went to school. One girl finished her Dip.Ed.; another, Sunitha, is about to complete a college degree. Sunitha concurred with the two women that her mother and aunt are powerful. Sunitha said, "We will not allow any person to dispossess them of their property when that person had not contributed anything toward improving their lives." Somaka and Shantava said they have heard of villages where women have been bullied, but such bullies will have no chance in their home. They also said they know about authorities they could contact if any person attempted to bully them.

The two agriculturalists have control over family land and their own production process. They make all their own financial and investment decisions. Their increased participation in the social world over the production process has enhanced their status and influence in their community. Their success as farmers is known in different parts of North Karnataka.

Their access to cash and their ability to make life choices including the education of their children, and to invest in growing more crops to diversify what they have and to buy shares in an NGO operation, are important indices of women who exercise their autonomy in a highly stratified society with strong sexual hierarchies. Their competence and courage and business acumen have been inspirational for Somaka's college student daughter.

It is partly accurate that most rural farmers do not pay attention to how their labor contributes to the national and global economy; they may, nevertheless, have status and recognition in their local communities. And some rural women assert that agricultural labor gives them value and status as useful and productive members of their society. Rural women shape reality within cultural and political contexts. "In the rural context, where women's agricultural labor force participation is widespread, employment is more likely to provide women with prestige and distinction" (Kagitcibasi 1986: 492).

In contrast to Shantava and Somaka's situations, some Muslim women in rural Pakistan experience a division of labor where women cultivate only vegetables in gardens close to home to help provide for their families, and the men go outside their villages to collect seeds or samples from other communities and bring them to the women to grow in the gardens.

While some scholars would describe the two farmers as powerful because of their autonomy, Shantava and Somaka's *shakti* embraces the respect and honor they have in their community and their courage and commitment to raise children by themselves. They have used their single-mother status, and, more precisely, their position as widows in rural India, to be industrious and supportive of others, including girls in their family. They have also used their resources to give their young female members a college education. As a result, Shantava and Somaka's hard work and responsible decisions have increased their status and dignity in their community.

The insights in *The Materiality of Social Power: The Artifact-Acquisition Perspective* by Walker (2006) help to clarify the relationship between social power and artifacts. Nielsen (1995: 49) also defines social power in terms of human practice "as the ability of actors to pursue goals" by acquiring and deploying "resources (objects, information, and other people's actions)." By focusing on an actor's power to mobilize resources according to his or her "position in society," Nielsen highlights the relational nature of power.

Once deployed in pursuit of an actor's goals, artifacts, especially architecture, have "multiple and often unintended effects ... on people's behavior" (Nielsen 1995: 53). Indeed, Nielsen (1995: 54) goes on to claim "that every artifact and material cultural attribute has specific and, to a certain extent, predictable effects upon social relations." Thus, social relations are reflected in, and consequently are affected by, for example, the capacity, accessibility, segmentation, and functional differentiation of particular social structures. Nielsen specifies the social correlates of these attributes in some detail, and concludes with a case study on the architecture in a pre-Hispanic community in the Argentinian Andes. He counsels readers to engage in further "studies of the active role played by material culture in the formation of power relations" (1995: 66). Nielsen's insights help us understand the relational power between Somaka and Shantava as they work together.

The two successful farmers' access to land was mediated through men who had been in their lives (i.e., their husbands, since deceased), but they have built on what they inherited and expanded their work. As they expanded their income base, they have simultaneously shaped people's notions of their role and status in their community and surrounding villages. They exercised the materiality of social power as they used and reworked material property to multiply their economic and social power. As Walker and Schiffer contend, social power has material consequences far beyond the identity-based inequalities that many artifacts come to symbolize (2006: 85). The acquisition of an artifact provides an example of social power transmitted to affect the activities of current users.

Shantava and Somaka creatively used the land they inherited to educate children in their family, advance their status in their community, and inspire other women in North Karnataka. It was not surprising that, when I contacted local NGOs and *sangha* officials in the Mundgod *taluk* about women who were successful farmers in North Karnataka, Somaka and Shantava's names were the first to be mentioned.

A newspaper article recently drew attention to another woman of *shakti* who is also a farmer. Deepak Jadimano wrote the story in the newspaper *Karavali Munjar*'s 28 June 2011 issue, about a woman farmer in the Sirsi *taluk*; the story is titled "See the Plowing Woman Omi."

Omi has no basic education but is an expert farmer, having been plowing her field for over 22 years. She does all the work pertaining to farming, including clearing her field, collecting manure to make fertilizer for the field, and the like. She has six children—one son and five girls. She has a 45-year-old daughter who is not married. Her husband is 80 years old. None of her children have received formal education because, they argue, the family is poor. Omi may at this stage (according to the reporter Jadimano) not consider formal education as valuable and productive.

The whole family is supported on the family's three acres of land. Omi plows, sows, transplants, and harvests, using no modern agricultural technology. She also harvests paddy rice. In her words, "Women are not helpless. They are capable. It is not only men who can stand on their own feet. Women can do the same [in Kannada, *Naari able ala mahele sabale*]." Mr. V. R. Hegde, who is the secretary of the Sirsi Cooperative Society and who sells retail seeds, manure, and tools, says that Omi is a source of inspiration for other women.

Women like Omi are not dependent on men. Omi started by taking a loan of 25,000 rupees from the cooperative society to transform her life and that of her family. She makes some money from farming; however, she came to the public's attention because she single-handedly farmed to support her family. Omi's ability "to stand on her own feet" became an inspiration and makes her stand out as a rural "plowing woman" with power.

4.8.1.3 A businesswoman

Women have expressed other forms of their *shakti* as well by running their own businesses. Ramijabi Madsab Bagwati Siddi, 45, a Muslim, lives in Kendelgari. She has three children who are all in school. She grows watermelons and lentils for sale. Ramijabi has bullocks that other farmers hire to plow their lands. She uses the income from renting the bullocks to support her household. She also makes bricks for sale.

As an entrepreneur, she commands respect (*izzath*) and envy from some men in her community. With a loan of 30,000 rupees from an NGO, Ramijabi began her business of hiring people to make bricks while others worked on her farm. She purchased a water pump and brick-making equipment. She is also the president of the Marikamba Sangha in Kendelgari.

Ramijabi said she learned business practices by observing how others grew crops, made bricks, and used water pumps to irrigate their fields. She said her business makes her travel to many places away from her immediate village, which allows her to meet people and socialize, which was not done by her mother and grandmother, who raised her in a traditional Muslim family. There are other women in her village who do not go out alone as she does.

In October 2012, Ramijabi was informed by the forest department that she was forbidden to use the soil with which she had been making bricks because the piece of land where she dug the soil belonged to the government. This challenge from the forest department, though not aimed only at Ramijabi, could undo much of her brick-making business; she therefore reported the case to the Mundgod *panchayat* office. The office sent the case to the Mundgod court; as of April 2013, she had suspended work and was awaiting the court's decision. The court had informed her that it had many land-dispute cases pending and that Ramijabi would be notified at the appropriate time. As of 16 May 2013, Ramijabi had been informed she could continue her brick-making business; she had won her case.

On the local level, Ramijabi was able to take a loan to run her business, but a branch of government then made it difficult for her to accomplish her development goals. Such frustrations and obstacles are often not addressed by NGOs and government intervention programs.

Undaunted by frustrations, Ramijabi began to maximize her economic opportunities by engaging in different types of production and by using her family network for labor. As she produced crops, she always looked for new markets for her wares. At the moment, she has access to equipment and tools, which were previously controlled by the Malayali/Keralite men who used to own the lands on which Siddis live in Kendelgari. Some of these lands have been given to the Siddis who live in Kendelgari. With her irrigation equipment, Ramijabi is able to prepare her land for crop production during the dry season. With the family network as a labor force, she has promoted her business and gained access to resources outside her village. While expanding her business opportunities, she became active in various *sanghas* as a leader with local political recognition, becoming the president of both the Marikamba and Shree (a variant spelling used by members) Shakti *sanghas*.

Ramijabi has control of material resources and socioeconomic control of decision making, which neither she nor most of the women in Kendelgari formerly had (Rose 1992: 206). She said, "I saw how Fatimabi, my mentor, who was president of three *sanghas,* ran meetings and, at times, she fought against forest department officials and the police." Ramijabi has drawn inspiration from Fatimabi, who was a senior member of her community. Also, when Ramijabi led a group of women to fight off some non-Karnataka men who wanted to dispossess Siddis of their lands, she began to build *izzath* (Hindi/Urdu for honor or respect) for herself.

Izzath (dignity, honor, respect, in Hindi) is one of the basic principles of family organization characteristic of communities in India, Pakistan, and Bangladesh, according to Ballard (1982). In addition to upholding the family honor, individuals' behavior and words are expected to uphold and increase the social standing, reputation, dignity, and respect of their family. In societies with institutionalized hierarchy and patriarchy, subordinates, especially women, bear the burden of building and maintaining the family honor or else are perceived as having brought shame to their families and community. The husband, family, or community usually punishes a woman or subordinate who challenges the authority of the husband or head of the family. Thus "honor killing" has received great attention in the news, and human rights activities and women's groups are raising their voices against all forms of violence against women. While honor can also mean male pride and the ability to protect the weak, honor and shame underscore the hierarchy of relationships in both family and community.

As Ballard (1982) argues, the asymmetrical relationship between the sexes is best illustrated by South Asian notions of *izzath* and shame. For instance, wives, sisters, and daughters, by being modest and obeying the cultural and patriarchal rules, uphold the male *izzath*. Honor can also accrue to the family based on their wealth, on members conforming to norms of the society, and on families' advancing their status through arranging marriages between their women and men from prestigious families (Ballard 1982). During my interviews, discussants 20-year-old Hamid Siddi and 28 year old Rajesab Siddi used the term *izzath*. In Kendelgari, this term also means the respect and honor that may result from the fearlessness and independence exhibited by Ramijabi.

Ramijabi was seen as a woman with courage, honor, and strength, aspects of *shakti*. She has demonstrated an ability to rally other women and men in support of social change in her community (see the description of her struggle to build a hostel for children, below). As a result of her power and influence, some of the women in Kendelgari are becoming bold enough to challenge men in their society and homes when they feel they are being treated unfairly. The confidence with which Ramijabi and other women approach matters in their community made one police officer in Mundgod once say, "Some of the women in Kendelgari are men" (personal communication, 20 June 2010). Thus, Ramijabi and the women are seen as courageous (*dairadith* in Konkani). Ramijabi has increased her sources of income and administrative skills by managing workers on her family land. These skills have been recognized by her community and surrounding villages.

While Ramijabi and other women who now control resources with their attendant power (*shakti*) may not directly confront gender inequity at all levels, their activities have helped some women to change their self-perceptions; some of the rules about gender roles are also beginning to change. Women's economic advancement may not correlate with their political activity, but Ramijabi and others are using opportunities to participate in political and economic activities as alternatives to reordering relations with men.

These women's family networks, their geographical mobility, and the force of their personalities have helped them to be influential in their communities. Thus, when Ramijabi championed the building of a hostel for children in 2012, she reported that she faced opposition from men who said a woman did not have the right to put up a building. The men, mainly Muslim and some Hindus belonging to the local *hiriyaru/pancharu* put obstacles in Ramijabi's path. In the face of this resistance, she organized other women in her community and went to court to redeem the deed to the land and get a permit to allow her to build the hostel. Such initiatives enhanced her autonomy and her visibility in her community.

Ramijabi said she had not been afraid of the men who objected to the building of the hostel. At a community meeting, Ramijabi informed the assembly that she had donated her land and was ready to sell the bricks she had made for the hostel before the stoppage by the forest department. She said, "I invited the other members of the village to contribute their labor and building materials such as sand, wood, and stones, so that we can build the hostel for our own children."

When asked what she thought about the opposition she faced, she said, "Whatever makes the men think they are powerful, I have that too. I'm a woman on the outside, but I too want the best for myself, my family, and my community just as a man may want" (Ramijabi, 10 August 2012). At one of the meetings at which some men objected to her building project, she pointed out that opponents were being shortsighted. For instance, she said, some men contended that the village did not need a hostel because parents often send their children outside the community. She explained that, about ten years ago, she took a loan for about 10,000 rupees to purchase the land on which the hostel now stands. She took that step because someone on a village *panchayat* had advised the women to buy land then because soon afterward it would become difficult for them to own land. Ramijabi said, "After buying the land, I was advised to register it. I did not understand the whole process, but I did it. Today, since I went to court for the deed on the land, I know that I have the court backing me and my claim to the land."

What Ramijabi did involved her ability to deploy a specific degree of power from multiple sources in an arena of negotiation to accomplish her objective. Ramijabi as an actor used tactics of negotiation to legitimize her *shakti* in a context of multiple agents in order to alter the events in her favor (Few 2002: 31). Giddens (1984) describes people's ability to mobilize resources in order to articulate their power as exemplified by Ramijabi.

Ramijabi motivated her community to build the hostel, which was completed in January 2012. She supplied bricks, donated her land, and invoked her property rights to build the hostel (Watts and Bohle 1993: 54) despite opposition. Not only that, she also mobilized legal and social support networks to ensure that the hostel was built.

While political economy is about the power dynamics of class relations in a society, Ramijabi and other women use multiple power bases to advance their goals. She has a daughter married to a relative, so her son-in-law, Huseinsab Siddi, is now also part of the family labor force. With their labor force, aside from making bricks, Ramijabi also grows green peas and watermelons, thus diversifying her business. When she incurs a loss from one source of income (she says), she may gain a profit from another, or take loans from *sanghas* to start other business ventures.

When a kindergarten teacher was hired five years ago and the community needed housing for the teacher, she and her family offered the teacher a room. She said, "Other people were behaving as if it was a strange idea to have a stranger stay with them—a teacher from another community or caste. I did not have those worries." Ramijabi argued that what mattered was that the teacher who was to educate children of their village would have a place to stay. That was her reason for agreeing to provide accommodation for the teacher. As a result, since she had rented to a teacher in the past, in January 2012 she and her family were willing to host the warden hired to work with the hostel's children.

Ramijabi's *shakti* is multifaceted. She is involved in rural enterprises of brick-making and vegetable farming and uses her adult extended and joint family members as a workforce. Her daughter and son-in-law in this matrifocal/local setting contribute to the growth, harvest, and sale of Ramijabi's farm produce. Since Ramijabi's business is family run, she takes small loans from the Sisters of the Holy Cross and from *sangha* groups to purchase seeds or seedlings from local nursery grounds. She and her family workers use their technical skills while she manages the business. Ramijabi's business acumen is an example of an entrepreneurial woman whose power is based on familial loyalties, the family's collective skills, and a limited loan cash investment as a resource (Ballard 1982).

As Ramijabi and other women engage in rural economic activities, they help create new opportunities for employment for their family members and those they hire to earn incomes to improve their living standards. Ramijabi's story helps us understand how some women adopt a counterideological stance to social hierarchies and create alternative structures of power and careers and new spheres of influence. Also, she is a local actor who uses strategies to mobilize and enlist the help of authorities that are sympathetic to her needs and can enforce the law to her benefit (Gaventa 2003). Ramijabi knows how to access resources to help her put up resistance against the patriarchal traditional power of her community.

With the help of *sanghas* and individuals as well as the women's own determination and hard work, they have established a more differentiated model of economic, social, and political mobility in rural South Asia.

As Few (2002: 29) argues, the tactical use of power in social interactions differs from decision-making/non–decision-making in society. Ramijabi is an actor who uses available power resources and her own knowledge and ability to address specific issues confronting her and her community. By so doing, she demonstrates actor strategies (Few 2002) of female transformative energy.

Another Muslim woman who is self-employed is Mirinam Gaskubi Musambi, profiled in the next section.

4.8.1.4 *An incense stick maker*

Most women who do other jobs describe agricultural labor and coolie work as tedious and unrewarding. Some rural women look for ways to advance beyond traditional roles and encourage their husbands and children to find alternative livelihoods, thus exercising power to effect change in their families' circumstances. The women may live in traditional societies, but they can also show they are in charge of their future through their foresight, hard work, and determination to take advantage of new opportunities. Women like Mirinam exhibit their own vision as social, economic, and political actors who try to achieve their goals in light of new government and NGO opportunities.

Unlike incense stick makers in Muslim households in rural Karnataka, where the women collect the paste and sticks as well as make the incense sticks, which are later collected by NGO representatives, Alavi (1988: 1329) reports that, in Pakistan, it is the men, as the heads of their households, who bring the materials for the women to work on at home, because the women are not allowed to go out in public because of the belief that respectable women do not mingle with men who are not their relatives. The men mediate with entrepreneurs. They bring home work orders and deliver finished products. The men control production as well as incomes.

Unlike such strict division of labor that privileges men in Pakistan, there are Muslim women in India who either share power with their husbands or wield much of the power at home. Though they belong to the same faith, some Muslim women who live in specified geographical areas are able to assert themselves differently from other Muslim women.

Mirinam Gakurbi Musaub, 51, lives in Karkinkoppa village. She belongs to a *sangha*, or SHG. She sells dried fish and makes incense sticks, with financial and training support from Dharmasthala, an NGO that works with rural women. Her surrounding villages provide a good market for her fish. According to Mirinam, she was selling dried fish when she saw women making incense sticks. Upon asking them, she learned that Dharmasthala had taught them the craft. She invited some women in her village to form the Basveshi SHG so they could ask for assistance from Dharmasthala. At present, she and the women make incense sticks. Neither her mother nor her grandmother had been involved in incense-stick-making, nor did they join a *sangha*. Her family members had always been coolies, she said. Their *sangha* gives them small loans and helps the women get savings accounts.

Since her husband was involved in a motor accident, he had not been able to go out to do his coolie work, so she now supports the family and takes care of her husband. She decides how to spend the family's money. She said, "It was when I was traveling to Sidapur, Yellapur, Ankola, Mundgod—where I sold [dried] fish—that I found women doing the incense-stick-making business." Motivated by a desire to improve her own and her family's material circumstances, she therefore sought more information about the incense stick business. To pursue the new business, she had to learn new skills beyond the sale of fish. According to her, "Dharmasthala agents come to collect the incense sticks after I have finished working on them. It is the SHG that puts perfume on the stick, and they sell the finished products. All I do is to put the not-yet-scented paste of charcoal mixed with masala, and roll the paste onto bamboo sticks." The sticks and paste are supplied to the female incense stick makers.

Being self-employed has given Mirinam self-confidence. In 2011, she said, "other *sangha* members and I needed ration cards, but a Havig Brahmin man took a contract from the ration card office to enable him to issue the cards." Ration cards are Indian state government documents issued to people below the poverty line so they may purchase food and other items at subsidized prices; the cards are part of the Indian government's policies to alleviate hardships on marginalized people. "When we the women came to know that a man had signed a contract to be the middle person for the ration cards, we boycotted what the ration contractor was offering. We women traveled to another village so we could be part of another ration card application system outside of our village. The man who took the bid on the ration card had to look for new clients elsewhere since the women discovered that he wanted to charge them an exorbitant fee for the issuance of the cards," Mirinam said. "Now he can eat the cards."

She said, "We women are no longer going to allow some rich and powerful men exploit us as in the past," she said (personal communication, 15 September 2010).

Though incense stick manufacture does not pay much, Mirinam's membership in a *sangha* helped give her and other rural poor women confidence to exercise their right to boycott the issuance of ration cards that would have cost them more than they could afford. Her economic power is linked with her ability to insist on her rights and challenge people who abuse power.

Mirinam derives joy and satisfaction (*kushe* in Hindi/Urdu) from the work she does. She is content and inspired by knowing that her products are "accepted, valued, and sold to people for *puja* [devotion/worship] or marriage," she said. The more the NGO collects what she makes, the more enthusiastic and innovative she gets. She gains respect and a name by making incense sticks, and she said, "I don't exert too much muscle power in the manufacture, as compared to coolie work. It is more skill and knowledge [*budhi* in Hindi/Urdu], this time."

Within the new opportunities provided by NGOs and government organizations, some rural women who take advantage of such opportunities are able to exercise power to effect change in their families' circumstances. Women like Mirinam exhibit their own vision as social, economic, and political actors working to achieve their goals in the light of new opportunities. By refusing to buy ration cards from a corrupt official, the women in Mirinam's *sangha* not only successfully defended themselves from exploitation, they also increased their self-confidence. They also took an action that, in its own small but significant way, threatened the larger social order of government official corruption and disregard for marginalized people. These women thus became agents of change.

Mirinam has taken control of the affairs of her family to deploy her foresight and determination, traveling and observing people as they make incense sticks. Having that information, she then joined an SHG that gave her a loan to set up an incense stick business, and now she is able to support her family. She believes that incense stick making has brought her recognition, status, and respect. Her *shakti* involves increasing her skills and knowledge, and challenging injustice.

In the context of governmental and NGO efforts to transform peoples' lives, there are some rural women who continue to perform their caste/tribe specific professions, but with a difference. Such women rework aspects of their traditional roles, such as basketry or pottery, to improve themselves and their material circumstances, in the process creating and exercising forms of power that illuminate parts of their heritage; at times they also depart from that heritage.

4.8.1.5 A potter

The ancient craft of pottery among the Kurumbar in rural India also provides opportunities for some women to express their *shakti* creativity and their transformative abilities. In Mosali lives Parvakar Gora Kumbhar, a member of the Kurumbar, a subcaste of the Lingayat caste; she is a potter, making cooking pots, bowls, flowerpots, and statues of Ganesh. She also belongs to the Dharmasthala NGO, mentioned earlier. She took loans from Dharmasthala to build a house and buy two milk cows.

Parvakar sells her products at festivals and markets to families planning a wedding. According to Parvakar, "My parents used to do coolie work as well as make cooking pots. Now, we potters are in competition with producers of plastic and steel cooking pots." While the family's traditional source of support and influence had been based on pottery, modern inventions pose a threat to her family's livelihood. Rather than changing her livelihood completely, she said, "I get more income and prestige from making Ganesh [elephant] statues. There are times when I'm able to make 200 items that my family sells during festivals."

Her customers either come to her house to place special orders or carry her wares for sale at pilgrimage sites.

People respect her in her community, Mosali, which has about a 1,000 people and where she and two other women are the only people engaged in pottery-making at home. Her husband, who used to work with her, is now employed by a company in Mundgod, where he uses his skill in making hot plates and other clay-based products.

Asked how she perceived her influence relative to her husband, Parvakar said, "Though I have power at home and in my community, I think [that], because my husband goes outside to work for a company while I'm self-employed, he may have more power than I do." Her response underscores local perceptions that those who work for a company and are paid a salary may wield more influence than someone who is self-employed.

Parvakar said that she used to be a *panchayat* member, her responsibilities covering her own village of Mosali, Katur, and two other villages. When asked how she was elected to the *panchayat*, she said, "It is true that the government wants various SCs and STs to be represented on the *panchayats*. However, I stood and won the election because people saw that I work hard and I'm someone who interacts with others outside of my home." She also said that when she was a *panchayat* member, she helped with the construction of a road to her village and ensured that a water tank was built for some of the communities. She admitted that the government procedure is always cumbersome. "That is why I don't seek aid directly from either the state or central government. The SHGs, on the other hand, provide direct aid," she said. "That's why I belong to the Mahila Mandel *sangha* in our village."

When asked about the difference between pottery-making and other jobs like coolie work and gathering firewood, she said, "Pottery always sells, people will want to cook. At present, people use flowerpots, and religious people will always purchase statues for *puja*. But it is not always that cows give enough milk." She said her parents made small statues of Ganesh, but now some customers ask for big-size Ganeshas.

Also, her parents and grandparents did not color the statues, but now she and her family paint their products. She said her children, who have formal education, send her calendars and center foldouts of magazines, from whose images she has learned how to paint multicolored images of Ganesh. She sells some of the products she makes, though her husband sells more because he has contacts with the outside world.

In 2010, a potters association was founded in the Mundgod *taluk*. Parvakar belongs to the association, and her husband is the president.

The Karnataka forest laws have affected them adversely, as potters can no longer get clay from lands belonging to the government. Hence, Parvakar and other potter women must buy clay from outside their village, the cost involved in travel and the price of the clay posing the potters with a new challenge.

Parvakar and other potters thus produce their commodities within contemporary social and economic relations that reproduce expectations, such as that a community's members who are expected to travel far, carrying heavy items, are men, not women (Hapke 2001: 225–249). The economic benefits of potters' lives foster situations in which cultural practices and economic activities shape, and are in turn shaped by, their cultural expectations (Hapke 2001: 225–249).

In Mosali, some women potters who belong to the potter caste use microfinance to raise cattle, run shops, and make bricks to improve their material circumstances. They are also able to send their children to school like upper castes and middle-class people. For example, today Parvakar's son has earned a bachelor's degree in education. She said this was made possible through her work as a potter.

As they construct their identities in India's attempt to bring equality to all castes and tribes, the potters work their consciousness and craft through cultural expectations about the division of labor between men and women. While the women work at home, the men may work outside the home on new products such as hot plates and modern utensils made from clay. Parvakar, for instance, makes Ganesh statues that bring her fame and prestige in her village, and her involvement in a *sangha* enhances her chances to get more financial assistance and more markets for selling her products (Natrajan 2005: 227–241).

Hapke (2013) asserts that the division of labor within a household is central to the system of production and the differential impacts on men and women. Though men and women may be engaged in similar economic activities, the relative bargaining power of men reverses the equal benefits that would accrue to both men and women (Iversen and Rosenbluth 2010: 29). Domestic activity and experience have important implications beyond the household domain. Thus, the creation and "distribution of jural and other formal rights belie the power of women, most ordinary and important interactions occur in the context of face-to-face community, where informal relationships and forms of power are at least as significant a force in everyday life as formalized, authorized relationships and power" (Rogers 1975: 730).

Both men and women "equally depend on each other economically, socially, politically, or in other ways" (Rogers 1975: 730). Both Parvakar's and her husband's incomes were used to raise their children and support their family. The apparent subordination of women to men may conceal or obscure the power of women to organize, lead, counsel, and protect men and control their own lives (Rogers 1975: 732–733.) even while they seem to play traditional roles.

Parvakar has expanded and diversified her role and products. At the same time, she has ratified elements of her caste-specific profession while simultaneously using *sangha* resources to advance herself and improve the lives of her children. Parvakar also depends on small loans with minimal interest that she takes from her *sangha* to meet the needs of her family.

Parvakar is employed in the informal sector to express her creativity and her ability to adapt to change by incorporating new depictions of Ganesh statues while using skills she inherited in a traditionally caste-based profession. There are, however, other women whose skills are also caste-based, whose jobs require them to work outside their homes for NGOs, businesses, government organizations, and schools.

The following case, about Bangladeshi garment factory workers, illuminates ways in which opportunities for work have unequal impacts on women who are differently situated.

4.8.2 Garment factory workers in Bangladesh

Ahmed (2004: 34–45) introduces insightful ideas about the opportunity for Muslim women to work outside of their homes. According to her, even when women in Bangladesh are employed in garment factories, work has different meanings for different classes since women's roles are shaped differently within their respective households. Ahmed's position raises the significance of how NGOs, governments, and global organizations that are committed to income-generating opportunities may not always empower the women they employ.

Ahmed argues that there are Bangladeshi women who, in spite of the deplorable and insecure conditions under which they work, are not able to quit their jobs. For such women, working under deplorable conditions is a means by which they are able to earn income to help support their families. This also means that social institutions, local leaders' power, and religious injunctions are not static. When rural women are employed in the factories, they tend to be less dependent on agricultural labor work (like coolies in India), where the land might be owned by local landowners (*matbars*). As women move from their local communities to find jobs, including domestic work, they use the work opportunities to establish domains of influence and self-development. But, Ahmed argues, these women do not have any bargaining power to unionize. Therefore, working in the garment factories becomes disempowering.

However, there are some women who work in the garment factories so that they would not become domestic servants, prostitutes, or workers in the fields. Some of the women, upon returning home, give their incomes to their husbands. In cases where the women refuse to give their incomes to their husbands, Ahmed reports that some husbands who have felt they were the breadwinners perceived their wives' economic powers as a threat and therefore victimized their wives or committed acts of violence against them. The behavior of these men reflects some long-held beliefs in conservative Islamic households.

At the same time, there are women who benefit from working in the factories because they are able to use their income to better their standard of living, especially young unmarried women who want status and economic independence for themselves.

The above provides examples of the multiclass and different responses to job opportunities provided for women by NGOs.

There are cases when some women have taken the initiative to assert their *shakti* in innovative ways. Such trailblazers have not only empowered themselves, but also inspired other women to break with tradition as part of their self-advancement.

Schuler et al. (1996) provide examples from Bangladesh to show that when, in the early 1990s, Bangladeshi women behaved in ways inconsistent with the norms of their society—by doing such things as taking jobs outside the home, using contraceptives, and going to health centers themselves (unaccompanied by a male relative)—their actions unleashed freedom for other Bangladeshi women to follow suit. Thus, the bold steps of a few women enabled other women to exercise their own notions of courage to take control of their own fertility or reproductive health and participate in local politics.

The women might not have changed all gender inequalities or social structures that subordinate women; however, they embodied *shakti*, and gradual changes have started to occur. As women begin to take control of their bodies, gain consciousness of their rights, and participate in decision making at home and in public spaces, they reflect the ripple or viral effect of what a few women have initiated in rural Bangladesh, India, and Pakistan. Also, when women acted in ways inconsistent with conventional expectations, their counterhegemonic attitudes generated new and alternative modes of behavior for other women (Schuler et al. 1996). Also, as Kabeer (2001) argues, women manifest power when they make strategic choices and face the consequences of those choices. They manifest power because they were previously disempowered. Bangladeshi women who used their newly gained power to break with norms and cultural expectations holding them back succeeded in transforming the informal and formal institutions that supported patriarchy and religious conservatism.

4.9 Violence against women

Another arena in which women deploy their *shakti* is how they handle violence against them. South Asian women suffer from a wide range of violence against their economic, social, and cultural rights. Many women face "sexual violence by family members, strangers and agents of the state; domestic abuse including spousal murder; being burned, disfigured with acid, beaten and threatened; ritual honour killings; and custodial abuse and torture" (Niaz 2003: 175). India, Bangladesh, and Pakistan have promulgated laws against violence against women, but the laws are not always enforced. The three countries also have activists whose grassroots political actions have made some headway in bringing attention to atrocities against women. But the violence persists.

Dowry-related violence involves atrocities that young brides face at the hands of their husband or in-laws. In such cases, the in-laws argue or contend that the young bride had not paid a fitting dowry to her husband's family. Because of a failure to pay a dowry consisting of cash, jewelry, cows, and, in some cases, cars to her groom's family, the bride may suffer verbal and physical abuse that sometimes leads to her death. Dowry-related deaths are often described as bride burning, because sometimes kerosene is poured on the victim, who is then set on fire. At times, the euphemism "a kitchen accident" is used to describe this type of violence. Stove-burning is another type of dowry-related violence. In Bangladesh insufficient dowry has resulted in husbands or their relatives throwing acid on the women. As discussed earlier, the honor of a woman is a necessary component of family and community honor. *Izzath* is gender neutral, and the lives of women are strongly affected by their honor and dignity.

Niaz (2003) points out that the violence women suffer tends to depend on their class, religion, and geographical location. For example, upper-caste men sometimes use rape to humiliate and silence lower-caste women; also, in rural areas, where local religious leaders and heads of communities are steeped in patriarchy and strong beliefs and wield unlimited powers, women tend to live more restricted lives than those of urban women. Although India, Pakistan, and Bangladesh have seats reserved for women at all levels of government and women's groups have been formed, women still face entrenched countervailing forces that limit women's rights (Kabeer 2001; Niaz 2003).

At times, family expectations and cultural norms are invoked by men and the extended family members to discriminate against women (Niaz 2003: 177). There are occasions when women tolerate the violence because their communities regard, for instance, wife battery as the norm. An example is among Lambanis.

Despite the Lambani communities' worship and veneration of female deities, Lambani women do not share equal status with men. Even though female goddesses are valorized and have positive constructions of femininity, some of the men use violence to subordinate their women and expect them to acquiesce. Some Lambani men, after selling their firewood, often drink and end up battering their wives and children. Incidences of violence against women and children have often been ignored by the *goar panchayats.* Asked why some of the men continue to abuse their wives, Laxman Lambani from Kamal Nagar stated that "women need to be put in their place, else there won't be peace in their homes" (personal communication, 5 July 2011). Customs and justifications of wife battery in other communities are discussed later in this section.

Sexual harassment and gang rape of women are becoming rampant in India, Pakistan, and Bangladesh. Social pressure and family honor are used as the excuse for not reporting most of the sexual violence against women.

There have been recent examples of how women have suffered forms of assault because they live in communities that do not regard them as citizens with equal rights with men. Although the examples seem extreme, they represent some deeply held attitudes about women in South Asian societies.

In the last months of 2012, the Pakistani girl Malala Yousafzai was shot by militants who opposed her efforts to promote girls' education; Bangladesh reported cases of women who have suffered forms of violence including debilitating acid attacks; in India, there have violent gang rape attacks on women, one of which led to the death of a 23-year-old physiotherapy student and another to the death of a 5-year-old girl. These are just a few of the many atrocities that are being committed against female citizens of South Asia despite programs South Asian governments and NGOs have embarked on to equalize rights for their people.

According to Vidya D'Acosta, a social worker in Mundgod in Karnataka, India, Vaddars in India have some of the highest incidences of violence against women. She said that when the men work in the quarries (Vaddars are traditionally stonecutters), some of them spend their income on alcohol instead of using the money for the upkeep of their families. When their wives complain, Vidya said, the men batter the women. Wife batterers, she said, "justify their violence as a disciplinary measure towards their disobedient wives." The women's mothers-in-law at times condone such cases of social injustice. For some of the mothers-in-law, their daughters-in-law would not have been beaten if they respected their spouses.

Senior women's complicity in violence against women, especially in joint family homes, is prevalent in rural Karnataka. Social justifications for the battering of women in patriarchal systems are often aimed at controlling or dealing with female disobedience, bad temperament, or the women's perceived irresponsibility (Mahajan 1990; Mohan 1990). In 2006, the central government of India passed the Protection of Women against Domestic Violence Act; however, as with many Acts, the test of the Act's effectiveness lies in how it is enforced.

While social workers encourage the women to report cases of abuse, most women tend not to report the violence against them. A common response has been that their husbands would inflict more punishment on them if they reported the abuse. This phenomenon is what Lukes (2005) has addressed as the fear that powerful actors induce in their victims: the victim weighs the cost of taking action against her abuser and chooses not to act in her interest. It is also the case that some victims become defiant in the face of the potential adverse consequence and therefore take action to break out of the cycle of violence against them.

Some of the women among whom Vidya works reported to her that their husbands subject them to sexual coercion.

The protests of Indian women belonging to *panchayats* against all forms of violence against women, as described by Lalita earlier, is similar to women's activism in Bangladesh that seeks to redress such violence; for instance, Anwary (2003) points out that there are Bangladeshi women activists who provide care for women victims of acid attacks by mobilizing civil society and government officials to bring health care and healing to the victims. Victims receive severe physical, psychological, and social scars and always need years to rebuild their lives through medical treatment and social support networks. Acid violence does not occur only in Bangladesh; there have been instances of this violence in Pakistan and India. Although the three countries have laws that forbid acid violence against women, some women still become victims at the hands of men and their families (Anwary 2003).

Anwary puts violence against women in a social context and argues that, in patriarchal cultures, women tend to be regarded as property (Anwary 2003: 307). The emphasis on a woman's facial appearance is critical because the face is believed to represent the woman, her personality, and her family's honor. When women are protected from sexual temptations in patriarchal societies, those who insist on such protective measures argue that marriage is the only way to maintain women's social status and ensure a woman's economic security; therefore, virginity and appearance are important resources for women (i.e., in the marriage "market") (Anwary 2003: 307). Thus, when a woman's appearance is attacked, the attacker is using the violence to "bolster their political power" (Anwary 2003: 307).

Anwary also points out that, when women activists in Bangladesh have confronted acid violence against women, they draw on local and international organizations, mobilizing civil society to fight women's oppression and to serve as an "agent of healing and healthcare" (Anwary 2003: 305).

Thus, not all South Asian women acquiesce in the face of male violence. Women activists who confront violence against women provide an example of the varied responses that women in South Asia have toward abuse or violence against women. The Bangladeshi example shows how women exercise actor strategies (Few 2002) by marshaling internal and external power resources to deal with local problems.

4.10 Women's resistance

Some women activists in rural Bangladesh and Pakistan confront men who sexually abuse girls, and report cases of violence to local officials. These women activists have thus enhanced their agency and expanded their social scope to take up issues that have gone unchecked for centuries.

They have their Indian counterparts in women like Lalita, the *panchayat* president, and Girija, the rural healthcare provider, profiled earlier. Indian women have formed their own courts to try men who commit violence against women. Such women create domains of informal legal systems to redress injustice against women.

The women use their dispositional power (Clegg 1989) to summon men to their female community court. They pronounce verdicts that are binding on men and women. For example, when they settle a case between spouses, they expect the parties to abide by their recommendations. If a male drunkard does not stop beating his wife, they inform him that the next step will be for him to appear in a formal court where there are judges, magistrates, and so on. If an abusive husband does not stop the battery, the women's court can recommend that the woman leave the husband.

As the women challenge their oppressors, they negotiate, concede, and maximize their interests in the "context of plurality and diversity" (Nyamnjoh 2002: 116). Their *shakti* has emerged in response to violence against women that was previously accepted as normative or otherwise condoned by male members of village councils.

Anjali Siddi, also profiled earlier, used her position as a *budavanta* to prevent a battered woman from returning to her husband's house. Lalita, as a *panchayat* president, used the influence of her office to mobilize a group of women, which dragged an abusive man from his house to shame him and eventually reported him to the police. Though without any formal education, she was able to deploy her *shakti* to protect a woman in an abusive relationship. Public humiliation, according to her, is effective in their communities. She further said that when a man is shamed, he could be ostracized until he stops beating his wife.

Domestic violence, including verbal and physical abuse, tends to be higher in conservative, rural communities in Pakistan, India, and Bangladesh, where the women are afraid that if they report the abuse, their husbands will divorce them. The unreporting of wife battery in South Asia also covers the violence and impedes women's progress. Koenig et al. (2003) cite the Sirajgonj area of Bangladesh. They show that, in this rural area, microfinance aid that was supposed to empower women sometimes has become the cause of domestic violence, because the financial success of some married women has caused their husbands to beat them (Cain 1979).

Atrocities against women became a context in which we saw some Pakistani women exhibit their *shakti*. Mukhtaran Mai's celebrated case is an example of how individual women defy patriarchy and social hierarchies. In June 2002, Mukhtaran Bibi, also known as Mukhtaran Mai, was brutally gang-raped by men from a neighboring village as punishment for her brother's crimes. Though Mai received no adequate formal education and was from a conservative family in a rural area, she refused to be silenced, filed charges, and took the case to court. The government of Pakistan awarded her a sum of $8,200, and with this money, Mai built a school for girls. She also linked up her endeavors with other women who belonged to networks and civil societies outside her local community. Mai embodied and demonstrated her strategic actor's power by enrolling other women facing similar repression (Few 2002; Gaventa 2006). Mobilizing the power of local women is therefore a component critical to the democratizing efforts of their respective societies (Omvedt 2005: 47–51).

Mukhtaran's personal story and her determination to challenge oppression blurred the boundary between private and public spaces. Since power is diffuse and productive and relies on social relations and diverse points of resistance (Foucault 1977), Mukhtaran deployed the subversive dimension of power to fight for her rights. By so doing, she also inspired other women.

From her *shakti*, we find an example of how some Muslim women engage in the discourse of social change that calls attention to entrenched patriarchy and religious norms that marginalizes women. Women like her, who put up resistance in order to free themselves and other women, are promoting the equality that some governments are not able to provide for them.

Despite the examples described, however, there are some senior women and other women who embrace the social values of gender inequality who do not share the views of the activists.

The above varied articulations of *shakti* among women between the ages of 20 and 60 do not cover all concepts of power among rural South Asian women. I will now turn to ways in which women above the age of 60 craft and manifest their forms of *shakti*.

5

The *Shakti* of Senior Women (60 Years of Age and Older)

Focusing on senior women allows us to unmask age differences between women as citizens in South Asia. In this chapter, I focus on how women of 60 years and above create alternative power positions to navigate social, political, cultural, and economic changes.

Rural senior women craft and articulate forms of power, to increase their competencies, at the edges of shifting societal values amidst long-held caste, age, and gender cultural expectations. At times, the senior women's manifestations of *shakti* challenge and disrupt ideals and practices that regard senior women as helpless and, thus, dependent on their male offspring to survive.

In this chapter, I examine the extent to which senior women are responding to the South Asian governments' efforts to expand women's capacity to make critical choices to shape their lives in ways that have not been available to them in the past (Kabeer 2001).

The identity and contributions of senior women to their respective communities are not just based on the fact that they have their own hopes, aspirations, and styles of advancing themselves. Rather, as we discuss senior women, their forms of power, and their contributions, we can understand how these women help reevaluate cultural practices, governments, and political officials' and patriarchal attitudes. As the senior women manifest their power, they simultaneously help create new ideas for their respective governments that may help their societies in their reform efforts to bring about equality that speaks to "differentiated citizens" (Young 1989) such as senior women in South Asia.

Senior women manifest different forms of *shakti* through the ways they order their lives, negotiate, and mediate their notions of power and influence in rural South Asia. It is in the lives of senior women that we observe the critical intertwining relationship between *shakti*, age, dignity, and respect. Some senior women are birth attendants; others are quilters; others are farmers and caregivers.

I also address sociohistorical roles and role norms in rural India to highlight people's notions of women's ideal roles and status, and examine whether ideals are changing or tend to be rigid. I also examine the social contexts in which senior women's roles and status are shaped as well as how the women act to change social relations.

Since age-based identities are formed through social relationships (Gardner 1995), I pay attention to how people define who is old, and the different ways in which seniors define themselves.

Age-based identities are not fixed. For instance, the multiple tribal, caste, and religious identities formed in South Asia are articulated differently, and at times they contain competing notions of the elderly. Thus, it is important to explore how societal law, religion, community, and self-perception shape the meaning and articulation of age and tribal identities.

In Europe and North America, life expectancy has risen, while in India and other Global South countries, life expectancy, though it has increased somewhat, is not as high as in the Global North. Worldwide, people tend to live longer, and fertility rates seem to be dropping. Increased life expectancy therefore poses a number of challenges and opportunities for the societies in which the elderly live. Demographers stress the increase in population and visibility of elderly women, and the marginalization of women among those populations and its implications for individuals, groups, and nations (Sankaram 2006: 55–61).

Senior women and men face opportunities and challenges to continue improving and monitoring their lives, sense of self-worth, and dignity. When the challenges include declining health, disruption in their ability to be in charge of their routine activities, and a dwindling network of support, some seniors contend that their sense of self-worth has diminished.

The apparent plight of senior citizens has given rise to scholarship focusing on the elderly as those in need of help to cope with life. There are, however, senior women who have accumulated experience and knowledge and live exemplary lives as advisors and counselors and caregivers, and as a result have gained the respect and recognition of people in their communities. Some of these seniors draw on the recognition, respect, and status they have to sustain and improve themselves.

Some of the seniors depend on local webs of social network and economic systems (Watts and Boehle 1993) to navigate their way through the highly stratified societies and entrenched cultural ideals of rural South Asia.

There are places where seniors are cared for when they have no relatives to support them, which happens when able-bodied family members migrate to look for jobs outside their natal communities. Retirement and nursing homes are some such facilities housing senior citizens.

5.1 Retirement and nursing homes in India

The Sisters of the Holy Cross of the Catholic Church have set up homes for seniors in different parts of India, including one in Trasi in Karnataka, and one in Kalyan in Maharashtra. The old people's homes were first established in 1969 to cater to seniors from the local community and surrounding villages, whose able-bodied family members no longer lived with the seniors in joint family households. At Trasi in Southern Karnataka, a Catholic hospital was modified into an old-age home in 1990. Sister Emmy, the Mother Superior of the Holy Cross Convent that runs the seniors home, said, "All castes and religions are represented. Residents are from different backgrounds—medium income and poor backgrounds. Nine members pay 1,000 rupees while others pay nothing."

The Sisters supplement the residents' contributions with private and NGO donations. Some family members who have seniors living at the Home for the Aged in Trasi volunteer their services when they come to visit the residents. Some of the visitors teach reading, songs, and crafts to the seniors. Few of such centers are administered by the state of Karnataka and other agencies. Not all seniors live in retirement or nursing homes. Some seniors live by themselves or with other family members.

5.2 Multiple articulations of senior status

Senior women select and express their age and identity differently from person to person (Cligget 2005: 15). Some senior women calibrate their status as elderly women by the ages of their children and grandchildren; for instance, Davita Siddi said, "My oldest son, who works in a construction business in Yellapur, is thirty years old, and my second is twenty-seven, while my daughter is twenty-five. I have six grandchildren." Others refer to changes that have occurred since the monetized economy was introduced in India, while some say they are old because they can no longer do hard work (personal communication, Nugubai, who is in her eighties in Basnal, 25 July 2009). Some women structure their status and power by referring to the sacrifices they made by having and raising children (Cliggett 2005: 11). Some senior women mobilize and deploy resources based on where they live (whether they live with sons and their wives or alone), make links with distant relatives, and use their livelihoods to support themselves and contribute to shape the lives of others. Most rural senior women who are key players in their households tend to tie their roles to their status; for instance, they argue that they take care of light duties in the house and that everyone comes to them for advice.

While some senior women are no longer field workers or coolies, they work at home as caregivers. Gowli senior women still tend their cattle, and Lambanis continue to fetch firewood and also care for their grandchildren. Other women are birth attendants with high repute in their communities. Some senior Siddi women have formed a quilt cooperative society that provides a source of income from which the members receive and grant loans to others in need. There are Koravar women who still weave baskets in their senior years. Senior women who are birth attendants, healers, and ritual specialists embody and express notions of sacred power for their household, for shrines in their local communities, and for the surrounding villages or towns. There are senior Muslim and Hindu women who perform ritual roles in festivals such as *Dasara* (Hindu) and *Bakir-Id* (Islam). Though some play minor roles, such women tend to be in charge of the *prasad* (consecrated) food, for Hindus. The senior women are the first to participate in preparing and ritually handling the food before others have access to it. In Muslim festivals the senior women supervise those who cook the meals that are offered at shrines and before it is shared with the festival's celebrants. Though senior Christian women may prepare meals to feed participants in Christian feasts, they do not play a ritual role in the Catholic sacrament such as Holy Communion or baptism; however, when a Siddi child is baptized, senior Siddi women perform a post-baptism ritual in the household of the child's family. Catholic priests and nuns are always invited to the household rituals, but it is senior Siddi women who carry the ritual power during the rituals.

Some senior women gain power and status by engaging in income-generating work. For those seniors, they feel valued and respected when they work "with their hands," as 70-year-old Nandita Siddi from Honshettikoppa pointed out (personal communication, 9 July 2009). In reality, however, the accumulation and control of resources, such as land, cattle, shops, and children, tend to be the source of power and influence for some senior women. While most senior women have limited access to cash and other resources, some have mediated access to land through deceased husbands or their families.

Das et al.'s (2002) book, *Status of Women and Reproductive Behavior,* is helpful in addressing women's control over their bodies, their increased autonomy, and their roles in their households. While the work stresses the connection between women's status, their empowerment, and their reproductive health, it is important to investigate if a woman's autonomy goes beyond her childbearing years. The discussion that follows speaks to how women beyond childbearing age redefine and use other symbolic and literal centers of power to enhance their well-being and the well-being of their families and communities.

Although people in villages tend to maintain traditional patterns of behavior, such as respect for elders or women deferring to their husbands and to sons having the right to property, women are creating their own distinctive spaces in which to assert themselves, which I discuss next.

While Ciscel and Health (2001) argue that, in feminist economics, social capital is the product of women's unpaid work, such as caring for elderly parents and doing domestic chores, it is equally important to indicate that labor, both paid and unpaid, is more complex than a reductionist approach to social capital. Paid work is often more valued than the unpaid female labor of caring, parenting, and attending to domestic responsibilities;

however, care and civil society are intertwined in the same economic and gendered spheres (Oppong 2004: 4). Also, unpaid labor may provide social cohesion and promote the pursuit of economic activities to enable those who do paid labor (Oppong 2004: 3). Where a senior woman's well being is important to the family and community, the household and kin group support provides security to her; some senior women reciprocate the care they receive by caring for their grandchildren in a joint household, as I show later. And, while some senior women are no longer field workers or coolies, they work at home as unpaid caregivers and heads of their household.

5.3 Bangladesh

Widows are among the marginalized people in South Asia; however, they are not a monolithic group. Cain (1991) provides a profile of a widow named Atorjan, from rural Bangladesh, who lives in a joint household with her youngest son and his wife and children. Atorjan is over 60 years old and does light work at home, but she wields significant power in the household. Cain (1991) contends that her *shakti* is tied to the "wealth and power of her sons and her close relationship to them, to age and experience," and to her force of personality. Her sons own land and, to work the land, employ people from their village; thus, the sons have economic and social influence in their community. Others often envy Atorjan because she maintains peace and harmony in her household as she relies on the material resources and social capital of her intergenerational network. In these communities, it is common for seniors to count on receiving their due through filial obligation from children and grandchildren (Cain 1991).

Nosaka and Andrews (2004) state that Bangladeshi senior women, especially widows, face many disadvantages. Nevertheless, in rural Bangladesh, 61-year-old Amina rises early in the morning for prayer, feeds the family chickens, and waters the plants; then she weaves mats and baskets, grinds spices, or harvests vegetables. When her daughter-in-law underwent surgery, it was Amina who took on unexpected responsibilities in the household by caring for her grandchildren and handling the chores by herself. Her son was able to go to work, and the family also saved money that might have been spent on hiring a domestic worker in Bangladesh. Amina's influence was manifest in her dexterity to combine her routine activities with taking on extra household chores that had been performed by her incapacitated daughter-in-law.

According to Nosaka and Andrews (2004), Majiba, at 61 years, had been widowed for 12 years and lives alone, though her son and daughter-in-law interact with her very often. When her daughter-in-law needs to leave her *bari* (place of residence or home), she often asks Majiba for permission; she also often asks what meals she should prepare for her household. Majiba's son often consults his mother on managing his household. According to

Majiba, her interactions with her son, her daughter-in-law, and their children had always been positive because she was happy to keep out of the daily interactions between her son's family members. Although Majiba admitted she was frail, she stated that she was not a burden for her daughter-in-law and her son.

As I point out later in this work, the relationship between daughters-in-law and mothers-in-law in coresidential households is not as simple as described by Majiba. What is absent from Majiba's narrative is her daughter-in-law's perspective about their relationship. Also, that the daughter-in-law had to seek permission from her mother-in-law to leave the *bari*, as mentioned, shows that Majiba is an extension of the patriarchal control that restricts female mobility, a common practice in most Muslim households in South Asia (to be discussed later). This, however, does not mean that all relationships between in-laws are fraught with contention and difficulty.

5.4 India

In Kendelgari, Fatimabi Siddi, who, at 70 years is a household head, is a community leader who until recently served as a *sangha* president in her village. Fatimabi is among senior women who live in households where there is a division of labor regarding food preparation, shopping, and pooling of resources and their distribution (Cain 1991: 522). Most households like hers combine their resources to protect the welfare of their members (Cain 1991: 523) when economic activity embraces daily wages, farming, trading, and shopkeeping (Cain 1991: 523) and caregiving. She still performs her traditional role as the administrator of the family finances (Bourque and Warren 1981: 183) but has also extended her influence beyond the domestic sphere, to playing a key role in local politics.

Fatimabi uses her social obligations and webs of obligations to enhance her status (Rao 2001: 85); for example, as a household head, she exercises jural and other formal rights that underscore the power of senior women as she is engaged in ongoing and important interactions that occur in face-to-face interactions in her community. Thus, her forms of power are important in the everyday articulations of power in both domestic and public domains (Rogers 1975: 730).

Fatimabi has 20 people living in her house: her 5 children, their spouses, and their children all live under the same roof (she threw her husband out of the house when he did not stop drinking). People often gather at Fatimabi's home, visiting, discussing *sangha* issues, or strategizing on issues that affect Siddis.

Certain power bases are created outside the public sphere, but their meanings and effects are felt in public. For instance, the number of daughters-in-law in Fatimabi's household tends to augment her status and power as a household leader in Kendelgari. Thus, in that community, while a senior woman may have stopped working in the fields, going to the market, or trading, her *gaurava,* or *shakti,* is produced, sustained, and represented by the domestic power dynamic that places her above her sons and their wives. Fatimabi's authority also resides in her ability to resolve family conflicts, counseling people in her community. She also advocates for the needs of her children and grandchildren.

Being head of the household does not always mean a senior woman like Fatimabi necessarily controls the family's land (if there is any) or finances. In the few cases where senior women are household leaders who themselves own land, their power and status are increased. Senior women who have money and are therefore respected tend to have greater power than some men. There are instances when male members of a family have taken loans from some of the family's relatively well-off senior women.

Though she did not receive a formal education, Fatimabi ensures that all her grandchildren are receiving one. She controls the resources of the income from the coolie work of her sons and their wives; at one time, she supervised the fieldwork done by her daughters-in-law, though at the moment she stays at home. Fatimabi is the "family bank" since they do not keep their money in a formal bank. She makes sure that all her children and grandchildren are fed. She further ensures that when the grandchildren's parents are at work, the children go to school, some in Pune, others in Bangalore, and others in Haliyal, all of which locations are outside her immediate community.

Fatimabi has the addresses and telephone numbers, where available, of where her grandchildren go to school. For example, she told me she has a grandchild in the seventh standard in a Urdu school and a sixth standard child in Pune. She uses her recordkeeping skills to ask people to interpret whatever documents she receives regarding her family, her community, or any matter that affects Siddis. She keeps, all in one box, records of finances for women's groups, municipal government transactions with Siddis in Kendelgari, and her grandchildren's report cards. Fatimabi said, "I learned that, through recordkeeping, non-Siddis have always cheated us in the past. Now I am going to keep records to protect our interests and to contest other people's claims" (personal communication, 10 January 2009).

Fatimabi derives her influence from multiple sources. She draws support and strength in the intergenerational family relationships with whom she lives (Cliggett 2005: 98). Like other senior women living in coresidential or joint families, Fatimabi demonstrates relational power (Loomer 1976) through caregiving as she is in turn cared for by the adult members of her family.

Many seniors tend to live alone despite poor health and other vulnerabilities. For those who are physically weak, it is difficult to receive the immediate care they need. In Fatimabi's case, the potential drop in the available social capital for seniors whose able-bodied family members have moved away from home has been offset through her ingenuity and foresight. For example, she encouraged her sons to build extensions to their family home (where she resided) to accommodate the sons, their wives, and their children.

Fatimabi provides care at home as she receives security and augments her prestige in her community by serving as a *sangha* leader. She contributes to the well-being of her extended family and the whole society by caring for children whose parents can go to work. The care she provides for her grandchildren is valued and gives her respect and dignity in the family and community. Her private contributions strike a healthy balance with the public-sector labor force. Thus, both directly and indirectly, she sustains the economy and social fabric of society.

Fatimabi's additional personal and political force came into focus when, on 22 October 2007, she led a group of Siddi and non-Siddi women from three villages—Kendelgari, Gunjavatti, and Mainalli—in a protest, setting up roadblocks (*rasta roko*) to resist the opening of liquor stores in those villages. In this way, Fatimabi, a senior woman, championed the noninstitutionalized power of underclass people—who, until 2007, had not had anyone to represent or fight for them—to challenge and subvert the economic ventures of influential upper-caste liquor store owners.

The women who embarked on the *rasta roko* at the instigation of Fatimabi were articulating their local understanding of their political power and agency against a perceived injustice. The men in the villages did not support Fatimabi and the other women, as they would have liked the liquor stores to be opened in their communities.

Fatimabi's caregiving is outside the paid labor sector, yet this economically unacknowledged labor contributes to the well-being of future children. As Waerness (2004) points out, an unskilled job is not for the unskilled—speed, patience, love, courage, perseverance, and strength are abilities required for both paid and unpaid labor. Fatimabi brings to her work an invaluable skill set, such as a predictable and reliable presence and experience in caring for her grandchildren.

Fatimabi seeks and sees her power and influence as resulting from how she has empowered others, particularly her offspring, to advance in life; this is an example of Boulding's "integrative power" (1990: 25).

This local version of power is similar to the perspectives of some *panchayat* and *sangha* women who say they derive power from helping others as they advance their own interests. Fatimabi's contribution captures elements of Foucault's (1977) point that power flows through all social interactions to connect all actors in a "web of mutual influence" (Karlberg 2005: 2).

Fatimabi's influence and prestige were structured in her family and her immediate community, and she expressed the care she displayed in her "power to" (Gaventa 2006) help her children and grandchildren.

The next discussion highlights the complex nature of mother-in-law and daughter-in-law relationships in patrilocal coresidence.

Babubi Siddi, 60, lives with her son and his family in Kendelgari. She helps to take care of the grandchildren. In the caregiving, Babubi provides support that enables her son and daughter-in-law to go out to work as coolies. According to her, her caregiving involves her paying meticulous attention to her grandchildren, including the sharing of stories and songs with them.

At her son's invitation, Babubi moved in with him and her daughter-in-law after the death of her husband. Her authority in the new house is thus realigned through her son. In the new household, she exercises authority over her daughter-in-law, Gausubi. Despite the apparent harmony in the house, harmony resulting from the fact that the adult members understand and perform their roles in most cases without friction, it is important to address the mother-in-law–daughter-in-law relationship as it exists there.

Coresidence with in-laws accounts for limitations exerted on daughters-in-law. A daughter-in-law like 20-year-old Gausubi moved, as a young bride, away from her natal family in Haliyal to live in Kendelgari with Babubi's son. Gausubi's parents and siblings were, and are, therefore cut off socially from her. She is expected to identify her views with those of her husband's family. It is her mother-in-law who regulates her movements and the people with whom she can socialize, and her right to spend money on herself. In an interview with Gausubi on 10 August 2012, she said, "My mother-in-law and I do not fight. We have peace, but when I want to see my parents or go to Mundgod market or hospital, she complains that I can't go with my female friends." Gausubi also cannot exercise her right to discretionary spending for the family or for her health.

Rew et al. (2013) argue that the normative aspect of patrilocality compounds the uneasiness between daughters-in-law and mothers-in-law when the young bride lives with her husband's family. Here it is the mother-in-law who perpetuates gender inequality because she acts by proxy for male constraints on a Muslim woman's body and freedom of mobility.

The senior woman Babubi embodies the traditional expectations of women as she expands her power in her son's household. Babubi is the one who now exercises spatial control over her daughter-in-law (Rew et al. 2013: 151). Therefore, in spite of Babubi being a widow and landless with no home of her own, her son's house has become the realm for her to assert her authority. Babubi's situation seems to confirm the cultural assumption that sons are a source of security for elderly women, and that assumption leads to influence fertility decisions (Cain 1991: 519). For instance, according to India's 2011 census data, the child ratio (0–6 years) declined from 927 females per 1,000 males in 2001 to 914 females per 1,000 males ten years later.

Das et al. (2002) argue that the continuing male preference in India, Pakistan, and Bangladesh is manifest in rampant feticide. Male preference is thus based on the expectation that sons always and necessarily take care of their elderly parents. Also, the economic aspect of a dowry to be paid by a bride's family fuels the antifemale child sentiment.

However, some sons fail to play their traditional role as a source of security for their aging parents, and there are situations in which it is daughters who, in effect, are the "sons" and thus pillars for the elderly in the latter's waning years.

Despite the above cultural expectation, Babubi's security and power are also based on the role she plays in her son's household. She might have come with a disadvantage since she is a widow, But in her new setting she exercises some control as household head and as one who must be obeyed. According to her, her power is not just because she is the household head but also because she has security and can depend on a daughter-in-law and her son to ensure that she is cared for. This security in a joint family enables her to exercise power and rights as a mother, as a mother-in-law, and as a grandmother.

Security comes from immediate family members who provide for the elderly before they ask. Babubi Siddi said that when she feels pain in her back or leg, her daughter-in-law takes care of her.

Babubi Siddi provides an example of how a senior woman contributes, through caregiving, to the well-being of others as she benefits in turn from a son's and daughter-in-law's care in an extended family. She has a safety network of young people who may reciprocate care because they feel indebted to the aged for the love they received as they were growing up.

This expectation of filial loyalty, Babubi was quick to add, does not always materialize. Children are not necessarily a means of security. "Land does not change its mind. There are children who pay lip service about care for old people, but once they marry or move away, some forget their promises. At times cattle can guarantee security while *poran* or *burugi* [Konkani for children] may refuse to care for their elderly," said Babubi Siddi on 16 July 2010. She said some children can be unreliable. Babubi Siddi asserted that she is fortunate to have a daughter-in-law who loves her, but she knows other senior women who have been abandoned or neglected by their children and in-laws in Kendelgari, Ugingeri, and other communities.

Lilabhai Shakirbai Ngelege, 83, is known in Mundgod and its surrounding areas as a freedom fighter. She has grandchildren, but they do not live with her; she draws her influence and articulates her power as a senior woman in different ways, finding her power situated in India's struggle for independence against British colonial rule.

Lilabhai was among the Indian freedom fighters jailed in 1942 in Belgaum, Karnataka, for agitating for Indian independence from British rule. Lilabhai said, "Our India was under Britain, and we wanted freedom for ourselves. When I and other young women were going to jail, we kept shouting, 'British, go back to your country' and 'We want our country back.'"

Although she was only in the seventh standard, she joined about 36 girls who agitated and were sent to jail. She was living in a hostel and marched through the streets in Hubli and Belgaum, carrying flags, talking to people, and shouting the slogan "*Hame Apna lo*" (Hindi for "You are our people"). She fought for freedom, she repeated, continuing, "Now India is free, and I was among the architects that engaged in the agitations against British rule."

She contended that she and other activists marched in the streets, traveling from place to place in defense of "Bharat Mata" (Mother India). As well as marching, Lilabhai and the other freedom fighters picketed liquor and foreign clothing shops or blocked potential customers from the shops. She said, "I attended all public speeches because it was there that we learned tactics that helped us to remain committed to the struggle to free India."

According to Lilabhai, she understood the entire anticolonial struggle as promoting *swadeshi* (Hindi for self-reliance) and *swaraj* (Hindi for independence). She said she belonged to youth leagues that organized activities that expressed aggressive, transformative, and disruptive aspects of *shakti*. Lilabhai said that the young freedom fighters performed underground activities that some adult woman might have refused to engage in.

She recounted how Mahatma Gandhi and later political officials visited their house to compliment her and some of her "jail friends." At the time, the girls (and later, as women) were praised for their dedication, courage, and persistence. According to her, their preindependence struggles provided a template for present-day activities for those who fight for their rights over land and other government facilities.

Mahatma Gandhi himself drew inspiration from women's agitation movements and later wrote, "Just as Hindus do not harm a cow, the British do not attack women as far as possible. For Hindus, it would be cowardice to take a cow in the battlefield in the same way it would be cowardice for us to have women accompany us" (Gandhi 1969: 12–13). Thus, when Gandhi later encouraged women to be involved in the freedom struggle, he believed that women could bring a sustained, disciplined, nonviolent tone to the movement, not that women would be used as human shields as some critics had accused him of doing (Kishwar 1988: 2754–2763).

Lilabhai informed me during my visit that "from time to time, some government officials visit my house to chat with me and to reminisce and to seek more information about how I and other young women succeeded in overthrowing the British."

In 1947 she met her husband, who was in the Indian air force. Her husband's work as an air force officer exposed her to national politicians on many occasions. She said that she hosted officials such as Indira Gandhi and Mahatma Gandhi. The fact that she knew Gandhi, Nehru, and other political heroes and pioneers of modern India accords her the great respect and importance she has in the eyes of the recent government officers who visit her.

According to Lilabhai, "a powerful person is one who has confidence, freedom, courage, and the wisdom to access resources or get others to provide the resources for one's use." She said, "Power is expressed when one with a good soul [good *atma* in Hindi] does something good for others. It is a person who makes sacrifices for others that is powerful." For instance, Lilabhai's daughter's profession enables her, as a doctor, to work for the poor. She said her son also helps poor farmers get loans for their agricultural work.

Her strength, she said, "comes from my commitment to social justice. As a result I sign up to participate in local and district events that create awareness for village people." She said, "After we succeeded in removing the British from India, I knew that I was ready to work with others to rid society of caste, gender, and economic inequalities."

Lilabhai's participation in protests at the national level has been converted to her passion to be involved at the local level, where she empowers marginalized people to gain political awareness to fight for their rights. Lilabhai has consolidated her experience and energy as she takes pride in fashioning her power in the face of cultural political ideologies that create landlessness and social and political deprivation. She uses her previous political consciousness and influence to deploy *shakti* to advocate for rural caste and tribal women and children who cannot access municipal and government resources.

In addition to her preindependence activities, Lilabhai served on a *panchayat* in the Mundgod area. Her last service on the *taluk panchayat* ended in 2000. As a *panchayat* member, she said she was instrumental in getting schools to such villages as Bachanaki, Nyasargi, and Jainmuri. She was responsible for inspecting government building projects under construction.

Although she drew status and power from the past as a freedom fighter, she said she is pleased that when the government of India introduced local governing bodies such as *panchayats*, she could serve in some formal capacity. She is an example of seniors who have evolved a power base stretching from preindependence to present-day India. She receives a pension as a freedom fighter and as a former inspector of *panchayat* projects. Project inspection was prestigious because only men had been inspectors. Lilabhai's political connections and influence and the fact that she has served on *panchayats* have contributed to enhancing her influence.

She situates her access to and use of power within the politics of India before and after independence. While she participates in the present-day Indian universe of discourse of attempts by both governments and NGOs to improve peoples' material circumstances and to enhance peoples' rights, Lilabhai said, "I tell a different story as one who saw, lived, and helped today's India to come into existence."

Lilabhai owns a property of 13 acres in Bachanaki, which she manages. She has workers who raise chickens, grow mango, paddy rice, and cashew nuts and has leased some of her land to farmers who live next door. The former freedom fighter inspects and supervises workers who are employed by her children to work on the family land. She does not live in a joint-family house. Instead of children and grandchildren, she has people who repair broken house items, run errands for her, and take care of her farms. Her children remit funds to her for her upkeep.

National political action and relationships with leading national heroes helped Lilabhai to express her influence, but there are other senior women whose roles in religious rituals and contributions to the social life of others have become the basis of their influence.

5.5 Sacred capital

Social, material, and sacred capital are imbricated in the concepts of power and status among rural senior women in South Asia. Gardner (1995) includes sacred capital in the factors that can enhance people's power and status. According to Gardner, women's religious observance and the role women play in ritual can build status and influence for themselves, for their households, and for their larger community (Gardner 1995: 219). Human relationships and affiliations are important for creating and sustaining power and status. Since relationships are created in social contexts, sacred capital benefits from moral, emotional, and cultural values in societies (Van Staveren 2001). For instance, Pakistani Muslim women are able to use mourning rituals to manifest their sacred power.

5.5.1 Pakistani mourning rituals

In writing about Shi'a Muslim women in Peshawar in Northwest Pakistan, Hegland (2003: 411–442) argues that Muslim women engage in traditional mourning rituals in order to use the performance to subvert traditional notions of patriarchal control and insert their own meanings and personal concerns into the rituals. Hegland continues that women construct alternative transcripts and gender definitions while at the same time affirming the Shi'a *majles* rites, lamenting the suffering and death of Imam Hussain, the grandson of the prophet Muhammed and third Shi'a Imam (2003: 433). While Pakistani women may find it difficult to openly resist gender systems, the Shi'a women perform the rituals to articulate their competence through practice (Hegland 2003: 420). Their spectacular ritual performances and ability to reach out to other women also help strengthen ties among themselves. For instance, the Peshawar women are able to bring women from different ethnic backgrounds such as the Pukhtuns, Qizilbash, and Mohejerin or migrants from India, in order to create a panethnic community.

Despite the conservatism and the fractured cultures and histories of minorities in Pakistan, the women's ritual activity provides cohesiveness and mutual empowerment. Hegland further states that the women are able to leave their homes several times to participate in the rituals and use these opportunities to develop their female social networks. Some of the women, during such mourning rituals, were able to develop skills as performers and public speakers. For instance, widowed Mohajerin and single women were able to preach to young women and teach them their religious duties. Through the rituals, some of the women gained status through having apprentices whom they taught how to speak in public and participate in and perform the rituals.

The context in which the women performed their rituals enabled them to operate outside the direct observation of male powerholders (Scott 1990: 4). On occasions when there were no men, Hegland (2003) states that female leaders or senior women were the participants who maintained the appropriate mourning practices.

Muslim women in Pakistan at times create alternative responses within Islamic rituals to address their needs. Muslim women in Pakistan may also use Islamic rules to protest abuse of power. For example, in January 2013, the militant group Kashkare Jhangvi claimed responsibility for a twin bomb attack in the city of Quetta, Pakistan, killing over 100 and wounding 121. Women took an active role in the protests against the killing by tapping into the Islamic custom of burying the dead within 24 hours; by refusing to bury the dead, they subverted the ritual, using it as a weapon. They sat with the men who also were mourning, in cold wintery weather, next to the caskets, until they succeeded in having Mawaz Aslam Raisani, the Chief Minister of Quetta, resign. The protestors also instigated other Pakistanis to demonstrate against government officials so that the governments would take stringent action against militants and perpetrators of sectarian violence. Thus the women's active participation in the street protest and refusal to bury their dead mobilized others to force the state and national government to listen to their demands.

The above examples of Muslim women in Pakistan help us to problematize Islam in the lives of women. Islam has changed historically because it is a dynamic culture. Muslim women are therefore able to use aspects of their faith to blur the personal and public domains in order to mobilize other women for political action. Ordinary Muslim women who succeed in imparting knowledge of their faith and other practices to one another exhibit their sacred power. Their strategies in mobilizing and blurring the spaces between public and private are devices they use to enhance their status and advance the conditions of other women. The women therefore create their own spaces by drawing on the Quran and their own ways of making sense of their present-day realities.

Pakistani upper- and middle-caste women are not the only religious people who create new domains both to express their faith and to build community.

Pakistani Sheedi Muslim senior women's power is manifest in how they create sacred spaces to deploy religious ritual power to redefine themselves as an ethnic minority and contribute to the religious landscape of their country.

Pakistani Sheedis have been engaged in traditional singing and dancing for centuries. Nizamani (2006: 61) gives an account of his interview with Waziran Sheedi to the effect that Sheedis inherited their singing and dancing, as well as their musical instrument, the *muggarmman*, from their ancestors. The drumming and dancing used to be performed by men only, but, over time, women took over the performance, so that now, some men may sing on some occasions while women play musical instruments and dance. The occasions on which the women perform include *shaadi* (wedding), *tohar* (circumcision), *chhatti* (a six-day ceremony), *aqiqa* (an event celebrated when a new mother takes her first bath on the 40th day after delivery), funerals, and festivals.

Another senior woman, Amina, shared with Nizamani that it is senior women who teach the new generation the music, dancing, and drumming involved in these and similar ceremonies (2006: 63). The senior women always invite the young women to accompany them to the different ceremonies so that the younger ones can participate in events as they observe the veteran musicians. They use the singing and dancing, according to Amina, for self-empowerment and also to improve their skills.

The Sheedi musical heritage is also used to enable the communities in coping with their marginalized status. In their songs, they also express their plight. They use the songs called *las bela* for entertainment. As they sing the *las bela*, they have a refrain in the words *Sheedi Basha Hambasha* (Sheedis are king). Sheedi senior women use their aesthetic and theatrical skills as important means whereby this marginalized group in Pakistan contribute money to their households and to themselves and also enhance their social status as Muslims in Pakistan.

During the *hambasha* dance (also called *jhumar*), the performers play a *muggarmman*. The women also play the *dhol* (a drum). Whenever Sheedi senior women are invited to perform at ceremonies, according to Amina, "it is the senior women that determine the fee for the performance, and at times the women who are also the managers and take advance payment before the event happens." They also charge the fee that consists in transport allowances and *bakhshish* (Nizamani 2006: 64).

The women perform either in someone's home or in the *ottaq* (a gathering place or community center). During the singing, some of the women go into a trance. The Sheedis also have built into their performance *ghor* (showering of money) and *mubariki* (congratulations). Members in the audience stick paper money on the foreheads of the dancers to acknowledge their skill, or they throw the money to the performer, and then some of the women collect the money.

The senior woman who supervises, teaches, and leads the group of dancers is called *ustani*. At times she is called *fahmi* or *sharu*. All these words mean either a leader or a teacher.

Sheedi senior women use their performing arts to draw attention to their sociohistorical and religious situations, while at the same time they encode their African–Pakistani values by reformulating notions of power relations in Pakistan.

In India as well there are individual senior women who have used their ritual roles to increase their status and influence. Sacred power is also tapped by a Siddi widow at a death anniversary to achieve status and reestablish links with her late husband's spirit.

5.5.2 Senior rural women and sacred capital in India

In Chipgeri, Gopal Babu Siddi, a 65-year-old widow, lives with her daughter-in-law and her grandchildren. This joint family has seven household members. According to Gopal Babu Siddi, she does not see herself as the leader of the household. Gopal and her husband built their house with help from their sons. In some cases, senior women who can work are integrated into their children's family because the family sees them as productive or income earners; thus, caring for them is not burdensome.

Gopal, in India, may be encouraged to perform lighter jobs such as caring for her grandchildren, but in her village, in October 2009, she created and deployed sacred power during an anniversary ritual at her home in Chipgeri.

When I visited the family before her husband died, Gopal was respected as a married woman who had a husband, daughters-in-law, and grandchildren living together. At the death of her husband, the widow Gopal had to support herself. She had lost a lot of respect that had been accorded her while her husband was alive. She was still a coolie, and she had to care for herself and her grandchildren when her daughters-in-law went to work outside the village.

Gopal's key role in performing her husband's death anniversary rite undergirded the people's belief that her husband's soul would come to bless her family. In the ritual, she provided a link between the living and the dead while she used ritual to honor the dead (Waerness 2004: 96). Also, while despair and depression may immobilize some elderly widows, Gopal Siddi's ability to exercise a ritual role at her husband's death anniversary shows that she was able to use the ritual to advance herself.

What Gopal Siddi did to honor her husband may not make economic sense at one level. However, Rao argues that some Indians may hold lavish festivals to shape their identities, maintaining "social reputations and webs of obligation and serve as arenas for status-enhancing competitions" (2001: 85). Within the Karnataka Chipgeri cultural economics, for example, the death anniversary feast has benefits beyond financial advantages. People use public events such as feasts to express notions of self and to shape how others perceive them. Since death anniversaries are socially sanctioned arenas, when Gopal Siddi and her family celebrated the event in honor of her late husband, they were rectifying social relationships, fulfilling obligations to the dead and the living, and enhancing their reputation as people who honor their dead in a fitting manner. Gopal's participation in webs of obligation by inviting large crowds (up to 300 people) to the feast despite her limited resources enabled the family to build and enhance networks of relationships in the community, to gain respect, and to build "coping strategies against" future risks and circumstances that will require assistance from others in their community (Rao 2001: 85–102).

Gopal and other senior women, aside from the fact that they play roles, of greater or less importance, in religious ritual, are more engaged in the everyday religious activity than their male counterparts. In fact, it is women who perform a household's daily ritual activities. Most senior Gowli, Siddi, Lambani, and Vaddar women tend to fill their lives and work with great social and religious symbolism. Such sacred and social capital is used by women to act in both private and public arenas in their communities. By so doing, the women create and represent their own prestige and influence because they have access to religious power.

Gopal deployed belief, ritual role, and the social significance of the anniversary to help improve her self-image and simultaneously enable her to assert her sacred power. In light of the manifestation of the sacred capital, the family fed everyone who attended, and the size of the crowd augmented the status and power of the leader of the ceremony, Gopal Siddi.

Women's ritual power extends beyond death anniversaries. The following discussion shows that female ritual acts, though often performed at home, are as important as public rituals conducted by men.

The Gowli Samubai Nagubai, 70, contends that women's religious practices are critical to the public performance of ritual. When women perform religious rituals at home among Gowlis in Chipgeri-Gautam, and when Gopal Siddi presides at her late husband's death anniversary, the women are "domesticating" their respective religions (Sered 1988: 506). Samubai stressed that, despite the public power that men seem to hold in their society, it is the women who facilitate and support the public ritual roles of men.

According to Sered (1988), when women participate in their domestic religion, they express their allegiance to the larger religion by personalizing/privatizing the institutions, rituals, and symbols, and by so doing, they safeguard the well-being of those with whom they are connected, the people for whom they enact the rituals. While women's domestic religious activities may reflect their everyday duties, Samubai said, "I regard women's ritual acts as powerfully spiritual and important for the existence and continuance of our religion and thus central to everything." Women therefore link those with whom they are "connected in webs of relationship" (Sered 1988: 508). By interpreting and approaching the sacred through personal relationships, women stress the core principles of their religions. Women's domestic religious expression "shares in the symbols, beliefs, ritual framework" myths and history of the "wider tradition" (Sered 1988: 516). In the confines of their homes, religious women address issues of life, suffering, success, failure, death, marriage, and birth in "relationship-focused" ways.

Samubai further said, "As an *aji* [senior woman], I'm respected in my community because I have *vajen* [power or 'weight'] authority." At the same time, she said, "the respect the person (male or female) receives depends on if they behave well in the society." She gave examples of some senior men who were irresponsible toward their children so that, when disputes arose in their community, some people preferred to come to her or other senior women to resolve their conflicts.

Her power contained respect and dignity, though *ajis* (senior women) and *ajas* (senior men) are equally respected. Men typically hold more political power. For ritual activities, however, she said the women prepare the offerings and clean the icons of deities before the men do the public ritual. Samubai said, "The men perform the public ritual once a year, but the women do daily *puja*. We senior Gowli women and other senior women are those that first touch the food and distribute the items before anyone cooks them."

The senior women always fast 30 days before Dasara. Their fast is a way of preparing the whole community for the festival. It is they, the senior women, who provide *kum kum* and coconut and perform the preparatory acts to foster the efficacy for the public rituals often led by men.

Samubai and other women are herbalists in the Chipgeri village. She argued that

> [t]emple *puja* is like sunlight or electric light that shines brighter, but home *puja* is a flame of a candle. Temple gathers all of the community. That *puja* is big. Home *puja* reflects deep and committed sentiments. Home *puja* is intimate, though, like a candle flame is powerful. When we pray with pure *atma* [heart], we can reach God anywhere, so we can reach God without going to the temple—at home or outside. We used to go to Maharashtra, and now we ask, "Why do we go far away before we pray to reach God?" We can reach God here in our house. Pandrapura and Saundatti are both important pilgrimage sites, but it is home *puja* that helps us in a deeply spiritual way because we feel God's protective power inside us. (Samubai, 13 July 2010)

These sentiments point out that "the daily puja performed by women is as important as the public one, which is often officiated by temple priests" (Samubai, personal communication, 13 July 2010).

In fact, the "efficacious moment is the moment when the channel of communication between human and God is most open" (Tapper and Tapper 1982) and is the moment when the devotee personalizes the encounter. The sacred moment is as immediate in the domestic space as it is in the nondomestic realm. Home *puja* is tied to domestic work and thus not valued as much as formal and public *puja*. However, the intimate knowledge base, the planning and organization of household *puja*, the ceaselessness, the meticulous thought and action can only happen from an insider who understands the details of each situation for which petitions, thanksgiving, and expressions of concern can be performed.

Gowli senior women's devotional activity for themselves, their families, and their communities is guided by flexibility and the ability to balance home care with religious duties. Their thinking and acting are "contextual and descriptive rather than public and abstract" (Waerness 2004: 97). Domestic *puja* is based on intimacy, interlocking relationships, and emotional knowledge. In their nonpriestly fashion, women perform sacred acts for others to underscore the relevance of being "relationship-oriented" (Sered 1988: 518).

Samubai and the women I interviewed did not tie their power to the mythic roles or ideals of Gowli culture. Rather, they pointed to their contemporary practical and indispensable ritual roles, which they combine with other domestic activities to sustain their families and the public ritual performances of male ritual specialists.

5.6 Traditional birth attendants/midwives (*dais*)

The role of birth attendants/midwives is receiving new emphasis in India, Pakistan, and Bangladesh. These women have been critical in delivering children. Birth attendants had been given much recognition in the past. The United Nations Children's Fund (UNICEF) recently teamed up with the central governments of India, Pakistan, and Bangladesh in providing training and setting up health centers to give prenatal and postnatal care for women. Women are trained for the profession of nurse midwife, and graduates from the programs serve urban and rural communities. In addition to such new professional midwives are the *dais* of rural South Asia, who have for generations been the birth attendants for their communities. *Dais'* roles in rural communities cannot be overemphasized.

5.6.1 India

Gangama Narayana, a widow at 70 and a *dai*, lives with her son and daughter-in-law. As a birth attendant, she helped in the deliveries of her grandchildren.

Gangama, and other traditional birth attendants (TBAs), have helped women have safe deliveries for many years in rural Karnataka, India. According to her, she has helped in delivering children who might not have survived without her intervention. At times, Gangama prescribed herbs that stopped profuse bleeding by some women who had just had babies.

She contends that her services have averted unnecessary infant and maternal mortality in communities in and around the village of Sobha, where she lives.

During my visit to Sobha, Gangama's family members and other groups in the village shared their stories about how Gangama had helped them. Forty-year-old Sunitha, who received help from Gangama during the birth of her two children, said, "Gangama is a fearless and skilled woman who has helped to bring babies into the world. They said that she is trusted by the society and is highly respected as a *dai*." She has comforted mothers and given helpful advice to families.

The advice Gangama gives mothers and family members, according to Sunitha, "empowered young mothers to negotiate with their families so they would not do heavy work before and immediately after delivery."

Twenty-year-old Sangetha, a woman who was in the house during my visit, was about to have her first child. She was living in a joint family with her parents-in-law, who were stern with her, and their word could not be challenged. Gangama visited Sangetha's home and spoke with the whole family, explaining why a woman who is about to have a baby should have her workload reduced. Thereafter, Sangetha's responsibilities were reduced; her in-laws did not expect her to do the heavy work of cleaning, going to the market, cooking for the family, and taking care of the paddy rice that had been harvested. Sangetha was also able to go to her mother's house for the birth of her first child, returning to her husband and in-laws' house only after the child had been weaned. Gangama is therefore powerful and respected, Sangetha said.

Gangama is one of the many *dais* who have assisted in over 70 percent of births in rural India over hundreds of years. Since she lives among the people she helps, unlike a nurse at a hospital or a doctor who sees patients only occasionally, Gangama said,

> The young men and women in Sobha trust me. They do because they know I know them and I may have helped to deliver some of them. I always make sure that pregnant women receive proper care so they can have safe deliveries. When a family invites me to their home for a delivery, I check the pregnant woman's lower abdomen and rub it to help position the baby to help with an easy delivery. I also talk to the woman to encourage her as she endures the labor and birth pains. When the baby is born, I cut the umbilical cord and bathe the baby. If the delivery is difficult, such as in a breach birth, I accompany the mother to the nearest health center. At the health center or hospital, I tell the medical people what I have done for the mother before she was brought to the hospital. (12 August 2010)

She asserts that she can take "the pulse of a woman to know if she is pregnant."

The difference between her practice and what others offer is that she takes time to listen and recommends the best place to go if the woman has a difficult childbirth. She discusses options with the woman and what medical care could help the woman to make informed decisions.

At 15, Gangama learned from her mother how to help people deliver babies. She was also trained in a government hospital in Sagar. After her training, she worked in Sagar for two years. Now, at 70, she has been doing *dai* work for over 40 years. She said, "Doctors and nurses in the area recognize and value my services as a *dai*, because I have been helping at hospitals on some occasions."

Gangama completed the fourth standard. "Better than third," she said. According to her, the fourth standard education, which she completed before her *dai* training, enabled her to understand the basics of the *dai* program. When she finished the *dai* training, she said she gained the trust of the doctors and nurses. Later, when she went to hospitals with an expectant woman or a woman in labor, she was respected for her knowledge and ability to handle cases that "even some of the doctors found difficult to deal with," she added. She has helped in the delivery of about 500 babies. Due to the fact that she has been a *dai* for a long time, doctors and nurses at the Manipal hospital know her. They call her *kaki*, like a grandmother.

Gangama said, "I keep a diary of the deliveries. It is important to do so because after helping with delivery, sometimes the parents come and ask what time the baby was born because they want to fix the times with the municipality on the birth certificates. They want the specific date, the particular time and place of the delivery," so she makes the information available. Without those details, some children have been refused entry into schools.

She takes about 200 rupees for a delivery. According to her, God blesses the good work she is doing, so she does not want to take risks that may harm any mother or baby, and is always careful and thorough.

Her husband was a goldsmith, of the *vivshwakarma* caste; she is of the same caste, therefore she learned to do *akasaliga* (goldsmith) work from him. She makes headbands (*basinga*) for marriages, and jewelry work, statues, and gold objects, most of which she did with her husband before his death. When her husband died, she combined selling jewelry with *dai* work to raise her children on her own.

She shared a story about how she almost quit delivering babies at the death of her husband. She said, "I did not want to go to the hospital anymore to work, and I resigned my position as a *dai* at a local hospital. Then one Dr. Prema called me and said, 'Don't stop this work, because you have helped children to come into the world, and you are doing worthwhile work.' The doctor's encouragement made me continue delivering babies."

According to Gangama, "*Akasaliga* [goldsmithing] is a job. It is a part of life for people to work. Although gold is valued a lot in India, a *dai* helps people. *Akasaliga* is a business. Being a *dai* is service. If you give service, the people bless you. Whenever I help a mother to deliver a baby, I feel I have gained some blessings because it's service and not business."

Gangama continued, "It is important that I do good work. If I am not doing good work, then I'm selfish and useless. I am doing good work. I come from a poor family, but I have raised my children, and I manage them and my grandchildren. Nobody goes to beg for food in this household."

Based on income she earns from doing the *dai* work and gets from land she has leased to a farmer, she is able to support herself and her family. Also, since she has grandchildren at home, she spends time with them.

Gangama benefited from a government-training program that qualified her as a *dai*. She interpreted what she does as service or good work (*olleya kelasha* in Kannada). The recognition she receives, the choice she made to stop selling gold products, and her courage to advocate for pregnant women's welfare, combined to make her a senior woman who uses her *shakti* to help bring children into existence. The training Gangama received has equipped her to save the lives of women and their babies, especially during delivery.

Not all *dais* receive the training Gangama had. Nor are they all given the respect that Gangama receives in India. I will address other stories from Bangladesh and Pakistan to add to my analysis.

5.6.2 Bangladesh

There are occasions when birth attendants have caused irreparable harm to infants at birth, or death to the mothers. In 2004, the government of Bangladesh began training community-based birth attendants at the village level. The training was similar to what prevails in India and Pakistan. Including the government-trained birth attendants, the majority of traditional midwives learned their skill from female relatives or neighbors. Khan and Amin (1989) argue that such rural birth attendants often impose strict dietary measures on mothers during pregnancy and postpartum, which is a health risk because the mothers do not get sufficient nutrition during those periods. Also, some of the tools they use for cutting the umbilical chord and placenta are not properly sterilized; as a result, the mothers, as well as the infants, often get infected.

Examples from some rural communities in Bangladesh show that ignorance, cultural constraints, and poverty make some families subject women who are about to deliver to unqualified *dais* whose services border on serious medical malpractice. This malpractice often goes unchecked because the victimized families are too poor and lack the knowledge to seek better care.

Pakistan's awareness of the high mortality rate of pregnant mothers led the government to increase its effort to address the problem; I discuss this in the following section.

5.6.3 Pakistan rural healthcare providers

Pakistan's Ministry of Health's Lady Health Workers Programme has been training TBAs and integrating them into maternal healthcare systems in rural

Pakistan since 2000. The program is aimed at curbing maternal mortality in Pakistan, which often happens at home. Such deaths occur at the hands of TBAs. Training is given in different communities, such as the Larkana district in the Sindh province of Pakistan (Jokhio et al. 2005).

"In contrast [to trained midwives]," Zofeen (2010) contends, "a traditional midwife may be completely unschooled, having learned her trade from her mother or mother-in-law, as is often the case among TBAs in rural villages, but without fully understanding the female anatomy."

Some *dais* do not know the health of pregnant women before labor. *Dais* may not be skilled to handle complications during delivery, and thus increase postpartum mortality for women (Khan and Amin 1989). The role of the TBA is one of the ways by which rural women achieve status and influence, but untrained and unscrupulous ones can abuse rural people's trust in them. Such birth attendants end up doing harm.

The training lasts from three days to several weeks. The trainers use "picture cards containing advice on antepartum, intrapartum, and postpartum care; how to conduct a clean delivery; use of the disposable delivery kit; when to refer women for emergency obstetrical care; and care of the newborn" (Jokhio et al. 2005).

The TBAs, as part of their training, were advised by the Ministry of Health's Lady Health Workers Programme coordinators to "visit each woman at least three times during the pregnancy (at three, six, and nine months) to check for dangerous signs, such as bleeding or eclampsia, and to encourage women with such signs to seek emergency obstetrical care. Lady Health Workers were trained to support the traditional attendants and record the data" (Jokhio et al. 2005).

Jokhio et al. (2005) report that some Pakistani women have gained confidence in themselves after they received training to deliver services to pregnant women. The following quotation from Afshan, a birth attendant living in a village in the Sanghar district in Sindh, clarifies some of the benefits of the Pakistani government's training programs: "We all learned to be hospital midwives. But the [community midwifery] training prepared us to deliver in villages using only the most basic facilities, or even without medicines" (Ebrahim 2010).

Amina from Lasbela, Baluchistan, is another woman who got a six-week training in practical skills to care for women in the pregnancy cycle, from conception to postnatal care. According to Amina, "I also learned about how to provide care for the psychological and social well-being of the mother and the family. This preparation involved how the whole family is equipped in dealing with a baby whose arrival may change the family dynamic" (Ebrahim 2010).

Some of the women express their newly gained power and confidence from the fact they learned the importance of sterilization during delivery. Overall, the training programs have enabled the women to gain confidence in themselves as they render their services to families.

As part of their training, TBAs are instructed to register all pregnant women in their communities and to inform the Lady Health Workers about the women under their care. Subsequently, the TBAs are issued delivery kits. The kits consist of "sterilized disposable gloves, soap, gauze, cotton balls, antiseptic solution, an umbilical-cord clamp, and a surgical blade" (Jokhio et al. 2005). The training of the TBAs also includes teaching them to recognize serious complications of pregnancy and delivery so they can refer women in labor to the nearest health center (Jokhio et al. 2005).

Since not all the *dais* have received adequate training, or become competent after training, TBAs who rely on their limited knowledge and use unhygienic devices continue to harm infants and women in labor. Also, poor families in Pakistan prefer to go to *dais* in their homes and villages and thus fall victim to untrained TBAs.

When South Asian countries improve the skills of birth attendants, the women increase their chances to provide better care for their families and their communities. As the women enhance their status and influence, they also improve trust among their members and strengthen their skills.

There are other senior women who use traditional crafts such as quilting (discussed in the following section) to increase their power and help their community in India.

5.7 Patchwork quilters: a collective enterprise in India

While other seniors show their *shakti* individually, Siddi Women's Quilt Incorporated deploy their collective power through their craft as quilt makers. Under the auspices of the cooperative, with seed money from Professor Henry Drewal, the distinguished scholar and researcher, and from myself, a group of senior Siddi women began commercial quilt-making in Mainalli, Kendelgari, and Gunjavatti in Uttara Kannada (North Karnataka) in 2003. The quilters had their first batch of patchwork quilts (*kawandi*) sold at the conference of Africa and the Indian Ocean Identity of the 13th Triennial Symposium of African and African Diasporic Art at Harvard University in Cambridge, Massachusetts, in April 2004. Since then, Dr. Drewal; Bani Singh, a colleague of Dr. Drewal and a lecturer in industrial design in Bangalore; and Dr. Sarah Khan have sold Siddi quilts in India and various cities in the US. Professor Drewal has given all sales revenues to the women in the cooperative for the setting up of a credit system, which the women opened with a bank in Mundgod, Karnataka, in May 2005.

The women determine how to use the cooperative's income. The collective thus presents a platform for the quilters to assert their independence, as they pursue income-earning projects, which previously were "domestic" and thus not valued. When they opened an account at the bank to lend money to others, these women became a new, informal group of self-employed workers with an economic power base that previously had belonged to Havig Brahmins and others like them who, as traditional land owners, controlled most of the economic activities in Karnataka and were therefore the moneylenders.

The quilters' newly found power is beginning to threaten some of their husbands. I learned that a man tried to borrow money from his wife after he heard she and the others had earned income that had been deposited at the bank. Upon hearing that his wife had made some money, he thought, and argued, that he had the right to whatever his wife earned. The other quilters and his wife invited him to one of their meetings and reminded him that the money was collectively owned and that no individual had the right to use it as she wanted. Prior to this, this man could have used his wife's income as he chose, but he cannot do so now.

Up to now, Siddi women have engaged in quilt-making within their households for home use only. However, in the villages of Mainalli, Ugingeri, Kendelgari, and Gunjavatti, about 20 women now make quilts with the intention of selling them outside their villages in big cities in India and the US. As mentioned above, the seed money given by Dr. Drewal provided the impetus to make marketable quilts. The infusion of foreign funds into this potentially successful cottage industry has empowered the Siddi women as, for the first time, their quilts are proving to have financial value.

Quilt-making, especially among senior Siddi women, can also be seen as a part of the socialization process; it can provide an opportunity for storytelling and exchanging of personal stories and village gossip. Furthermore, the presence of young women around senior women who are doing patchwork and sewing fosters intergenerational interaction, during which the young learn from the veteran quilters. The social power at work among the women entails their ability to impart technical knowledge (Giddens 1984).

Since a savings account has been set up to finance more quilting, they are no longer worried that their commercial activity will come to an end any time soon. They see themselves building on their experience, and they seek to continue and expand this new economic activity to earn additional income. How will this affect their status in society and in their immediate families? A personal communication with one quilt-maker, Aminabi Siddi, on 15 June 2004 revealed that, unlike previous times, when she made quilts only for personal and family household use, her quilts are now being appreciated outside the boundaries of her village and are a source of income for her, and these things make her glad. She said this with deserved pride, as she showed me quilt after quilt in her home.

Patchwork quilts are being used to empower women who are helping themselves and other Siddis break away from the shackles of exorbitant interest and debt that have become burdensome over the years. A local cottage industry like quilting is sharing in a transnational production process, connecting the work of village women to a global economic and cultural system in which the quilts earn money from abroad and are appreciated by people in other global communities.

These quilt-makers have an internal vetting formula for determining poor from good quality work. When the quilts are collected, some of the women go through them and reject quilts that are subpar. In addition to the women's self-vetting, Bani Singh, Dr. Drewal's associate, who knows the market very well, helps the quilters to select products that will sell well outside the quilters' own communities. Thus, the products go through rigorous inspection before they are shipped. Though the quilts do not have labels, the quilters, using a self-monitoring method and a distinctive triangular patch called a *phula* that each woman uses to designate the quilts she has made, can tell who made which quilt. These cottage industry manufacturers provide quilts that compete with other quilts, thereby opening the global market to the Siddis.

At present, the quilters are able to award scholarships or grant loans to students from their communities to pay their tuition up to the college or university level. The incomes they earn are also a source of loans for farming or to meet home needs. The incomes from the collective quilting have also helped members pay off previous debts. As Dumgi Moshi, a member of the quilters group, said, "We now have *svatantra* [freedom in the Kannada language]."

The power of the collective has multiple bases. They give loans to people to go to school, they are able to pay their own debts, they are engaged in a cottage industry that sells their products on a global market, and they determine how to spend the money they have collectively made. With this newly gained financial power, they and their relatives no longer need to take loans from moneylenders like the Brahmins mentioned above, who charge interest rates as high as 20–30 percent. The quilters, on the other hand, charge interest of only two percent on their loans.

Their power also stems from their freedom to determine the uses toward which the money they earn is put; for example, one of the first rules the collective made was that they would not lend money to anybody to perform an elaborate wedding. All requests for money are discussed openly by the collective's members before the money is given.

By itself, quilting brings prestige, as does being a member of an income-generating group of rural women, and the women's quilting group provides a support network for its members.

Other senior women benefit from other forms of social capital. I will now profile a senior woman and quilt-maker who does not have land or children and, therefore, depends on the goodwill of the community members.

5.7.1 An independent patchwork quilter: Community support

Bishebi Raseem Naik Siddi, 70, is landless and childless. She lives in Gurlihali in Karnataka and makes baby quilts for expectant mothers.

During feasts such as *Bakir-Id* and *Muharram*, the community under the guidance of the *mullah* and village group leaders provides for Bishebi and other elderly people. Bishebi said she has confidence in Allah and her village community. She has memories about her village that she shares with the other residents. She knows how to cooperate with others and promotes collaborative work among women engaged in sewing and quilting in her community. Over the years Bishebi's personal contacts, her networks of support, and her personal contributions to her community as one who has stitched quilts for expectant mothers and as an advisor became a critical form of social capital for her. The women in her community have confidence in her abilities, and they trust her for the intangible but important gifts she shares with them.

She may not reciprocate in equal value the resources she receives from her society; rather, Bishebi participates in a "generalized reciprocity" (Das 2004) because her community stands in solidarity with her without expecting to feed or clothe other seniors in Gurlihali.

Since she lives alone, she relies on the goodwill of her community. The Islamic practice of almsgiving has been a source of security for her and other aged people. As D'Souza (1982) points out, the religious underpinnings of filial obligations that also promote piety are extended to seniors at the community level. Such pious gestures provided Bishebi with respect, honor, and security.

Social change is occurring in her community as in other rural areas. Some able-bodied members of the community have moved to other places in search of jobs. In previous years, the community chose suitors for its members, but, Bishebi said, "the society is changing, and some youngsters marry for love alone. However, when mothers are going to have babies, they often contacted me to make quilts for their babies. I only take a fee of 150 rupees in such situations. For each quilt, it takes about six weeks to finish."

Bishebi acknowledges that her society is changing, and yet expectant women still consult her for her quilts. She said that when she can no longer thread a needle to stitch, she knows she has a Muslim community that provides communal social capital embedded in the Islamic ethos. She said she is respected in her community, and even in death she will have *aram* and *kushe* (health and happiness in Kannada). She also said she has faith in Allah that her community will give her a good burial when she dies. She prays to Allah, and her daily devotion is another source of security. Bishebi Raseem Naik's personal piety, her community's support, and her work for expectant mothers provide her with hope and status.

In societies with meager resources, and especially in economically and socially deprived areas, apparently "nonproductive" people such as senior women are treated with ambivalence (Paul 1992: 1). Seniors and children are often perceived as anomalous minors that are dependent on the able-bodied adult productive members of society. But in Bishebi's community, the Islamic ethos of almsgiving and the people's practice of mutual support destigmatize seniors. Also, in Gurlihali, the norms that are used to order social relations, membership, and meanings attached to belonging to the community are examples of "the circuit of social integration" (Clegg 1989). The constructive use of norms in this society fosters harmony and mutual support.

The above examples have focused on the efforts or resources that senior women draw on for personal advancement. The discussion has also shown obstacles that some of the women face as they negotiate their way through cultural expectations, physical weakness, and social change. The incident described in the next section elucidates how cultural belief in malevolent forces, or *mata mantra* in Kannada, plays out to adversely affect some senior women.

5.7.2 *Mata mantra* (sorcery or harmful occult power)

H. F. Siddi (initials are used to keep the person's identity anonymous), 66, is a widow whose son had just died. H. F. Siddi argues that if she is not able to support herself, she will have to beg to survive. She maintains that she and her husband had two acres of land that, when her husband died, were transferred to their son, K. Siddi. After the sudden death of K. Siddi, the land came into the hands of H. F. Siddi, the bereaved mother.

Unlike parts of continental Africa where senior women are often accused of using magical powers to hurt others, and are humiliated publicly and sometimes ostracized, such accusations are rare among the communities where I have done my fieldwork. Yet they do sometimes occur, and allegations of *mata mantra* (sorcery, or the use of malevolent spirits) have been made against both men and women.

When K. Siddi, then 35, died in April 2008, some people in the community alleged that his mother, H. F. Siddi, had been responsible for his death, using sorcery to redirect K. Siddi's resources to support herself in her old age, as the ownership of land by a senior widow without children may give her security and investment (Agarwal 1994). (The doctor said that K. Siddi died of jaundice.)

Also, access to and control of land can be a source of status, wealth, and economic security among people in South Asia. At age 35, K. Siddi had four children and was a coolie, working in the field and supporting his family. Some members of the Gunjavatti community, when trying to make sense of the tragedy, alleged that K. Siddi's mother had used a negative spiritual force—sorcery or *mata mantra,* the religious practice of bringing misfortune on others who least expect it—to bring about his death. By killing her son, K. Siddi's mother would then have access to wealth and status in her community.

Other incidents in Siddi communities adjacent to Gunjavatti provide examples of how inexplicable events tend to be blamed on malevolent power. For example, when two men and a woman in the same family in Mainalli became mentally unstable, some Mainalli residents said this was a punishment because the family's senior members had used *mata mantra* to divert the bountiful harvest of crops from their neighbors' adjacent farms. Neighboring farmers claimed their crops did not flourish as much as those of the family that was believed to have used spirit methods to siphon off the good yields to their farms, that the affected family had used *mata mantra* to generate money, and that the mentally affected men and woman suffered from mental illness and their families faced misfortune as a punishment for their ill-obtained profits. The above cases were shared with me on 25 July in Gunjavatti and on 27 July 2010, respectively, in Mainalli.

In both cases, senior men and women were accused of having used *mata mantra*. It is important to note that the accusers were both men and women from the accused people's community.

The above examples of accusations of *mata mantra* show that, besides the power and influence addressed earlier, some seniors are believed to possess spiritual powers that manifest in antisocial acts. Since the problem of evil is addressed differently in all societies, the rural Indians' response conceptualized in *mata mantra* gives us a lens for understanding the complex perceptions people have of senior men and women. It is in the context of cultural practices, beliefs, and social hierarchies that senior women continue to craft their *shakti*; while some seniors are accused of using their power and prestige for evil, there are senior women whose activities are valued immensely in their communities.

Mata mantra refers to an ability of humans to change their reality for good or for evil outside the established system, norms, and order of society, and discussing it opens up new understandings of powers that appear to operate outside the manageable boundaries of everyday life. Seniors who are accused of using *mata mantra* are feared and at times shunned by their immediate societies because they are believed to have the ability to act outside the established system or order; thus, their power is perceived to be subversive and deviant. The cultural construction of beliefs about agencies that lie outside people's control and established systems also helps us to understand sources of tension in social relationships. Accusations of sorcery can also lead to tensions and to scapegoating within the broader context of how people address conflict.

Stewart and Strathern (2004) argue that accusations of sorcery point to the significance of rumors and gossip in society. Rumors and gossip can lead to accusations against individuals or groups perceived as having done wrong to others. The consequences of such allegations vary from society to society. The senior woman H. F. Siddi was perceived to have a spiritual power that could not be contained or managed within the structure of people's personal and social lives; thus, this alleged power was counterproductive, in her community's view. Although to H. F. Siddi, she had *lost* her son, to her accusers, she had used sorcery to *kill* her son to gain wealth and prestige.

While such accusations may be used by people to understand a tragedy, it is increasingly critical to address their impacts on the dignity, human rights, and status of senior women in South Asia.

It is therefore timely that recent scholarship on accusations against women of sorcery is focusing on how local notions of magical power, patriarchal social systems, and norms are used to violate the human rights of women (Latimore 1997; Preston and Wong 2004; Chaudhuri 2012).

6
Conclusion

The women of rural South Asia are by no means helpless pawns of an oppressive society and culture: the discussion in this book helps us to understand the various domains in which these women manifest their power (*shakti*) even when they face daunting challenges from inhibiting traditions, exploitation by males (and in some cases by other women) in their society, and the actions of corrupt officials of governments legally and constitutionally dedicated to removing exploitative and oppressive policies and behavior based on distinctions of caste, ethnicity, and gender. The women in this study have been shown to be strategic actors who identify and use opportunities to create changes for their self-advancement and to empower others. These rural women have taken initiatives to enhance their autonomy, create alliances, and challenge restrictive social hierarchies in order to increase the visibility of women in public and private spaces. Rural South Asian women have been engaged in complex negotiations about their status, have enhanced their self-esteem, and have increased their capacity to effect more changes than previously, when they looked up to men to bring about such changes.

This study uses cross-regional approaches to analyzing gender power in order to examine how women of various ages, faiths, cultural backgrounds, and multiple geographies in South Asia have used (or in some cases failed to use) the democratizing opportunities that India, Pakistan, and Bangladesh and NGOs have provided.

I will now summarize the key issues raised in the analysis provided in this book that pays attention to how gender relations, caste, and geographic location are interrelated (Srinivas 1996; Dube 2001).

The rural women of South Asia have multiple identities, articulated differently and variously structured according to caste, tribe, religion, age, and geography. This work has addressed how it is important to explore ways in which societal law, religion, community, and self-perception shape the meaning and articulation of tribal identities and the articulation of women's power. By framing women's abilities to shape aspects of their destiny and transform their society, this study has called attention to fierce compassion, courage, determination, respect, and dignity, and the ability to take charge of resources and control outcomes as important dimensions of women's power.

The analysis focused on women between the ages of 20 and 60, and women aged 60 and above, to unearth their ingenuity in using opportunities provided by nongovernmental and governmental institutions for the advancement of themselves and others. While most scholars have only defined power in the light of autonomy, the acquisition and control of resources, and decision-making capacity, this work has included and stressed women's social power, power to accomplish specific objectives, and power to subvert and transform entrenched patriarchal and cultural power.

In this work I have examined various forms of rural women's *shakti* within the social production and distribution of status and power in South Asia. I have focused on forms of social distinction and formation of personal and collective interests that exist within ideological, religious, and cultural contexts in rural South Asia. The study demonstrated how rural women use governmental and nongovernmental resources and their own ingenuity to resist injustice and to advance themselves and their communities in the three countries under study. Also, I pointed out that, as Giddens (1984) contends, power unfolds in a complex social context in which human agency and social structures have intertwining relationships.

At times, in the interplay between agent and social systems, the powerless may resist their exploitation (Bourdieu 1977); on the other hand, they may acquiesce, because they have internalized a distorted consciousness that favors the dominant (Lukes 2005). For instance, when Girija Shankarapa Kalavai, from India, was fighting for women to be included on her village council, some women thought it inappropriate for women to be on the council. On the other hand, some Pakistani young women have refused to succumb to threats from their families when they chose to marry for love and not enter into an arranged marriage.

I have also shown how female *panchayat*, union *parishad*, and *sangha* members are using their newly gained power to facilitate development projects in their communities, for instance, helping to set up water tanks and schools in their jurisdictions. Some women who hold formal power have succeeded in raising awareness of women's rights and of how women and other minorities can fight for those rights. Despite the fact that most of the women have limited or no formal education, some have advocated for their communities to take possession of land that was under threat to be taken away from them by government officials or the rich and powerful who until recently could not be politically or legally challenged.

Marginalized South Asian women face a variety of challenges, including social norms that impede their advancement, weak and ineffective local and district institutions, and corrupt local officials who exercise formal and informal powers to disempower marginalized people. This analysis elucidated the social values and religious and political structures that have restricted women's lives and their economic and political participation in Pakistan, Bangladesh, and India, and how in culture-specific arenas and through religious traditions women have demonstrated their ingenuity, courage, and determination.

Muslim women in Pakistan and Bangladesh were shown to be a heterogeneous group. While some Muslim women might acquiesce to male dominance, others defied norms and other social hierarchies to advance themselves and to help others; also, some Pakistani Muslim women have used mourning rituals to create space for themselves and to teach women self-confidence and how to fight for their rights.

While some studies have not addressed the minority groups that emerged after the British-led 1947 partition of the Indian subcontinent, this work has touched on how communities became fragmented after partition, a fragmentation that led to the emergence of many different groups of minorities in India, Pakistan, and Bangladesh that continue to face challenges. I addressed this creation of multiple–minority societies that resulted from the fracturing of the Indian subcontinent. By commenting on the minorities that emerged from the partition, I showed how women were affected in ways that were both adverse and unequal.

Thus, I have focused on how women belonging to castes and tribal people in South Asia who may have migrated to their present locations have used their social memory to change some of their practices (e.g., Lalita Krishna Bhovi Vaddar, the *panchayat* president from Mainalli in India), reinforce old ideas, or leave behind important practices (e.g., Chennama Lambani, an Indian *panchayat* member) and the meanings of those practices, meanings embedded in the prestige of the past (e.g., the Indian Parvakar Gora Kumbhar, a member of the Kurumbar subcaste). I commented on the cultural geography of these distinct groups and how they benefit and contribute to the cultural practices of their respective societies. The discussion also explored the rural communities' respective notions about, and attitudes toward, women's sources of power.

The discussion contextualized women's *shakti* in sociohistorical contexts where communities have been classified according to caste, tribe, religion, gender, and class. I addressed the interplay between women's desires and aspirations, on the one hand, and, on the other, traditional expectations for women in rural South Asia. I have done a brief comparative gender analysis of some of the castes and tribes to highlight power relations between men and women in order to link the discussion to the complex ways in which power plays out in rural South Asia.

This work has also addressed differently configured local institutions within which women have deployed their *shakti*. I also touched on the many ways in which formal and informal political processes interact at the local, district, and national levels. The analysis also pointed out that, at times, government officials, such as police officers and politicians, who represent formal institutions, use their influence to undermine the informal roles and power structures of women (Bhatt 2006). The formal institutional power exercised by some politicians in Bangladesh and by some police officers in India was, at times, too formidable for rural women to handle. For instance, I drew attention to how police officers, forest department representatives, and male *panchayat* leaders used their positions to exploit the people they were expected to serve and protect. I commented on corrupt ration card officials to illustrate how some men with formal power impede progress in the lives of people at the local level.

However, this work also provided examples of women who defied most of the apparently invincible authority structures, such as Ramijabi Madsab Bagwati Siddi of Kendelgari in India and Mukhtaran Mai of Pakistan. I have explored the shifting power bases among rural women by highlighting how women combine their notions of *shakti* with roles that used to be played by men. Despite the barriers, some women have used or created spaces to increase their *shakti*, gain access to resources, and finally improve the conditions of their families and communities. In the process, the women's display of power has drawn attention to the importance, in our understanding, of power, of honor, strength, respect, dignity, collaborative skills, and the capacity to achieve goals. I touched on examples of "power to" (Gaventa 2006), whereby women use power as a productive force for themselves and for their society. The analysis has expanded the notion of women's power to focus on the different ways in which women fashion and craft *shakti* in the face of violence against women and children.

One area of violence against women discussed in the above analysis involves accusations of sorcery against senior women. In South Asia, as in other parts of the world, such accusations are sometimes used to understand a tragedy or psychological, social, and economic instability. It is, however, becoming increasingly clear that such accusations are underpinned by patriarchal norms that violate the dignity, human rights, and status of women (Latimore 1997; Preston and Wong 2004; Chaudhuri 2012).

It is thus timely that this book's discussion of accusations of sorcery adds to recent scholarship focusing on how local notions of mystical power and patriarchal social systems and norms are used to violate the human rights of women. In the face of such violence, there have been women activists who have set up counterhegemonic political actions to bring about justice in their societies.

This study has explored other forms of violence against women in cases of rape, incest, and wife beating. Under violence against women, this work described the different ways that women at the grassroots level define violence and work toward fighting it. In the face of such injustices, the work also focused on women's sexual power and their informal networks of friendships to galvanize one another to use symbolic and literal power to fight injustice (Bourdieu 1977; Giddens 1984; Clegg 1989).

I addressed the local perceptions of women's roles and of the new governmental and nongovernmental institutions where women have status and of women's entrepreneurial activities in rural South Asia.

This analysis also examined the three countries' efforts to create equality for all their citizens by reclassifying communities that live in socially and economically isolated places; thus, I profiled Indian women belonging to groups classified as STs, SCs, and OBCs. I used the Indian government's reform efforts to provide a comparative lens for exploring Pakistani and Bangladeshi central governments' reform programs to empower women and other minorities. The central governments of the three countries have instituted quota systems and enterprising projects for disenfranchised rural people to enable them to create or find income-generating jobs.

Panchayats, sanghas, and union *parishads* were discussed to show how each of the three countries' quota provisions allowed women to play active roles in local- and district-level politics. I explored how rural women are acquiring new roles to increase their self-determination for self-empowerment and the development of others. I problematized the quota systems to show that despite the opportunities that India, Pakistan, and Bangladesh have given to women, ineffective implementation of government policies and entrenched cultural norms about women have prevented some women from exercising their rights and authority as representatives or members of their respective local governing bodies. On the other hand, I have touched on the local perceptions of women's roles and of the new governmental and nongovernmental institutions where some rural women have succeeded in effecting change in their communities and on how, at times, women have done a delicate dance between remaining feminine and modest while at the same time challenging structures and ideas that have subordinated them (Sa'ar 2006). I also described context-specific ways in which women have embodied and deployed female power.

I have profiled a woman basket weaver and a potter to demonstrate that, though not all women have stopped performing caste-specific professions, some have refashioned aspects of their traditional professions. For instance, women belonging to the basket weaver caste such as Shobana Koravar, who lives in Ambedkarhoni, Mundgod, in India, may continue to follow their craft but produce new items for new uses. Potters like Parvakar Gora Kumbhar of Mosali in India continue pottery-making but have learned to paint and reshape their products to meet the needs and tastes of contemporary consumers.

After discussing how women between the ages of 20 and 60 acquire power and deploy it in multiple ways, I touched on ways in which senior women order their lives in rural societies. This work thus also examined the roles and statuses of senior women in contemporary society. Since age-based identities are formed through social relationships (Gardner 1995), my study has paid attention to rural senior women and how they expand their roles to empower themselves by enhancing the well-being of their family and community. For instance, I examined senior women's responses to efforts by the Indian government and Karnataka state government to expand women's capacity to make critical choices to shape their lives in ways not available to them in the past (Kabeer 2001). Some senior women, no longer able to work outside the home (e.g., in the fields as coolies) work instead at home as caregivers; some Gowli senior women still tend their cattle; and some Lambanis continue to fetch firewood and also care for their grandchildren. Other senior women are birth attendants with high repute in their communities. Some Siddi women have for the past six years formed a quilt-makers cooperative society that provides a source of income from which members are able to receive loans and grant them to others in need.

The above discussion also addressed how senior women tap various resources including their own enterprising spirit to improve themselves. By focusing on how senior women deploy their sacred power in ritual activity, the discussion illuminated the complex, gendered religious roles in rural South Asia.

Senior women have further been shown to make use of their resources to reposition themselves in their present-day rural societies. For instance, some senior Pakistani women use their cash-earning ability to engage in stitching quilts and sweaters, collecting and selling firewood, basket weaving, and selling vegetables and dried fish to enhance their well-being. Eating at relatives' houses is another strategy some senior women in Gowli villages in India use to order their lives so they can assert their independence and pride. Some senior women choose to live in their own houses especially when their sons live in houses adjacent to them. Other senior women construct social networks as the main support as they also provide "food, household assistance and general care" (Cliggett 2005: 95). Some senior women in private and less visible ways invest in their grandchildren, such as paying for their school fees, household needs, and medical costs, since they rely on getting support from the grandchildren. I also commented on the uneasy relationship that may exist beneath the apparent harmony between mothers-in-law and daughters-in-law in coresidential households when mothers-in-law are the heads of their households.

There are also senior women who staff small shops, selling condiments, sweets, and plastic objects. Thus, these senior women use their economic benefits to improve their lives in communities where they would have been expected to depend on their sons or other male members of their families.

This work has focused on different local understandings of power—including *vajen* ("weight," authority, influence, and courage), *izzath* (dignity, honor, and respect), and *gaurava* (respect and importance)—to clarify and develop a conceptual framework for understanding the various constructions and articulations of rural women's influence in South Asia. This framework will benefit policymakers and social theorists because it takes seriously the experiences of rural women within their daily social interactions. This conceptual tool enables us to understand the mutual influences of interlocking and overlapping spheres of economics, caste, social ideologies, sexual hierarchies, and politics and how they are subject to manipulation by rural women in their everyday social interactions (Bourque and Warren 1981; Clegg 1989; Gaventa 2003).

Finally, this work contributes to rethinking theorizing notions of gender, age, religion, caste, tribe, politics, and agency, and the broad contemporary research on indigenous and rural populations in South Asia.

Bibliography

Agarwal, B 2004, *A field of one's own: gender and land rights in South Asia*, Cambridge University Press, Cambridge, England.

Ahmed, FE 2004, "The rise of the Bangladesh garment industry: globalization, women workers, and voice," *NWSA* [National Women's Studies Association] *Journal*, vol. 16, no. 2, pp. 24–45.

Alavi, H 1988, "Women in a changing society," *Economic and Political Weekly*, vol. 23, no. 26, pp. 1328–1330.

Ali, O 2011, "The African diaspora in the Indian Ocean world," *Schomburg Center for Research in Black Culture* (The New York Public Library), accessed 20 August 2013, Blackpast.org.

Allen, A 1998, "Rethinking power," *Hypatia*, vol. 13, no. 1, pp. 21–40.

Allen, A 1999, *The power of feminist theory: domination, resistance, and solidarity*, Westview Press, Boulder, Colorado.

Alpers, EA 1967, *The east African slave trade*, African Publishing House, Historical Association of Tanzania, Nairobi.

Amin, R & Khan, AH 1989, "Characteristics of traditional midwives and their beliefs and practices in rural Bangladesh," *International Journal of Gynecology & Obstetrics*, vol. 28, no. 2, February, pp. 119–125.

Anwary, A 2003, "Acid violence and medical care in Bangladesh: women's activism and carework," *Gender and Society*, special issue: "Global perspectives on gender and carework," vol. 17, no. 2, pp. 305–313.

Bachrach, P & Baratz, MS 1970, *Power and poverty: theory and practice*, Oxford University Press, New York.

Ballard, R 1982, "South Asian families," in RN Rapoport, MP Fogarty & R Rapoport (eds), *Families in Britain*, Routledge and Kegan Paul, London.

Banerjee, S 1996, "The feminization of violence in Bombay: women in the politics of the Shiv Sena," *Asian Survey*, vol. 36, no. 12, pp. 1213–1225.

Bansal, IJS 1984, *Anthropology in Indian context*, Today & Tomorrow Printers & Publishers, Delhi, India.

Basu, A (ed.) 1998, *Appropriating gender: women's activism and politicized religion in South Asia*, Kali for Women, New Delhi.

Basu, A (ed.) 2010, *Women's movements in the global era: the power of local feminisms* [Reissue], Westview, Boulder, Colorado.

Basu, AM 1992, *Culture, the status of women and demographic behavior: illustrated with the case of India*, Clarendon Press, Oxford.

Batliwala, S 1993, *Women's empowerment in South Asia: concepts and practices*, ASPBAE (Asia South Pacific Bureau of Adult Education), New Delhi.

Batliwala, S 1994, "The meaning of women's empowerment: new concepts from action," in G Sen, A Germain & L Chen (eds), *Population policies reconsidered: health, empowerment and rights*, Harvard University Press, Cambridge, Massachusetts.

Batliwala, S 1996, "Transforming of political culture—Mahila Samakhya experience," *Economic and Political Weekly*, vol. 31, no. 21, pp. 1248–1251.

Batliwala, S 2011, *Feminist leadership for social transformation: clearing the conceptual cloud*, CREA (Creating Resources for Empowerment in Action), Bangalore, India.

Bennett, C 2010, *Muslim women of power: gender, politics, and culture in Islam*, Bloomsbury, New York.

Bhatt, ER 2006, *We are poor but so many: the story of self-employed women in India*, Oxford University Press, Oxford.

Bhattacharyya, H, Sarkar, P & Kara, A 2010, *The politics of social exclusion in India*, Routledge, London.

Bokil, M 2002, "De-notified and nomadic tribes—a perspective," *Economic and Political Weekly*, vol. 37, no. 2, pp. 148–154.

Boulding, KE 1990, *Three faces of power*, Sage Publications Limited, London, UK.

Bourdieu, P (trans. R. Nice) 1977, *Outline of a theory of practice*, Cambridge University Press, Cambridge, England.

Bourque, SC & Warren, KB 1981, *Women of the Andes: patriarchy and social change in two Peruvian towns*, University of Michigan Press, Ann Arbor.

Brinton Lykes, M, Banuazizi, A, Liem, R & Morris, M (eds) 1996, *Myths about the powerless*, Temple University Press, Philadelphia.

Butalia, U 2000, *The other side of silence: voices from the partition of India*, Duke University Press, Durham, North Carolina.

Cameron, MM 1995, "Transformations of gender and caste divisions of labor in rural Nepal: land, hierarchy, and the case of untouchable women," *Journal of Anthropological Research*, vol. 51, no. 3, pp. 215–246.

Cain, MT 1991, "Widows, sons, and old-age security in rural Maharashtra: a comment on Vlassoff," *Population Studies*, vol. 45, no. 3, pp. 519–528.

Chaudhary, IS & Nosheen, F 2009, "The determinants of women empowerment in southern Punjab (Pakistan): an empirical analysis," *European Journal of Social Sciences*, vol. 10, no. 2, pp. 216–229.

Chaudhuri, S 2012, "Women as easy scapegoats: witchcraft accusations and women as targets in tea plantations of India," *Violence Against Women*, vol. 18, no. 10, pp. 1213–1234.

Chhibber, P 2002, "Why are some women politically active? The household, public space, and political participation in India," *International Journal of Comparative Sociology*, vol. 43, no. 3–5, pp. 409–429.

Chowdhry, P 2004, *The veiled women: shifting gender equations in rural Haryana*, Oxford University Press, New Delhi.

Chowdhury, N 2002, The implementation of quotas: Bangladesh experience—dependence and marginality in politics, paper presented at the Regional Workshop on "The implementation of quotas: Asian experiences," International Institute for Democracy and Electoral Assistance (IDEA), Jakarta, Indonesia

Ciscel, DH & Health, JA 2001, "To market, to market: imperial capitalism's destruction of social capital and the family," *Review of Radical Political Economics*, vol. 33, no. 4, pp. 401–414.

Clegg, S 1989, *Frameworks of power*, Sage Publications, London.

Cliggett, L 2005, *Grains from grass: aging, gender, and famine in rural Africa*, Cornell University Press, Ithaca, New York.

Cohen, C 1999, *The boundaries of blackness: AIDS and the breakdown of black politics*, University of Chicago Press, Chicago.

Collier, P 1998, Women in development: defining the issues, Policy, Planning and Research Working Paper #129, Population and Human Resources Department, The World Bank, Washington, D.C.

Das, M & Maru, V 2011, Framing local conflict and justice in Bangladesh, Social Development Department, The World Bank, Washington, D.C.

Das, NP, Gandotra, MM, Pandey, D & Shah, U 2002, *Status of women and reproductive behavior*, Hindustan Publishing Corporation, New Delhi.

Das, RJ 2004, "Social capital and poverty of the wage-labor class: problems with social capital theory," *Transactions of the Institute of British Geographers*, New Series, vol. 29, no. 1, pp. 27–45.

Desai, M 2010, "Hope in hard times: women's empowerment and human development," Human Development Research Paper, United Nations Development Programme (UNDP), New York.

Dixon, RB 1982, "Mobilizing women for rural employment in South Asia: issues of class, caste, and patronage," *Economic Development and Cultural Change*, vol. 30, no. 2, pp. 373–390.

Dovi, S 2010, "Preferable descriptive representatives: will just any woman, Black, or Latino do?" in Krook and Childs (eds), *Women, gender and politics: a reader*, Oxford University Press, New York.

Dowding, KM 1991, *Rational choice and political power*, Edward Elgar Publishing, Aldershot.

D'Souza, VS 1982, The aged in India, paper presented at the *World Assembly on Aging*, Vienna.

Dube, L 2001, *Anthropological debates in gender: intersecting fields*, Sage Publications, New Delhi.

Dumont, L 1980, *Homo hierarchicus: the caste system and its implications*, University of Chicago Press, Chicago/Urbana, Illinois.

Eck, D 1985, *Darsan: seeing the divine image in India*, Anima Publications, Chambersburg, Pennsylvania.

Edlefsen, JB 1960, "Makranis, the negroes of West Pakistan," *Phylon*, vol. 21, no. 2, pp. 124–130.

Edmondson, L 2007, *Performance and politics in Tanzania: the nation on stage*, Indiana University Press, Bloomington.

Fabre, G 1994, "African-American commemorative celebrations in the nineteenth century," in G Fabre & R O'Maeally (eds), *History and memory in African-American culture*, Oxford University Press, New York.

Farzana, B 2002, "Women's Representation in Legislatures: The Way Forward." Islamabad: Ministry of Women and Development, January, p. 11

Farzana, KF 2008, "The neglected stateless Bihari community in Bangladesh: victims of political diplomatic onslaught," *Journal of Humanities and Social Sciences*, vol. 2, no. 1, pp. 1–19.

Few, R 2002, "Researching actor power: analyzing mechanisms of interaction in negotiations over space," *Area*, vol. 34, no. 1, pp. 29–38.

Foucault, M (trans. Alan Sheridan) 1977, *Discipline and punish: the birth of the prison*, Vintage, New York.

Freeman-Grenville, GSP 1971, *The Swahili coast, 2nd to 19th centuries: Islam, commerce and Christianity in eastern Africa*, Variorum, London.

Friedl, E 1967, "The position of women: appearance and reality," *Anthropological Quarterly*, special issue: "Status and roles of women in Mediterranean societies," vol. 40, no. 3, pp. 97–108.

Gandhi, M 1969, *Collected works of Mahatma Gandhi*, Ministry of Information and Broadcasting, Government of India, New Delhi.

Gardner, K 1995, *Global migrants, local lives: travel and transformation in rural Bangladesh*, Clarendon Press, Oxford.

Gaventa, J 1982, *Power and powerlessness: quiescence and rebellion in an Appalachian valley*, University of Illinois Press, Urbana, Illinois.

Gaventa, J 2003, Power after Lukes: an overview of theories of power since Lukes and their application to development, first draft.

Gaventa, J 2006, "Finding spaces for change: a power analysis," *IDS* [Institute of Development Studies] *Bulletin*, vol. 37, no. 6, pp. 23–33.

Gazetteer of the Bombay Presidency: Kanara District 1991, vol. XV, part 1, DK Gaokar, Kanvar, India (originally published by Government Printing Press, 1883), pp. 1396–1407.

Ghadially, R (ed.) 2007, *Urban women in contemporary India: a reader*, Sage Publications, Thousand Oaks, California.

Ghatak, NK & Singh, KS (eds) 2003, *Gujarat, part 1*, Popular Prakashan, Mumbai.

Giddens, A 1984, *The constitution of society: outline of the theory of structuration*, Polity Press, Oxford.

Gold, A 1994, "Gender, violence, and power: Rajasthani stories of Shakti," in N Kumar (ed.), *Women as subjects: South Asian histories*, University of Virginia Press, Charlottesville (Virginia) and Calcutta.

Goodburn, EA, Gazi, AR & Chowdhury, M 1995, "Beliefs and practices regarding delivery and postpartum maternal morbidity in rural Bangladesh," *Studies in Family Planning*, vol. 26, no. 1, pp. 22–32.

Gooptu, N 2002, *India and partition*, accessed 4 November 2012, http://www.sant.ox.ac.uk/areastudies/lectures/gooptu.html.

Gupta, D 2005, "Caste and politics: identity over system," *Annual Review of Anthropology*, vol. 34, pp. 409–427.

Haider, Z 2003, "Repatriation of the Biharis stranded in Bangladesh: diplomacy and development," *Asian Profile*, vol. 31, no. 6, p. 525.

Hapke, HM 2001, "Petty traders, gender and development in a South Indian fishery," *Economic Geography*, vol. 77, no. 3, pp. 225–249.

Hapke, HM 2013, "Theorizing patriarchy: development paradoxes and the geography of gender in South Asia," *Gender, Technology and Development*, vol. 17, no.1, pp. 1–29.

Haque, MS 2002, "The changing balance of power between the government and NGOs in Bangladesh," *International Political Science Review*, vol. 23, no. 4, pp. 411–435.

Harish, R & Harishankar, BV 2003, *Shakti: multidisciplinary perspectives on women's empowerment in India*, Rawat Publications, New Delhi.

Harris, JE 1971, *African presence in Asia: consequences of the East African slave trade*, Northwestern University Press, Evanston.

Harsha, VH, Hebbar, SS, Shripathi, V and Hedge, GR 2003, "Ethnomedicobotany of Uttara Kannada district in Karnataka," *Journal of Ethnopharmacology*, vol. 84, no. 1, pp. 37–40.

Hegland, ME 2003, "Shi'a women's rituals in northwest Pakistan: the shortcomings and significances of resistance," *Anthropological Quarterly*, vol. 76, no. 3, pp. 411–442.

Henderson, S & Jeydel, A 2007, *Participation and protest: women and politics in a global world*, Oxford University Press, New York.

Henningham, S 1981, "Autonomy and organisation: Harijan and Adivasi protest movement," *Economic and Political Weekly*, vol. 16, no. 27, pp. 1153–1156.

Hiremath, RS 1993, Life, living, and language among Siddis of North Kanara district, doctoral dissertation, Department of Anthropology, Karnatak University, Dharwad, Karnataka.

Iversen, T & Rosenbluth, F 2010, *Women, work and politics: the political economy of gender inequality*, Yale University Press, New Haven.

Jejeebhoy, SJ 2002, "Convergence and divergence in spouses' perspectives on women's autonomy in rural India," *Studies in Family Planning*, vol. 33, no. 4, p. 4.

Jejeebhoy, SJ & Sathar, ZA 2001, "Women's autonomy in India and Pakistan: the influence of religion and region," *Population and Development Review*, vol. 27, no. 4, pp. 687–712.

Jokhio AH, Winter, HR & Cheng KK 2005, "An intervention involving traditional birth attendants and perinatal and maternal mortality in Pakistan," *New England Journal of Medicine*, vol. 352, pp. 2091–2099.

Kabeer, N 1999, "Resources, agency, achievements: reflections on the measurement of women's empowerment," *Development and Change*, vol. 30, no. 3, pp. 435–464.

Kabeer, N 2001, "Reflections on the measurement of women's empowerment," in Sisask, A (ed.) *Discussing women's empowerment: theory and practice*, SIDA (Swedish International Development Cooperation Agency), Stockholm.

Kabeer, N 2005, "Gender equality and women's empowerment: a critical analysis of the third millennium development goal," *Gender and Development*, vol. 13, no.1, pp. 13–24.

Kabeer, N & Huq, L 2010, "The power of relationships: love and solidarity in a landless women's organization in rural Bangladesh," *IDS* [Institute of Development Studies] *Bulletin*, vol. 41, no. 2, pp. 79–87.

Kagitcibasi, C 1986, "Status of women in Turkey: cross-cultural perspectives," *International Journal of Middle Eastern Studies*, vol. 18, pp. 485–499.

Kanitkar, A 1994, "Entrepreneurs and micro-enterprises in rural India," *Economic and Political Weekly*, vol. 29, no. 9, pp. 25–30.

Karlberg M 2005, "The power of discourse and the discourse of power: pursuing peace through discourse intervention," *International Journal of Peace Studies*, vol. 10, no. 1, pp. 1–23.

Kasturi, L & Mazumdar, V (eds) 1994, *Women and Indian nationalism*, Vikas Publishing House, New Delhi.

Kaur, R 2007, *Since 1947: partition narratives among Punjabi migrants of Delhi*, Oxford University Press, New Delhi.

Kazir, S 1999, "Gender inequalities and development in Pakistan" in SR Khan (ed.) *Fifty years of Pakistan's economy: traditional topics and temporary concerns*, Oxford University Press, Karachi.

Kelkar, G & Krishnaraj, M 2013, *Women, land and power in Asia*, Routledge, London.

Khan, AH & Amin, R 1989, "Characteristics of traditional midwives and their beliefs and practices in rural Bangladesh," *International Journal of Gynecology & Obstetrics*, vol. 28, no. 2, pp. 119–125.

Kelkar, G, Nathan, D & Jahan, R 2004, "Redefining women's 'samman': microcredit and gender relations in rural Bangladesh," *Economic and Political Weekly*, vol. 39, no. 32, pp. 3627–3640.

Kerns, V 1997, "Women and the Ancestors: Black Carib Kinship and Ritual," no. 19, University of Illinois Press, Urbana.

Khan R, Khattak, SG & Kazmi S 2005, *Hazardous home-based sub-contracted work: a study of multiple tiered exploitation*, Oxford University Press, Karachi.

Khattak, SG 2010, "Women in local government: the Pakistan experience," *IDS* [Institute of Development Studies] *Bulletin*, vol. 41, no. 5, pp. 52–61.

Kishore, S & Gupta K 2004, "Women's empowerment in India and its states: evidence from the NFHS," *Economic and Political Weekly*, vol. 38, no. 7, pp. 694–712.

Kishwar, M 1988, "Nature of women's mobilisation in rural India: an exploratory essay," *Economic and Political Weekly*, vol. 23, no. 52/53, pp. 2754–2763.

Knott, K 1998, *Hinduism: a very short introduction*, Oxford University Press, New York.

Koenig, MA, Ahmed S, Hossain, MB & Khorshed Alam Mozumbder, ABM 2003, "Women's status and domestic violence in rural Bangladesh: individual- and community-level effects," *Demography*, vol. 40, no. 2, pp. 269–288.

Kothari, R & Manor, J (eds) 1995, *Caste in Indian politics*, Longman Orient, Hyderabad, India.

Kronstadt, KA 2010, Pakistan—key current issues and developments, CRS Report for Congress, R41307, Congressional Research Service 7.

Kumar, N 1994, *Women as subjects: South-Asian histories*, University of Virginia Press, Charlottesville, Virginia.

Lakshmi VK 2007, "Hindu women and property rights: role of religion and society," *Women's Link*, vol. 13, no. 3, pp. 23–27.

Latimore, C 1997, Gender, justice and development: women and development in Ghana, doctoral dissertation, University of Pennsylvania, Philadelphia.

Lawrence, BB 1994, "Women as subject/women as symbol: Islamic fundamentalism and the status of women," *The Journal of Religious Ethics*, vol. 22, no. 1, pp. 163–185.

Lewis, D & Kanji, N 2009, *Non-governmental organizations and development*, Routledge, London & New York.

Lobo, CH 1983, "Socio-economic changes in a Banjara community," in Bansal, IJS (ed.), *Anthropology in Indian context*, Today & Tomorrow Printers & Publishers, Delhi, India.

Loomer, B 1976, "Two conceptions of power," *Process Studies*, vol. 6, no. 1, pp. 5–32.

Lowitz, L & Datta, R 2005, *Sacred Sanskrit words*, Stone Bridge Press, Berkeley.

Lukes, S 2005, *Power: a radical view* (2nd ed.), Palgrave Macmillan, Basingstoke, England.

Lukes S & Haglund L 2000, "Power and luck," *European Journal of Sociology*, vol. 46, no. 1, pp. 45–66.

Madan, TN and Dumont, L 1971, "On the nature of caste in India: a review symposium on Louis Dumont's *Homo hierarchicus*," *Contributions to Indian Sociology*, NS. 5, p. 181.

Mahajan, A 1990, "Instigators of wife battering," in S Sood (ed.), *Violence against women*, Arihant Publishers, Jaipur, India.

Malhotra, A, Schuler, SR and Boender, C 2002, Measuring women's empowerment as a variable in international development, Gender and Development Group, The World Bank, Washington, DC.

Mathai, RJ 1979, "Perceived risk and rural entrepreneurship," in TV Rao & TK Moulik (eds), *Identification and selection of small scale entrepreneurs*, Indian Institute of Management, Ahmedabad.

Mba, C et al. 2007, "An in-depth analysis of socio-demographics, living arrangements and health conditions of Ghana's older population," *Institute of African Studies: Research Review*, vol. 23, no. 2, 61–70.

Mbembe, A 2001, *On the postcolony*, University of California Press, Berkeley.

Mehdi, SS 2007, "Pakistan: conflict, migration and peace," *Asteriskos: Journal of International and Peace Studies*, vol. 3/4, no. 4, pp. 55–84.

Menon, R 1999, "Cartographies of nations and identities," *Interventions: International Journal of Post-colonial Studies*, vol. 1, no. 2, pp. 157–166.

Metry, KM 2002, *Budakattu kulakasubugalu (tribal occupations)*, Prasaranga Press (Kannada University), Hampi, India.

Metry, KM 2007, Budakattu Adhyayana, *Tribal Studies, Bi-Annual*, vol. 4, no. 1–2.

Moffatt, M 1979a, *An untouchable community in South India: structure and consensus*, Princeton University Press, Princeton.

Moffatt, M 1979b, "Harijan religion: consensus at the bottom of caste," *American Ethnologist*, vol. 6, no. 2, pp. 244–260.
Mohan, V 1990, "Is there hope for battered wives?" in S Sood (ed.), *Violence against women*, Arihant Publishers, Jaipur, India.
Mohiuddin, Y 1989, "Female-headed households and urban poverty in Pakistan," *Pakistan Development Review*, vol. 28, no. 4, pp. 759–775.
Muhammad, ZA 2009, "Migration, settlement and identity: a cultural theme of the Muslim diaspora after partition of India—1947" in J Fernandez (ed.), *Diasporas: critical and interdisciplinary perspectives*, Inter-Disciplinary Press, Oxford.
Mullen, RD 2012, *Decentralization, local governance, and social wellbeing in India: do local governments matter?* Routledge, Abingdon, England.
Mumtaz, K & Noshirwani, MM 2007, "Women's access and rights to land and property in Pakistan," Scoping Study, International Development Research Centre (IDRC), Ottawa, Canada.
Mumtaz, K & Shaheed, F 1987, *Women of Pakistan: two steps forward, one step back?*, Vanguard Books, Lahore, Pakistan.
Naik, DB 2000, *The art and literature of Banjara Lambanis: a socio-cultural study*, Abhinav Publications, New Delhi.
Naik, DB 2008, *Banjara-Lambanis: origin and culture*, Regional Resources Centre for Folk Performing Arts, Udupi, India.
Nasr, S 2002, "Islam, the state and the rise of sectarian militancy in Pakistan," in C Jaffrelot (ed.), *Pakistan: nationalism without a nation?*, Zed Books, London.
Natrajan, B 2005, "Caste, class, and community in India: an ethnographic approach," *Ethnography*, vol. 44, no. 3, pp. 227–241.
Niaz, U 2003, "Violence against women in South Asian countries," *Archive of Women's Mental Health*, vol. 6, no. 3, pp. 173–184.
Nielson, AE 1995, "Architectural performance and the reproduction of social power," in JM Skibo, WH Walked & AE Nielsen (eds), *Expanding archaeology*, University of Utah Press, Salt Lake City.
Nizamani, SA 2006, Sheedi community of Sindh, Pakistan, doctoral dissertation, Quaid-E-Azam University, Islamabad.
Nosaka, A & Andrews, BW 2004, "Institutionalized powerlessness in context: the static and dynamic nature of women's status in rural Bangladesh," *Journal of International Women's Studies*, vol. 6, no. 1, pp. 149–167.
Nyamnjoh, FB 2002, "'A child is one person's only in the womb': domestication, agency and subjectivity in the Cameroonian grassfields," in R Webner (ed.), *Postcolonial subjectivities in Africa*, 11–137, Zed Books, London.
Obeng, P 2007, *Shaping membership, defining nation: the cultural politics of African Indians in South Asia*, Lexington Books, Lenham, Maryland.
Oommen, TK 1970, "Rural community power structure in India," *Social Forces*, vol. 49, no. 2, pp. 226–239.
Omvedt, G 1993, *Reinventing revolution: new social movements and the socialist tradition in India*, M.E. Sharpe, Armonk, New York.
Omvedt, G 2005, "Women in governance in South Asia," *Economic and Political Weekly*, vol. 40, no. 44/45, pp. 4746–4752.
Oppong, C 2004, "Social capital and systems of care: some contrasting evidence," *Research Review Supplement*, vol. 16, Institute of African Studies, pp. 1–18.
Ortner, SB 1974, "Is female to male as nature is to culture?" in MZ Rosaldo & LL Lamphere (eds), *Woman, culture and society*, Stanford University Press, Stanford, California.

Oxfam International 2010, Women in Pakistan: "I felt the power of my money!," accessed 10 February 2013, http://www.oxfam.org/en/emergencies/pakistan-floods-2010/women-power-money.

Pal, M 2004, "Caste and patriarchy in panchayats," *Economic and Political Weekly*, vol. 39, no. 32, pp. 3581–3583.

Panday, PK 2008, "Representation without participation: quotas for women in Bangladesh," *International Political Science Review*, vol. 29, no. 4, pp. 489–512.

Pandey, G 1991, "In defence of the fragment: writing about Hindu-Muslim riots in India today," *Economic and Political Weekly*, annual issue.

Pandian, A 2008, "Pastoral power in the postcolony," *Cultural Anthropology*, vol. 23, no. 1, pp. 85–117.

Paul, BK 1992, "Female activity space in rural Bangladesh," *Geographical Review*, vol. 82, no. 1, pp. 1–12.

Paul, V et al. 1972, *Chapter 6: major actors and their current roles relevant to biodiversity*, Centre for Management in Agriculture Indian Institute of Management, Ahmadabad, India.

Pitkin H 1972, *Wittgenstein and justice*, University of California Press, Berkeley.

Preston, V & Wong, M 2004, "Geographies of violence: women and conflict in Ghana," in W Giles & J Hyndman (eds), *Sites of violence: gender and conflict zones*, University of California Press, London.

Rahman ATR 1993, *Volunteerism and nation-building for Bangladesh*, Academic Publishers, Dhaka.

Rajan, SR 1998, Is the Hindu Goddess a feminist?, *Economic and Political Weekly*, vol. 33, no. 44, pp. WS34–WS38.

Rao, V 2001, "Poverty and public celebrations in rural India," *Annals of the American Academy of Political and Social Science*, special issue: "Culture and development: international perspectives," vol. 573, pp. 85–108.

Rege, S 2004, "Dalit women talk differently: a critique of 'difference' and towards a Dalit feminist standpoint position," in M Chauduri (ed.), *Feminism in India*, Kali for Women, New Delhi.

Rew, M, Gangoli, G & Gill, AK 2013, "Violence between female in-laws in India," *Journal of International Women's Studies*, vol. 14, no. 1, pp. 147–160.

Rogers, S 1975, "Female forms of power and the myth of male dominance: challenges a model of male/female interaction in person/society," *American Ethnologist*, vol. 2, no. 4, pp. 727–756.

Rose, K 1992, *Where women are leaders: the SEWA movement in India*, Zed Books, London.

Sa'ar, A 2006, "Feminine strength: reflections on power and gender in Israeli-Palestinian culture," *Anthropological Quarterly*, vol. 79, no. 3, pp. 397–430.

Sadeque, N & Zeenat, H 2009, "Economy initiatives 2009: poverty and environment," in Report of the consultation on 'revising the national plan of action for women', Shirkat Gah, Lahore.

Sangari, K & Vaid, S (eds) 1989, *Women essays in colonial history*, Kali for Women, New Delhi.

Sankaram, K 2006, "Women, work and improvement," in A Gandhi (ed.), *Women's work, health and empowerment*, Aakar Books, Delhi.

Sathar, ZA & Kazi, S 1990, "Women, work and reproduction in Karachi," *International Family Planning Perspectives*, vol. 16, no. 2, pp. 66–69, 80.

Sathar, ZA & Kazi, S 1997, *Women's autonomy, livelihood and fertility: a study of rural Punjab*, Pakistan Institute of Development Studies, Islamabad.

Sathar, ZA & Shahnaz K 2000, "Women's autonomy in the context of rural Pakistan," *Pakistan Development Review*, vol. 39, no. 2, pp. 89–110.

Schuler, SR, Hashemi, SM, Riley, AP & Akhter, S 1996, "Credit programs, patriarchy and men's violence against women in rural Bangladesh," *Social Science and Medicine*, vol. 43, no. 12, pp. 1729–1742.

Scott, JC 1990, *Domination and the arts of resistance: hidden transcripts*, Yale University Press, New Haven and London.

Sered, S 1988, "The domestication of religion: the spiritual guardianship of elderly Jewish women," *Man*, New Series, vol. 23, no. 3, pp. 506–521.

Shaheed, F. 2010. "The women's movement in Pakistan: challenges and achievements," In Basu, A. (ed.) *Women's movements in global era: the power of local feminisms*, Boulder, CO: Westview Press.

Sharma, S 2011, *"Neoliberalization" as betrayal: state, feminism, and a women's education program in India*, Palgrave Macmillan, New York.

Singh, KS (ed.) 2004, *People of India: Maharashtra*, vol. XXX, part I, Popular Prakash, Mumbai.

Singh, RK 2011, "Disappearing daughters" (editorial), *Women's Link*, vol. 17, no. 2 April–June 2011.

Sirajul Hassan, S 1989, *The castes and tribes of H.E.H. the Nizam's dominions*, Asian Educational Service, Delhi.

Srinivas, MN 1977, *The Changing Position of Indian Women, Man*, New Series, vol. 12, no. 2, pp. 221–238, Royal Anthropological Institute of Great Britain and Ireland.

Srinivas, MN 1996, *Village, caste, gender and method: essays in Indian social anthropology*, Oxford University Press, Delhi.

Starveren, I. van 2001, *The values of economics: an Aristotelian approach*, Routledge, London.

Stewart, PJ & Strathern, A 2004, *Witchcraft, sorcery, rumors, gossip*, Cambridge University Press, New York.

Streefland, PH 1979, *The sweepers of slaughterhouse: conflict and survival in a Karachi neighbourhood*, Van Gorcum, Assen, Netherlands.

Subramaniam, M 2006, *The power of women's organizing: gender, caste, and class in India*, Lexington Books, Lanham, Maryland.

Subramaniam, M 2009, "Capability building as potential to protest gender and caste injustice: poor women in rural India," *Theory in Action*, vol. 2, no. 1, pp. 1–22.

Sultana, P & Thompson P 2007, "Community-based fisheries management and fisher livelihoods: Bangladesh case studies," *Human Ecology*, vol. 35, no. 5, pp. 527–546.

Talbot, I 2006, *Divided cities: partition and its aftermath in Lahore and Amritsar 1947–1957*, Oxford University Press, New York.

Tapper, N & Tapper, R 1982, "Marriage preferences and ethnic relations among Durrani Pashtuns of Afghan Turkestan," *Folk*, vol. 24, pp. 157–177.

Visaria, L & Visaria, P 1996, *Prospective population growth and policy options for India*, The Population Council, New York.

Waerness, K 2004, "Epilogue: the study of care in cross-cultural, interdisciplinary perspective," *Research Review Supplement*, vol. 16, Institute of African Studies, pp. 108–114.

Walker, WH 2006, "The materiality of social power: the artifact-acquisition perspective" *Journal of Archaeological Method and Theory*, vol. 13, no. 2, p. 67.

Wartenberg, TE 1990, *The forms of power: from domination to transformation*, Temple University Press, Philadelphia, Pennsylvania.

Watts, M & Bohle, HG 1993, "The space of vulnerability: the causal structure of hunger and famine," *Progress in Human Geography*, vol. 17, no. 1, pp. 43–67.

Weiss, AM & Gilani, SZ 2001, *Power and civil society in Pakistan*, Oxford University Press, New York.
Williams, R 1972, *The East Pakistan tragedy*, Drake Publishers, New York.
Woodroffe, JG 1918, *Shakti and Shakta: essays and addresses on the Shakta Tantra Shastra*, Luzac & Co, London.
Young, M 1989, "Polity and group difference: a critique of the ideal of universal citizenship," *Ethics*, vol. 99, pp. 250–274.
Zahoor, MA 2009, "Migration, settlement and identity: a cultural theme of Muslin diaspora after partition of India–1947," accessed 25 September 2013, interdisciplinary.net/ati/diversity/diasporas/d1/Zahoorpaper.
Zulfiqar, B 2010, *Women and economy: the politics of empowerment*, Lambert Academic Publishing, Saarbrucken, Germany.

Newspapers and News Services

Agarwal, B 2005 "Hindu Succesion (Amendment) Act," *The Hindu*, 25 September 2005.
"American aid" (editorial), *Dawn*, 8 September 2009, Karachi.
Constable, P 2009, "Pakistan's Zardari holds off his political foes—for now," *The Washington Post*, 1 December 2009, Washington, DC.
GlobalSecurity.org, accessed 10 December 2012, http://www.globalsecurity.org/military/world/india/hg.htm.
Ebrahim, Z 2010, "Pakistan: community midwives gain recognition but concerns remain," *Inter Press Service*, 7 February 2010, Karachi, Pakistan.
Haque, I 2007, "Informal sector grows by 20pc," *Dawn*, 2 September 2007, Karachi.
Jahangir, A 2008, "Pakistan to focus more on women empowerment to improve growth," accessed 3 October 2012, http://www.allvoices.com/contributed-news/145691-pakistan-gender, Islamabad, Pakistan: PulsePoint.boul.
Ladly, MD 2009, "Defying parents, some Pakistani women risk all to marry whom they choose," *The New York Times*, New York City, NY, 9 September 2009, http://www.nytimes.com/2012/09/09/world/asia/some-pakistani-women-risk-all-to-marry-for-love.html?, accessed 9 September 2012.
Mohandas, P 2009, "Rural India gets a livesaving cookstove," *Mint*, 22 April 2009, Delhi, http://www.livemint.com/Politics/BpfJdNf2nyByjX46pvgsPM/Rural-India-gets-a-lifesaving-cookstove.html.
"NGOs press U.S. government in Pakistan aid packages," Reuters, 11 November 2009, Washington D.C.
"Siddis urge forest land regularization," *The Times of India News Service*, 21 February 1990, Karwar.
Tunio, H 2010, "When the crocs come to play at Manghopir," *The Express Tribune*, 14 June 2010, Karachi, Pakistan, http://tribune.com.pk/story/21111/when-the-crocs-come-to-play-at-manghopir/ accessed 15 October 2012.

Index

Printed and bound in the United States of America